AF658803

John Keats & Mirza Ghalib
(A Comparative Study as Poets)

John Keats & Mirza Ghalib

(A Comparative Study as Poets)

Z. Hasan

ABD PUBLISHERS

Jaipur ■ New Delhi

ABD PUBLISHERS

Regd. Off. "Bony Residency", Gate No. 2
Opp. Tilak Public School, Vishweswariya Nagar,
Gopalpura Road, Jaipur - 302018, India
Ph: 0141 - 2761280, Telefax: 2761381
Email: abdpublishersjpr@gmail.com

Delhi Office: 102, 1st Floor, Satyam House,
4327/3, Ansari Road, Darya Ganj,
New Delhi - 110002, India
Ph: 011-45652440

visit us: www.oxfordbookcompany.com

Distributed By
KEYA INTERNATIONAL PRESS LLP
E-mail: keyainternationalpressllp@gmail.com

First published in India, 2023

© All Rights Reserved

ISBN: 9788183762243

All Rights Reserved. Neither this publication nor any part thereof may be reproduced, stored in a retrieval system, or transmitted, in any form or by any means, electronic, mechanical, photocopying, recording, scanning or otherwise, without the prior written permission of the copyright owner.

Typeset by Shivangi Computer, Jaipur

Printed and bound in India by Thomson Press Ltd.,
New Delhi

Great poetry is the utterance of that to
which the human soul responds, of that
which the human soul endorses.
So that the history of the souls of the
great poets is the most essential
history of the human soul itself.

John Middleton Murry
in *Keats* and *Shakespeare*.

PREFACE

The idea to make a comparative study of an eminent Urdu poet and an equally eminent English poet came to me while researching for the Supplementary Dictionary of National Biography. I wrote about twenty-five research entries and noted that a comparison between an Urdu poet and an English one would prove a fruitful venture since in place of cultural animosity the people of the world have started talking in terms of cultural homogeneity and anthropological invariables. I embarked on a plan of studying Mirza Ghalib and John Keats. After my preliminary studies I contacted Qazi Abdul Sattar,Professor of Urdu, Aligarh Muslim University, Aligarh and (now late) Professor Zoe Ansari of Bombay University. They encouraged me and I presented my plan of study before the Research Degree Committee of Agra University, Agra.

Many critics of Ghalib have compared his thought and art with that of many a man of letters of the West like Shakespeare, Hegel and Wordsworth. I found a close kinship between Keats and Ghalib. I understand that a comparative study of the two poets of the stature of Keats and Ghalib definitely heightens the aesthetic pleasure of man and provides him with a better feel of life and time.

I noted that Keats and Ghalib tread the same ground, think the same thoughts, suffer the same miseries and misfortunes and seek shelter into almost a similar world of beauty. They provide a solace and comfort to the generations who live amid different sorrows and seek shelter and find it only in works of art. Unfavorable reviews of his early efforts, pecuniary problems and other temporal misfortunes could not drag Keats from the bower of the muse of poetry. Pressing monetary problems and social and political upheavals could not drag Ghalib form the bewitching veils of Ghazals.

The two poets went to the past, adopted the best of tradition and endowed their works with the native talents of their own. They learned much from the past masters, remained ever indebted to them and yet had a way of their own, created a world of their own and peopled it with their branched thoughts and sublime imaginings. Keats had a very short span of life and the Urdu poet lived longer. Ghalib definitely suffered longer at the hands of time. As a result, his experiences, observation, intellectual moorings and questioning spirit have a deeper probe and wider sweep. For study I have taken only the Urdu Ghazals of Ghalib since his complete works will be too much for Keats.

The political works of Keats and Ghalib are an adventure of the individual mind in search of Truth and Beauty. Their search is great and equally great is the communication of their experiences. They uttered the truth of life in a way that the world will never forget them and their verse. In this study I have tried to show that Mirza Ghalib and John Keats suffered greatly at the hands of time, they realized the sufferings of the world through their own sufferings and finally put forth works of art which provide solace and comfort to the wounded heart of mankind. They appeal to us because the wordings of these poets are an echoe of the voice of our own soul.

A word about the script. I have tried to put Urdu couplets of Ghalib into Roman script without caring much for niceties. My main concern was to make his verse intelligible to one who does not know Persian script. Spellings of Urdu words when put into English will have personal bearings of the translators . for example, I could never bring myself to use 'Hali'; I always write it as 'Haali'.

The letters of Ghalib are in Urdu and so are most of the critical books on Urdu poet. Quotations and references from these books have been rendered into English by me.

Z. HASAN

ACKNOWLEDGEMENTS

I have gone through a number of books on Mirza Ghalib and John Keats besides their works and consulted several eminent persons in the field; I find it quite difficult to express my sense of gratitude in words to all of them. The biographies of Keats by Dorothy Hewlett, Amy Lowell, Walter Jackson Bate and Robert Gittings were my constant company. In the case of Ghalib I had the books of Altaf Hussain Haali, Sheikh Mohammed Ikram, Gulam Rasool Meher and Sayyid Fayyaz Mahmud with me. I greatly depended on Yusuf Hussain's translation of the Urdu Ghazals of Ghalib.

I am indebted to the research Degree Committee of Agra University for the approval of my topic. Dr. R.P.Tewari, Ph.D.litt., Head of the Department of English, R.B.S. College, Agra and Dr. Harish Ralzada (retired) Professor, Department of English, Aligarh Muslim University, Aligarh gave me useful guidelines and I added one chapter on the poetic art of Keats and Ghalib to my original plan as suggested by them.

Qazi Abdul Sattar, Professor Department of Urdu, Aligarh Muslim University, Aligarh, gave me useful hints and (now late) professor Zoe Ansari sent me a useful list of books from Bombay. I stand highly indebted to them.

I have been consulting Dr. R.C. Seth (retired), Head of the Department of English, K.R.college, Mathura and Dr. N.N. Misra, the present Head of the Department from time to time. I owe them a debt of gratitude.

I am thankful to the Librarian of Agra University Library for lending me some useful books on Keats and Ghalib. My visit to the library of Ghalib Academy, Hazrat Nizamuddin, New Delhi was made fruitful by the members of the staff there who made some rare books on Ghalib available to me. I am equally grateful to the staff of K.R. College Library who allowed me a free hand in consulting books at any time and every time. I must express my indebtedness to the librarians of British Council Library, and Raza library, Rampur, U.P. who were kind enough to send me useful bibliographies on Keats and Ghalib respectively.

I shall be failing in my duty if I do not make a mention of my mother and wife who allowed me full freedom from domestic cares so that I could devote my self whole heartedly to my studies.

Last but not the least, a word of thanks to the publisher of this book who published it nicely and promptly.

Z. HASAN

CONTENTS

1
INTRODUCTION

Interest in comparative literature is neither new nor confined to any particular literature or country. The fast changing literary situation inspires poets and critics from time to time to make a comparative evaluation of their objects of study. Going back to Greek literature we note that the poets and writers delighted in comparisons. Simonides (Sixth century B.C.) made a comparison between Homer and Hesiod. "Simonides called Hesiod a gardener, Homer a maker of garlands. Hesiod created stories about gods and heroes. Homer wove them into garlands—*the Iliad* and *Qdyssey*."[1] Aristphanes made an analytical but interesting comparative study of Euripides and Aeschylus in his play Frogs. The play ends with Aeschylus returning triumphant to Athens. Plato compares poets and poetasters in *Ion* but Aristotle does not seem to be inclined this way. He makes a passing reference to the comparative action and duration of tragedy and epic. The comparative method or '*sun crisis*' was popular with the Romans.

---

1. Quoted by Rosmary Harriott, *Poetry and Criticism before Plato* (London: Methuen& Co.1969), p. 138.

Turning to our own English literature we find Dryden, the Father of English criticism, exhibiting an acumen for comparative criticism on a wide scale. He goes beyond the national frontiers to compare Greek drama with English and English drama with French. He analysed and compared the individual merits of Ben Jonson and Shakespeare and Beaumont and Fletcher and Shakespeare. In his preface to the *Fables* he widened his scope when he put before us a comparative estimate of Homer and Virgil and Chaucer and Boccaccio. The comparative studies could not catch up fast but during the Victorian age it again took up. By this time science had put poets and scholars in a better position to see not only their own works in literature but those of the foreign countries also. Matthew Arnold did not personally take interest in any comparative study but advised critics "to learn and propagate the best that is known and thought."

This line of thinking produced scholars like T.S. Eliot and Ezra Pound who explored the possibilities of studying literatures of the East also. It was Matthew Arnold who took up the question of literary studies across geographical and cultural barriers. The twentieth century has put poets, writers and critics on a vantage ground wherefrom they can see, appreciate and study their counterparts spread over distant lands all through the world. Analysing literary contacts between different cultural groups, Sisir Kumar Das pointed out:

> One can think of the Romans coming in contact with Greek literature, the Medieval Christian Europe with the pagan Europe, Persian with Arabic, Japanese with Chinese and Indians with the literature of Europe. All these contacts have resulted in certain changes, at times marginal, and at times quite profound and pervasive, in the literary activities of the people involved and have necessitated an enlargement of critical perspective. One realizes that diversities of literature do not necessarily prevent one from discovering deeper affinities between them. [2]

---

2. Sisir Kumar Das, "Comparative Literature in India : A Historical Prespective," in *Aspects of comparative Literature: Current Approches* (ed.), Chandra Mohan (New Delhi), India Publishers and Distributors, 1989) p. 1.

Now studies in comparative literature are progressing well in the United States, Canada, Soviet Union and India. There are still problems before the comparatists regarding their methodology. The fact is that comparative studies are very much here, sometimes in the form of Keats and Shakespeare and more prominently in the form of full fledged departments of comparative literature in the universities of West and in quite a few universities in our country. Comparative literature has started making its presence felt in literary circles in Delhi, Calcutta, Lucknow, Aligarh and other seats of learning in India. Urdu lovers in the early stages of literary criticism in Urdu did not approve of comparison between the poets of East and West.

Professor Asloob Ahmad Ansari reacted sharply to Asar Lucknavi's statement about Majaz Lucknavi when he said that 'a Keats was born in Urdu poetry who was kidnapped by the revolutionary wolves.' Professor Ansari pointed out ' that comparing an Urdu romantic poet with Keats and Shelley is really nothing but a display of one's learning and misguiding ignorant people. There is great difference of taste and temperament between our Urdu poets and werstern poets. Then it is also no less important that our life is not so enriched with the multi-coloured complexity, novelty and new intellectual and cultural movement as the life of western people is.'[3] Then, professor Ansari admitted that Ghalib and Iqbal were the only poets who exhibited paradoxes, inclusiveness and a picture of the different aspects of society which is found in most of the distinguished English Poets'.[4] And yet he did not suggest that the comparative studies of these poets with those of the West should / might be undertaken.

Sharib Rudolvi condemned Kalimuddin Ahmad for his idolatory of Western literature since he wrote that Mir, Sauda, Dard, Ghalib and Momin would have been great poets if they had been acquainted with any western literature.[5]

---

3. Asloob Ahmad Ansari, "Majaaz" *Aligarh Magazine* (1955-56) P. 55 (translation from Urdu by the present researcher)
4. *Ibid.*
5. Sharib Rudolvi, *Jadid Urdu Tanqeed: Usul-o-Nazaryat* (Lucknow: Uttar Pradesh Urdu Akademi, 1981), p. 414

Sharib Rudolvi asserted that only an acquaintance with English Literature can not become yardstick of great poetry. Rudolvi is greatly in favour of comparative studies where one compares and contrasts the works of two artists on the basis of the beauty of expression. It is natural for human beings to compare and contrast two objects and go for the better. Rudolvi pointed out that a comparison and contrast between two poets of one age or of different ages will prove useful, is desirable, and will bring out meaningful results or not is an important question. Secondly, it is also notable whether comparative criticism can be included in our critical methodology. He asserted that "Comparison is the best example of aesthetic criticism."[6]

India has a long tradition of comparative criticism because it is a multilingual country. The early Indian scholars must have studied their Sanskrit along with the Prakrit texts. It can be safely assumed that medieval Indian scholars studied their literature with reference to Sanskrit as an inter-relationship between different languages on the one hand and Sanskrit on the other, was inevitable. It was there in the middle ages that Telegu, Malyalam, Marathi, Gujrathi, Punjabi and Sindhi languages were developing and producing their own literature. The interactions between neighbouring literatures, however, continued throughout the Medieval period resulting in the growth of new genres and themes and occasionally style. The Persian language and literature made its presence felt in the country during the fifteenth and sixteenth centuries. Their influence on various Indian literatures becomes apparent. It is at this time that Urdu language emerged out of an interaction between Persian and Khadi Boli which was being used between Delhi and Agra. Urdu became a means of literary expression by the end of seventeenth century. The Urdu poets borrowed their themes and poetic forms from Perso-Arabic literary traditions. During the eighteenth century Urdu flourished well but it was in the nineteenth century that Urdu came to its perfection in the works of Mir, Sauda, Dard, Zauq, Momin and Ghalib.

---

6. *Ibid.*, p. 456

Comparative criticism in Urdu is of a very recent origin. During the modern times it entered our country in 1785 when Warren Hanstings, the first Governor-General of India, in his introduction to Charles Wilkin's translation of the *Gita* into English wrote," I should not fear to place, in opposition to the best French version of the most admired passages of *Iliad* or *Odyssey*, or the 1st and 6th books of our own Milton, highly as I venerate the latter, the English translation of the *Mahabharata*".[7]

The British Sanskrit scholar H.H. Wilson had a great admiration for Kalidas. In the works of Kalidas he found a poetical design, a poetical description of nature in its variety and all the human feelings and keener sensibilities, and noted that Kalidas was the fellow and kinsman of the great masters of ancient and modern poetry.[8] Matthew Arnold was the first to give us the idea of comparative literature, though the idea of a world literature was already with Goethe. Saint Beuve, a French critic, emphatically asserted the unity of world literature:

> Homer, as always and everywhere should be first, likest a god, but behind him, like a procession of the three wise kings of the East, would be the three great poets, the three Homers, so long ignored by us, who wrote epics for the use of the old people of Asia, the poets Valmiki, Vyasa of the Hindus, and Firdousi of the Persians, in the domain of taste; it is well to know that such men exist and not to divide the human race.[9]

In India it was Rabindranath Tagore who pleaded for a comparative study of literature. The National Council of Education, Calcutta invited him in 1907 to give a talk on comparative literature. The title of his talk in Bengali was *Visva-Sahitya* which means World Literature, Tagore said"

> What I am trying to say amounts to this. Just as this earth is not the sum of patches of land belonging to different people,

7. Quoted by Sisir Kumar Das, op. Cit., p.5
8. See Sisir Kumar Das, *Sahibs and Munshis, An Account of the College of Fort William* (Delhi, 1978), pp.113-14.
9. Quoted by Sisir Kumar Das in "Comparative Literature in India: A Historical Perspective," pp.6-7.

> and to know the earth as such is sheer rusticity, so literature is not the mere total of works composed by different hands. Most of us, however, think of literature in what I have called the manner of the rustic. From this narrow provincialism we must free ourselves; we must strive to see the work of each another as whole, that whole as a part of man's universal creativity, and that universal spirit in its manifestations through world literature. Now is the time to do so.[10]

The comparatists start with the simple proposition that human beings are everywhere the same. At the lower level they have hunger, sex and lust and at the higher level they have intellect and sympathy. When stirred by pleasure or pain, they are moved to an expression and communication of their thoughts and feelings. No language is good or bad, vulgar or refined for the spontaneous expression of the inherent human feelings. Every language, even of the tribal, is adequate to convey the thoughts and feelings of the people who use it. Languages may be rich or poor depending upon the creativity of their men of letters. So when a comparatist goes to two poets of the same literature or to two poets of two different literatures, he fulfils a natural human curiosity to see life and see it whole.

All human beings face problems concerned with life, death, love, food, sex, greed and shelter. They all react to these and find out solutions in their own way. A study of literature of different poets of different times and cultures provides us with better and wider understanding of human life and keener appreciation of human efforts.

Longinus, the famous romantic critic of antiquity, wrote that the sublime literature crosses the boundaries of race and time. The cultural barriers and geographical frontiers do not stand in the way of appreciation of a work of art which lifts the reader out of himself. Defining the true sublime he wrote:

> In general we may regard those works as truly noble and sublime which always please and please all readers. For when the same book always produces the same impression on all who read it

10. Quoted by Sisir Kumar Das, *op. cit*., p. 10.

> whatever be the difference in their pursuits, their manner of life, their aspirations, their ages or their languages, such a harmony of opposites gives irresistible authority to their favourable verdict.[11]

That which is sublime pleases all the readers whatever be the differences in their faiths, languages, ages and countries. As a matter of facts, the great literature, or what Longinus calls 'true sublime'. is an expression of the human heart and mind in its highest revelations and in the best possible way. There are some human invariables like love, honour, death, greed, jealousy, anger and hatred and out of these men of letters pick-up themes of their own choice. In this respect poets, writers, essayists and novelists of the whole world belong to one fraternity and therein lies the meaningfulness of comparative studies. When a literature comes into contact with another literature, in the early stages there is always a reaction because of cultural distance and at times due to certain political causes. The conquering race always thinks its literature better than the one of the conquered people. It was so with Macaulay when the Britishers imposed their system of Education on India and compared all the literature of the Orient to one shelf of English literature.

There may be certain cultural animosities because the conquered race feels humiliated under the white man's burden, if the burden amounts to conversion. R.K. Ramanujan asserted that colonization by a foreign language results in an inventive coping, co-opting and incorporating on the part of the writer.[12] In such cases it is the imitation of the ruling models which does the most harm. A sympathetic study of the literary achievements and cultural heritages will do good to both. This is possible only through a comparative study which may further strengthen bonds among different cultures.

In a multi-lingual society and a poly – lingual world comparative study is a *sine qua non.* Comparative study of different poets and

---

11. "On the Sublime" in D.K. Chopra, ed., *Literary Criticism: An Anthology* (Meerut: Loyal Book Depot, 1974), pp. 136-37.
12. Guy Amirthanayagam, ed *Writers in East-West Encounter: New Cultural Bearings* (London: The Macmillan Press, 1982), p. x.

writers, of the same age or of two different ages, of the same continent or of different ones, of the same faith and religion or of different faiths and practices, will enable us to appreciate how they react to the conditions around them, how they present the world in which they live and, most important of all, how they give expression to the permanent passions of mankind, the eternal subjects of fine arts all through the ages and all over the world. It is keeping in view these facts that I take up a comparative study of an English poet and an Urdu poet.

The Institute of Historical Studies, Calcutta asked me a few years back to write articles on Urdu poets and litterateurs for the Supplementary Dictionary of National Biography. I wrote twenty articles on, *inter alia*, jigar Moradabadi, Shakil Badauni, Majrooh Sultanpuri, Qurratul Ain Hyder, Saghar Nizami, Hayatullah Ansari, Kaifi Azmi and Sardar Jafri. The idea to make a comparative study of an eminent Urdu poet and an equally eminent English poet came to me while researching for the Supplementary DNB. Thus germinated the idea of a comparative study of John Keats and Mi rza Ghalib.

Keats, the great romantic poet of the younger generation and Mirza Ghalib, the great Ghazal- writer of Urdu literature apparently do not appear to be going together for long. Many Urdu critics in India have already compared the art and thought of Ghalib with that of many a western poet, philosopher and writer. It may appear queer to certain scholars like professor Ansari[13] because of the rich back ground in social, political and literary tradition available to the writers of the west which is denied to the Urdu poets. Literature is, indeed, a matter of tradition and literary tradition in the West may be quite different from the one in the East. What is being established these days is a literary and cultural synthesis of mankind into a wider literature and culture of the world. From this point of view poets and writers of different ages, races and nations constitute one single community and, I believe that such a study, in the Arnoldian phrases,

---

13. *Vide supra*.

will be capable of higher uses. It is in these studies that modern world, torn by struggle and strife, hatred and discrimination, greed and violence, will find a 'consolation and stay.' Urdu lovers may not approve of a comparison between Ghalib the mature man, profound thinker and poetic genius, and Keats, just a romantic youngster, I have already found Ghalib being compared with many a poet and philosopher.

Dr. Abdul Rahman Bijnori in his scholarly study of Ghalib, *Mahasin kalam-e-Ghalib,* brought out the salient charecterstics of the art and thought of Ghalib.[14] In the beginning he did not like the idea of Ghalib being compared with Shakespeare, Wordsworth and Tennyson by the English knowing students of India.[15] He pointed out that Salahuddin Khudabakash compared Ghalib with Hein Sich Heine, a German poet who sang of love in a very musical and melancholy tone but, Dr.Bijnori pointed out,Ghalib carries the whole world with him: he has a wider vision.[16] It was Iqbal who compared Ghalib with Goethe, the famous poet of Germany. Dr Bijnori says that Ghalib and Goethe present the ultimate in human imagination and the last word in poetry. The works of Goethe brought name and fame to him as well to his country and that is what the works of Ghalib are doing now.[17]

The two are the emperors in the domain of poetry and interpret civilization, culture, education, nature- almost every aspect of human life. There are many things in *Faust* which defy interpretation and analysis and such is the case with many couplets of Ghalib. The readers are simply wonderstruck at the energy, imaginative penetration, creative faculty and the power of expression of the Urdu poet. It is the element of philosophy in the two which stirs our sense of wonder and appreciation. Philosophy is not just an abstract speculation, it is also a thoughtful presentation of the reality of life

14. Abdul Rahman Bijnori, *Muhasin Kalam-e-Ghalib* (New Delhi: Anjuman Taraqqi-e-Urdu, 1983).
15. *Ibid.*, p. 8.
16. *Ibid.*
17. *Ibid*, p. 9.

and that is what Keats too did. Keats is nothing, it has been well said, if not a poet of thought. According to Bijnori, Ghalib is not satisfied like Saadi and Wordsworth with the beauty of spring and autumn, forests and wells, mountains and fountains. Ghalib is on the bank of the river or on the foot of the hill wherefrom he observes the hustle and bustle of human activity and the interplay of passions. From time to time Dr. Bijnori picks up stray sentences from Kant, Paul Verlaine and Baudelaire and finds similarities in Ghalib. Sometimes he finds close relationship between Mallarme and Ghalib on the one hand and Ghalib and Alfred Mombert on the other.[18] While talking of the philosophy of Ghalib, he finds parallel in Spinoza, Hegel, Berkley and Fichte.[19] There are just references in Bijnori, no detailed study. He seems to raise Ghalib sky high in comparison with the poets and philosophers of the West without making a close or comprehensive study.

Ram Babu Saxena, in his *History of Urdu Literature* pointed out that the delicate thought and noble expressions in the early works of Ghalib resemble the European poets of the Middle Ages known as the school men, as there is much borrowing from the Persian masters. Saxena then compared Ghalib with Robert Browning who analysed the inner working of the heart and soul of his characters. He compared him with Heine also as the latter has a rich element of melancholy and dejection. Comparing Ghalib with Goethe, he says that Ghalib has all the qualities which Goethe possessed. Then unconsciously, Saxena adds 'beauty is truth and truth is beauty.' He quotes Keats unawares and makes no mention of him.[20] Sayyed Mahmood had already noted that "Ghalib is a combination of the flight of Shelley, ludicity of Kearts, insight of Goethe, nobility of

18. Abdul Rahman Bijnori, *Muhasin Kalam-e-Ghalib* , p.46
19. *Ibid.*, p.55
20. RB Saxena, *History of Urdu Literature*, Mirza Mohammad Askari, tr. (Lucknow: Munshi Nawal Kishore, 1929) p.395-96

thought of Schiller, imagination of Thompson, melancholy of Momin, humour of Sauda and simplicity of Mir."[21]

Sayyad Fayyaz Mahmood analysed the native talents of Ghalib and said that, it is strange that neither Hali, nor any other biographer of Ghalib has reported any spells of introspection, or any meditative tendencies in him, but though Mirza was a pronounced extrovert, he must have had a very observant mind. His sense perceptions were keen; he appears to have been sensitive to light and fire, to colour and fragrance, but from any standard, the spontaneous combustion of feeling and thought, which we are going to observe in his early verse, in which a keen and very percipient mind upreaches towards Reality, is a rare phenomenon. It has happened, perhaps, only in the case of John Keats in poetry and Mozrat in music.[22]

Aziz Hasan in his study of Ghalib [23] found parallels of Ghalib in Keats (p.40), Victor Hugo (42), Sir Walter Scott(p.52) Alexander Pope (pp.11,18), Cowper (p.119), Coleridge (P.120) and Shakespeare (pp. 38,127,158) and others. But then his study too gives us only passing references and there is no systematic effort on his part to compare Ghalib with a particular poet. He studies Ghalib's poetic art and quotes parallels from the Western poets. Majnoon Gorakhpuri studied *Hero and Hero worship* of Carlyle and found that Ghalib was one of the Heroes of the world because of his poetic qualities.[24] He does not approve much of Dr. Abdul Rahman Bijnori as there is

---

21. Quoted by Sayed Salahuddin Abdul Rehman in *Ghalib Madah-o-Qadah ki roshni mein*, Dr Yusuf Husain Khan, ed. International Ghalib Seminar (New Delhi: Sad Salah Yadgaar Ghalib Committee, 1969), p. 305.
22. Sayyed Fayyaz Mahmood, *Ghalib: A Critical Introduction* (Lahore: University of the Punjab, 1969), pp. 168-69.
23. Mohammad Aziz Hasan, *Tasawwrat-e-Ghalib* (New Delhi: Ghalib Academi, 1987).
24. Majnoon Gorakhpuri, *Ghalib: Shakhsh aur Shair* (Aligarh: Educational Book House, 1976), p. 64.

much exaggeration in him. [25] He admits that while studing a great work of a great person, ideas and thoughts of other writers and thinkers of eminence naturally come to our mind. (Ibid). Dr. Yusuf Husain Khan compared Ghalib's art of condensing thought into words with Shakespeare's 'brevity'.[26]

Having gone through a score of books on Ghalib I found that he remains supreme in the domain of Urdu literature. His predecessors, contemporaries and successors cannot be compared with him if we take into account every aspect of his art and thought. By virtue of his thought and expression and consequently his appeal to readers, Ghalib will always be read and admired by those who know Urdu. Further, I noted that many Urdu critics compared the matter and manner of Ghalib with many a Western man of letters and brought out some revealing, rather fascinating parallels. I found that no Urdu critic has made a systematic study of Ghalib with reference to any Western counterpart. There are some pleasing but only passing references. While studying Keats I found in him a picture of pain, misery and sufferings, privations and aspirations and a rich thoughtfulness along with a criticism of life, love of beauty and lucidity of expression and these qualities I noted are there in abundance in Ghalib. They go together and cover up quite a long span of art and thought but then the life –span of the English poet was cut short in his twenty sixth year while the Urdu poet lived longer, upto the age of 73 plus to enrich not only Urdu literature but to add much to our understanding of the world, of the working of the human mind, its frustrations, its struggles, its ambitions and aspirations. The two poets created a world of beauty out of this world of misery, suffering and deprivation and left for the generations to come works of art which will sustain them, console them, inspire them and tease them out of thought.

While embarking on a comparative study of Keats and Ghalib I know I am taking a risky path because no one at home or abroad

25. *Ibid*, p. 65.

26. Yusuf Husain Khan, *Ghalib aur Ahang-e-Ghalib* (New Delhi: Ghalib Academy, 1971), p. 263.

has attempted a comprehensive comparative study of Ghalib with any other poet of the West. I don't have the sense of being a pioneer in an unknown country or of having embarked on a voyage of discovery but I know that my task is one of research and investigation, of comparison and contrast and, I hope, will add much to the understanding and appreciation of both Ghalib and Keats. It will heighten aesthetic pleasure and help readers find new meanings in the writings of the two poets.

I tried to contact some Urdu scholars like Malik Ram, an eminent Urdu scholar, but he pooh – poohed at my idea and wrote to me that Keats is a child before Ghalib and that the comparison will not hold good.[27] Dr. Zoe Ansari of Bombay University, an eminent scholar of Urdu and critic of Ghalib, encouraged me, he appreciated the idea of this comparative study and sent me a comprehensive list of books on Ghalib.[28] Dr. Sayyed Qazi Abdul Sattar, Chairman and Professor, Department of Urdu, Aligarh Muslim University, Aligarh was much pleased with the idea and gave me certain guidelines for my study. I was equally encouraged by Professor Harish Raizada, Retired Professor, Department of English, Aligarh Muslim University, Aligarh. The Research Degree Committee of Agra University, Agra was equally encouraging and approved of the outlines of my project.

Coming closer to Ghalib and Keats, I found that the two great poets explore the permanent passions and 'Anthropological invariables' and quite often tread the same ground, think the same thoughts, suffer the same miseries and misfortunes and seek shelter in almost a similar world of Beauty. They provide solace and comfort to the generation of people who live amid different sorrows and seek shelter and find it only in the world of beauty, the world of art and the world of thought. They were born poets: poetry was in their blood. They took to their divinely ordained task irrespective of failure and frustrations, unfavorable reviews and comments and pecuniary

---

27. Malik Ram, see his letter, Appendix I

28. Dr. Zoe Ansari, see his letter Appendix II.

problems. The industrial and the French revolutions did not sway Keats but the social and political upheavals in India gave an intensity and poignancy to the art and thought for Ghalib which raises him above Keats. The two poets had their rich share of poverty and privations but that resulted only in the flowering of their poetic geniuses. The two looked to the past, their ancestors in the domain of art and beauty but exhibited a freshness and originality of their own. They did not blindly adhere to tradition: they honoured and respected traditions but chalked out a way of their own. Both learnt from their classics, remained ever indebted to them, frankly confessed the debt and yet had a way of their own, created a world of their own and peopled it with their branched thoughts and sublime imaginings.

Keats had a very short span of life: twenty five years, four months and twenty two days. Ghalib lived longer. He definitely suffered longer at the hands of time. As a result his experiences, observations, intellectual moorings and questioning spirit have a deeper probe and wider sweep.

Keats wrote poems, Sonnets, Odes and few longer poems like The Eve of St. Agnes, Endymion and the two Hyperions. Ghalib wrote Ghazals, Masnavis and Qasidas long narrative poems in praise of some lord, prince, King or queen. Keats, as Garrod noted, found his true genius in Odes. So did Ghalib find his true genius in Ghazals. The Odes of Keats have been studied separately as well as a single composition in various facets. There is a close "connection of thought" in the Odes as noted by Garrod [29] and Halloway.[30] This is said of the ghazals of Ghalib also. Every couplet is a unity and complete in itself but the whole ghazal also has an organic unity. It is the gradual development of thought that bewitches the readers, enlightens the scholars and puzzles the critics.

---

29. HW Garrod, *Keats* (London: Oxford University Press, 1950) p. 94.
30. John Halloway, "The Odes of Keats, in Judith O' Neill, ed. *Critics on Keats* (London: George Allen and Unwin, 1967), p. 59.

The two poets wrote letters – a unique treasure in the history of their respective literatures. The letters may be read for sheer pleasure as well as for biographical information and critical acumen of the writers. Keats does not tell us much of the socio-political syndrome while Ghalib does and touches on some vital issues of life and death, of appreciation in literature, poetic faculty and literary excellence of a work of art.

Both were men of ideas and had something original, vital and powerful to say about life and love, truth and beauty, time and death. The two poets put before us a *magnum opus* that will ever fascinate, transport and tease us out of thought. Keats discovered the secret of beauty and truth through his own sufferings. His words find a path through the sad heart of mankind and sprout there. Ghalib had to suffer and much more than that he saw sufferings around him during the 1857 imbroglio and presented a picture of pain and suffering which will ever find an echo in every heart. Ghalib saw life as a vale of unending tears and noted that the poor candle must burn and melt the whole night to remove the darkness around and spread light all around – that is what suffering does. That is what Ghalib did.

They are neither philosophers nor moralists, nor are they preachers. They definitely hate poetry that has a palpable design on us. They led neither a religious and pious life nor did advocate such but one cannot find better philosophy, better morality, more ethical values than in the works of Ghalib and Keats. 'Taste is the only morality', said Ruskin and Ghalib and Keats were poets of taste and that too of a higher, moral and universal order. They were humanitarians and preached human values through aesthetic venture and human relationship.

2

THE PERSONAL NOTE

John Keats was born on the 31st of October 1795 at Finsbury in the North-eastern London. His parents provided horses for hire and possibly even for coaches. The family was not a Londoner by origin. The father Thomas Keats had come as a boy from Cornwall near Land's End. Much is not known about the ancestors of Keats. In 1805, the father died of an accident and the same year his mother remarried. John Keats, along with his two brothers and a sister, moved to the home of their grand-parents, John and Alice Jennings at Enfield. The mother of Keats died from tuberculosis in 1810. Alice Jennings appointed guardians for the Keats children. At an early age John Keats, the elder brother, is left an orphan and so are his brothers and sister. It is the grand-mother who looks after the children but then she too died in 1814 when our poet was nineteen. He had already been sent to Thomas Hammond, a surgeon and apothecary of Edmonton. The younger brother George was in the counting house of the guardian Richard Abbey where Tom the youngest joined him soon. John was an apprentice from 1811 to 1815 and by mid July 1816, he qualified at Apothecaries Hall.[1]

---

1. Walter Jackson Bate, *John Keats* (New York: Oxford University Press, 1966), p. 43.

The grandfather of Keats, John Jennings, had a flourishing business at the Swan and Hoop and Thomas Keats, the son-in-law as 'khana-damaad'[2] took over the business as the parents-in-law left for a nearby village. The Keats children passed their early life in the 'nani haal'[3]—We will note almost similar facts in the life of Mirza Ghalib. The Keats children will fight for long and will suffer much on account of the Jennings will which allowed them a satisfactory amount for maintenance when they came to maturity. The will was very obscure. John Keats and Tom could not get much of their share of property. George and Fanny Keats were able to get only a part when the other two brothers were already dead.

Keats started his attempts at writing poems sometime in 1814 when "Imitation of Spencer" came out. His friend Charles Brown noted "Though born to be a poet he was ignorant of his birthright until he had completed his eighteenth year.... It was *The Faery Queen* that awakened his genius... enamoured of the stanza, he attempted to imitate it and succeeded.[4] The same year he rejoiced at the happy end of war with France in a sonnet entitled "On Peace". It is an irregular Shakespearen sonnet and extols peace and freedom. The thoughts of Keats have already started taking shape:

O Europe! Let not sceptred tyrants see
That thou must shelter in thy former state;
Keep thy chains burst, and boldly say thou art free;
Give thy king's law- leave not uncurbed the great.
So with the honours past thou 'lt win thy happier fate.[5]

---

2. The son-in-law who stays put with the parents-in-law.
3. The household of the grand-parents (maternal).
4. Quoted by Miriam Allott, ed., *Keats: The Complete Poems* (London: Longman, 1980), p.3.
5. *Ibid.*, p. 6. All references from the text of the poems of Keats are from Miriam Allott's edition and the page number will be given immediately after the text.

The same year we find one more interesting poem which indicates that the young apothecary apprentice is no more interested in surgery and ointments. The poem beginning with "Fill for me a brimming bowl" promises that the young poet will go to higher realms of art and thoughts. The poem is written at the sight of an unknown woman whose beauty left a mark on the young mind of Keats. Turning to Ghalib we note that unlike Keats, he came of a family of warriors who came to India in the days of Emperor Shah Jahan, the builder of the Taj Mahal, and frequently shifted from one court to another winning one battle after the other and thus established as feudal lords commanding a huge cavalry. Ghalib was always proud of the fact that his ancestors wielded the sword effectively and earned name in the war annals. Mirza Abdullah Beg, the father of Mirza Ghalib, married Izzatunnisa, a daughter of Mirza Ghulam Husain khan, an army officer of Agra. He was also a 'khana – damaad' like the father of Keats and lived at Agra wherefrom he was called to military campaigns. Ghalib (born 27th December 1797) was only five when his father died in a military campaign fighting for the potentate of Alwar in 1802. Nasrullah Beg khan, the younger brother of his father, who ruled over Agra on behalf of the Marathas became his guardian. In 1803, he surrendered the Agra Fort to Lord Lake and then died in 1806. Thus our Ghalib is also an orphan and so are his brother and sister. The descendants of Nasrullah Beg khan used to get a pension from the British government. Ghalib started versifying at quite an early age. The latest researches show that his earliest poem was on a kite which he wrote at Agra.[6] It was sometimes in 1807 when he was just a child of nine. There is a Persian couplet at the end of the poem suggesting that Ghalib had already started his studies into Persian poetry. For some time Ghalib studied at the school of Maulvi Mohammad Muazzam at Agra. Quite possibly he studied Persian grammar and literature here. Ghalib adopted the pen-name 'Asad' and started writing poems. These days he was brought into the presence of Mir Taqi Mir, the grand old Urdu poet,

---

6. Kalidas Gupta Raza, ed., *Diwan-e-Ghalib kamil: Tarikhi tartib se* (Bombay: Sakar publishers, 1988), p. 28.

who, according to khwaja Altaf Husain Haali,[7] pointed out, "If this boy gets a good teacher, he will become a great poet otherwise he will spoil himself. "

When Ghalib was fourteen, he came into contact with a zorostrian of the name of Hermuz who later on became a Muslim and changed his name to Abdul Samad. He stayed at Agra for a couple of years and instructed Ghalib into Persian language and literature. Ram Babu Saxena noted that "it is due to the efforts of Abdul Samad, who was a great scholar of Persian language and literature, that Ghalib became a great master in the use of Persian idiom."[8]

Haali, the disciple and first biographer of Ghalib, and Malik Ram,[9] an eminent Ghalib scholar of today, assert and establish the presence of Abdul Samad with Ghalib at Agra. Abdul Samad was a past-master in the use of Persian language. The chaste, pious and idiomatic Persian that Ghalib wrote came to him through the efforts of this man. Some critics point out that there was no man like Abdul Samad: Ghalib simply concocted a tale to assert his superiority to the contemporary poets and writers. Both Haali[10] and Ghalib[11] make a clear mention of Abdul Samad and leave little scope for speculation.

Umrao Begum, the eleven year old bride of thirteen year old Ghalib, was the daughter of Ilahi Bukhsh Khan Maroof, an eminent lord and an equally eminent poet. It was in 1812-13 that Ghalib shifted to Delhi, started attending poetical gatherings and after struggling hard became a force to reckon with.

---

7. Khwaja Altaf Husain Haali, *Yadgar-e-Ghalib* (Lucknow: Uttar Pradesh Academy, 1982), p. 98.
8. Ram Babu Saxena, *History of Urdu Literature*, translated into Urdu by Mirza Mohammad Askari (Lucknow: Nawal Kishore, n.d.), p. 376.
9. Malik Ram, *fasana-e-Ghalib*, (New Delhi: Maktaba Jamia, 1997), pp. 13 & 52-77.
10. *Yadgar-e-Ghalib*, p.13.
11. Sheikh Mohammad Ikram, *Ghalib Namah*, (Lucknow: Ehsan Book Depot, n.d.) p. 26.

In 1826, Ghalib went to Calcutta for the release of his pension which had been stopped due to certain political causes. There he became a victim of literary controversy since he could not admit the superiority of any one in the sphere of Persian language and literature. He cut a sorry figure in literary squabbles and had to return empty-handed also. In Delhi, life was not a pleasant affair for him. He used to get some money from his grand-mother at Agra, some pension from Loharu and then he started getting one hundred rupees from the Nawab of Rampur also. His wife was a pious and God - fearing woman. One after the other she gave birth to seven children but none survived. Mirza Ghalib was always hard- pressed because of his princely extravagant habits. He became tutor to Bahadur Shah Zafar, the last Mughal emperor, when Zauq expired in 1854 and now he had free access to the royal court.[12] The poetical gatherings or 'Mushairas' were frequently held in the court and Ghalib was there to recite his Ghazal. In the early gatherings, his verses were much denounced. At times he was condemned for his composite words and Persianised expression which he had derived from Bedil, an eminent Persians poet. The listeners and the poets present there could make neither head nor tail of his highly-worded couplets. Ghalib was carried away by the charm, meaningfulness and diction of Bedil whom he praised in many a couplet. Bedil's style is intricate, elaborate and knotty: there are metaphysical nuances which defy understanding but then if we take some pains, we will find affluent meaning and rich suggestions there. It is only in the early phase that Ghalib is 'Bedilian' and loads every rift with an excess of ore but by and by he takes to his Urdu couplets seriously and came to develop a syntax and style of his own unmatched by any other Urdu poet.

His early listeners could not find any meaning in his intricate coinage, persianised vocabulary, peculiar expression and somewhat far-fetched conceit. The poet with all his manliness about him could valiantly retort:

---

12. Pavan K. Verma, *Ghalib: The Man, The Times* (New Delhi: Penguin Books, 1989), p. 135.

Na sataesh ki tamanna, na sile ke parwah,

Na sahi gar mere asha'ar mein maini na sahi.

I aspire for no praise and care for no reward;

If my couplets are meaningless, be it so.

He did not care for the adverse comments on his verses. It is sometimes during 1816-1820 that Ghalib wrote a number of Urdu Ghazals and had a full 'diwan' to his credit.

We may shift our attention to John Keats during the years when he had already embarked on a poetical career neglecting all his medical studies. The first volume of his poems came out in 1817 which was reviewed quite sympathetically in the *champion* of March 9, 1817[13] but the *Eclectic Review* of September1817, *Edinburgh Magazine* of October 1817 and the *Blackwood's Magazine* brought out harsh reviews on the early poems and *Endymion* of Keats. The *Blackwood's* made some highly unbecoming observations about the young poet. He is presented as suffering from *Metromonie*—the madness of versification.

The subject matter, the diction and expression, every thing was condemned: "It is better and a wiser thing to be a starved apothecary than a starved poet; so back to the shop Mr. John, back to 'plasters, pills, and ointment boxes,' & c. But for heaven's sake, young Sangrado, be a little more sparing of extenuative and soporifics in your practice than you have been in your poetry."[14] Keats was naturally unhappy with these scathing comments but he took all these assaults valiantly and in one of his letters addressed to his publisher James Augustus Hessey, he wrote,

> Praise or blame has but a momentary effect on the man whose love of beauty in the abstract makes him a severe critic on his own works. My own domestic criticism has given me pain without comparison beyond what Blackwood or the Quarterly would

---

13. John Haydon, ed., *Romantic Bards and British Reviewers* (London: Routledge and Kegan Paul, 1971), p.297.

14. *Ibid.*, p.322-23.

> possibly inflict, and also when I feel I am right, no external praise can give me such a glow as my own solitary reperception and ratification of what is fine.[15]

It was the popular idea about Ghalib that his early efforts were meaningless and carried nothing but a jumble of words and phrases brought in the from obscure recesses of literature. The oft-quoted quatrain about him is:

> *Agar apna kaha yeh aap hi samajhe to kiya samjhe,*
>
> *Maza kahne ka jab hei ek kahe aur dusra samjhe;*
>
> *Kalaam-e-Mir samjhe aur zubaan-e-Meerza samjhe*,
>
> Magar apna kaha yeh aap samjhein ya khuda samjhe.

If you alone understand what you say, it's nothing to us. Better it is that one says and the other one understands.

We understand the poems of Mir Taqi Mir and the language of Mirza Sauda but what he says he alone understands or God does;[16]

The early efforts of both the poets had almost a similar share of condemnation at the hands of their readers and listeners. Both the poets put a good fight. Ghalib swallowed it hard but he would never compromise. He had his own authority in the classical Persian literature and could easily stand by himself. His manliness, vast study and strenuous efforts stood him in good stead. So it was with Keats. The young poet would never compromise. Richard Abbey, the guardian of Keats, reacted sharply to his poems. The account is recorded by John Taylor:

> I took it and said I would look at it because it was his writing, otherwise I should not have troubled my Head with any such thing—when we next met I said well John I have read your

---

15. Maurice Buxton Forman, ed., *the Letters of John Keats* (London: Oxford University Press, 1952), p.221.
16. All translations from Urdu or Persian are by me, if not otherwise mentioned.

> Book, and it reminds me of the Quaker's Horse which was hard to catch, and good for nothing when he was caught—so your Book is hard to understand and good for nothing when it is understood. Do you know says the old man, I don't think he ever forgave me for uttering this opinion, which however was the truth.[17]

In English literature we do not have a tradition of having a mentor or 'ustaad' to instruct one in the art of versification. So there was no guide, superficially speaking, before Keats to whom he could put his efforts and get his pieces corrected or improved upon but as we noted above, he was the best judge of his own works.

He was carried away by the sweetness and imagery of Spenser and thrilled to great delight by Champman's Homer. He exhibited his reverence for the Greek master and the unbounded joy that he felt while reading the great epics. Above all, there was a seven-volume Shakespeare with him, a permanent companion, mentor, guide and philosopher which he always carried with him as a 'talisman or charm'. He learned much from Spenser, Shakespeare and Milton but he alone was the judge of his works.

John Keats had no mentor but he had the 'presiding genius' of Shakespeare with him. We know he never showed his verses to anyone for correction. He did it himself because the genius of poetry was in him as he wrote to Hessey when there was an adverse comment on his *Endymion*, "I will write independently.—I have written independently *without judgment*.—I may write independently, and *with judgment* hereafter. The genius of poetry must workout its own salvation in a man: It cannot be matured by law and percept, but by sensation and watchfulness in itself. That which is creative must create itself —."[18]

It may be safely affirmed that Ghalib never showed his verses to any 'ustaad' for correction or improvement. Haali quotes Ghalib

---

17. Quoted by Walter Jackson Bate, *John Keats*, and p.118.

18. *The Letters of John Keats*, p. 221

saying that' he was instructed by none but God.'[19] the classical Persian poets were very dear to Ghalib and he had an inherent love for Persian language and literature. He used to say that the best of his work was in Persian:

Farsi been ta ba beeni naqsh ha-e-rang rang,

Dar quzar az rekhte ki be rang-e-man ast.

See my Persian couplets if you want to see the colourful variety of my work. Leave Urdu aside: it doesn't have my true colour.

The fact is that Ghalib lives in India as an Urdu poet though he is great in his Persian ghazals also. His popularity in India and greatness in Urdu depends on, and is established by, his Urdu Ghazals.

He loved Mir Taqi Mir and appreciated his works for their simplicity and a genuine display of emotion therein. First he followed the diction of Bedil, a Persian poet of the Mughal court era and then walked into the footsteps of Urfi and Naziri.[20] Ghalib did not attach much importance to the Persian scholars of India since he was well-founded on the best of Persian poets whose works he, to borrow the words of Bacon,' chewed' and digested' to such an extent that he became an adept in the use of Persian idiom and soon came to develop an acumen of writing Persian verse and prose unmatched by any poet in India before or after him.

Even in his own day Persian had started showing signs of decline. On the one hand, English, the language of the ruling class after 1857, was coming up and, on the other, Urdu, the language of the masses, was acquiring a popular character. Urdu verses of Ghalib came to acquire a freshness and refinement so much so that Ghalib himself was soon carried away by his own effortless efforts in Urdu:

Jo yeh kahe ki rekhta kyonki ho rashk-e-farsi,

Gufta-e-Ghalib ek bar padhke use suna ki yoon!

---

19. *Yadgar-e-Ghalib*, p.13.

20. Sheikh Mohammad Ikram , *Ghalib Namah*, p.52.

If some one says how Urdu can compete with Persian, read him out a verse of Ghalib and say 'like this'.

Marriage and Love

What has conjugal bliss to do with creative writing? There will always be two or more opinions on this issue. We are almost sure that it had nothing to do with Shakespeare and in the case of Milton, the absence of conjugal bliss provided him with the adventures of mind and soul. In our own century Scott Fitzgerland, an American novelist and D.H.Lawrence, the British one, were greatly inspired and encouraged by their respective spouses. Generally speaking, a happy married life leads to luxuries and comforts and finally to a host of children and grand-children. Keats had nothing of the conjugal bliss in his life and Ghalib was married at an early age when he did not know what marriage meant. Both the poets were deprived of a happy family life and may be said to be belonging to almost broken homes.

The British society allowed, as it does now in a freer way, the free mixing of boys and girls. Keats might have got many a chance to be quite close to the members of the opposite sex. What did he feel? In a letter to Bailey, he wrote in July 1818, "when among Men I have no evil thoughts, no malice, no spleen—I feel free to speak or to be silent—I can listen and from every one I can learn—my hands are in my pockets I am free from all suspicion and comfortable. When I am among women I have evil thoughts, malice spleen—I cannot speak or be silent – I am full of suspicions and therefore listen to nothing – I am in hurry to be gone."[21] In December the same year he wrote to George and Georgiana Keats that he had been once delighted by Mrs. Tighe and Beattie.[22] We then read that he soon almost falls in love with Jane Cox who had rich eastern look, fine eyes and manner. Her beauty haunted him only for a couple of days and then he came into contact with Mrs. Isabella Jones.[23] He flirted with her timidity and was much impressed with

21. *The Letters of John Keats*, p.191.
22. *Ibid.*, p.258.
23. Walter Jackson Bate, p. 382.

her beauty and good manners. He went to her house where she behaved in the kindest manner and even sent some game for Tom. He was in close touch with her for about four months. It was she who suggested the legend of the Eve of St. Anges as a subject for romance.

The third woman and, indeed, the most important one is Fanny Brawne, the beloved of Keats. It is in his December 1818 letter that we first read of a daughter of Mrs. Brawne, "Mrs. Brawne who took Brown's house for the summer, still resides in Hampstead – she is very nice woman – and her daughter senior is I think beautiful and elegent, graceful, silly, fashionable and strange we have a little tiff now and then – and she behaves a little better, or I must have sheered off – " [24] She had her interests in clothes and dances and belonged to a richer family. His love letters to Fanny Brawne began in 1819 and continued till the last year of his life.

He could not even think of marriage because of Tom's illness and then his death, departure of his brother George and his wife to America and his own financial burdens. But then the affair had already started and the girl was very much there before him. She was energetic, knew several languages of the continent and loved a fashionable life. "Blue eyed, she would select ribbons for her brown hair that would match her eyes; and she carefully curled her hair everyday. She not only studied the colours and textures of cloth and every change in design of dress, but also had begun to pride herself on her knowledge of historical costume."[25]

The Victorian idea was very unkind towards Fanny Brawne. By that time most of her letters addressed to Keats and his sister were neither traced nor studied. Moreover, it is difficult to judge the feelings of a woman if she marries a person other than the one she loved. Amy Lowell was the first biographer to come to know of the letters of Fanny Keats, the sister of our poet and after reading these she concluded that Keats was not at all killed by the unkind beloved,

---

24. *The Letters of John Keats*, p248.

25. Walter Jackson Bate, p.428.

rather a happy relationship went on between the two. Miss Lowell opined that Fanny and Keats became engaged at Christmas 1818.[26] The letters of Fanny Brawne reveal that the engagement took place sometimes after September 1819. Walter Jackson Bate surmises that the engagement was made sometimes between October 1819 and January 1820.[27] There is no indication of the engagement in the letters of John Keats. Keats was not in a position to marry since he knew himself and the things around him fairly well. "I must work. I must read. I must write ". That is what he should do before he could think of any matrimonial alliance.

The letters of Keats, Fanny Keats and Fanny Brawne indicate that the relations between Keats and his beloved were cordial. Now we know it for certain that they were engaged, evidently to get married at some happy future date.

We know Keats had his own worries around him and the words of Fanny proved a balm and soothed his wounded sprit. In his very first letter of July 1,1919 we find Keats complaining against the miseries of life as well as her own playfulness and imploring her to "write immediately and do all you can to console me in it –make it rich as a draught of poppies to intoxicate me—write the softest words and kiss them that I may at least touch my lips where yours have been. For myself I know not how to express my devotion to so fair a form...: I want a brighter word than bright, fairer word than fair. I almost wish we were butterflies and lived but three summer days—three such days with you I could fill with more delight than fifty common years could ever contain."[28]

The happy correspondence continued up to August 1820 when the disease took a fatal turn and he could no longer bring himself to write to her. He is in fever; there is an easy spirit, an unguessed faith which spread a veil between the two. Consumption was in the

---

26. Amy Lowell, *John Keats* (London: Jonathan Cape, 1925), vol .II, pp.148-49.

27. Walter Jackson Bate, p.430.

28. *The Letters of John Keats*, p.352

family and there was no escape. There is still firmness and a resolve in him and a powerful manliness which enabled him to sustain himself all the time. These are the times when his poetic faculty is at its best and then comes the illness with a mighty blow.

With his medical knowledge about him, he knew what was happening to him . On February 3, 1820 he happened to sit on the top of the coach in order to save money. He entered his house at eleven in the night and spat blood. He knew it was arterial blood and it was his death warrant. Fanny Brawne and her mother did all they could. He was sent to Rome so that he might recover in a warmer climate and it was understood that on his healthy return, they would be married. The expected did not happen.

Ghalib had a long married life—he was married at the age of thirteen and his wife survived him by one full year. It was a conjugal life alright but was there any conjugal bliss in it? It is difficult to say. The marriage was an arranged one and he had no say of his own. In our country where women were strictly confined to separate quarters, we cannot imagine Ghalib having access to women. For Muslim women communication with the outside world was possible only through servants. The letters of Ghalib reveal some interesting details about his married life and his relations with a couple of women outside wedlock. Ghalib often makes clear references to his unhappy life. It was like an 'imprisonment' to him. The second wife of Umrao Singh, a common friend of Ghalib and Munshi Har Gopal Tufta, died and Ghalib wrote to Tufta that "Umrao Singh was lucky that he had been liberated twice from the imprisonment while he himself (Ghalib) had been hanging on the gallows for the last fifty-one years. The gallows did not break nor did he die."[29]

Ghalib seems to be highly critical of his married life. We note frequent satiric comments against the poor wife. Once he went to see a house since he had no house of his own and then his wife went to approve of the house. She came to know that it was a

29. *Yadgar-e-Ghalib*, p. 87.

haunted place that is, inhabited by evil spirits. She told it to her husband. "As if there were any greater evil spirits than the wife:" Ghalib quipped.[30]

Ghalib knew that he was poor and had practically no resources. At times he tried to be kind to his wife. Mostly he spent his time in the room away from the ladies quarters. There the friends and disciples came and talked of life and literature. The wife had nothing to do with the literary life of the poet. She was a pious lady, observed fasts and offered 'Namaaz' very regularly. Ghalib, on the other hand, was given to drinking and wine is strictly prohibited in Islam. We also find that his eating utensils were also kept apart.[31] The pious wife never caused any irritation to the husband. She knew the poor plight he was in and in her own way tried to lessen his sufferings although most of her efforts were confined to the prayer- carpet.

Ghalib had no issue of his own. His wife gave birth to seven children but none survived for more than fifteen months. He then adopted Zainul Abidin, a nephew of his wife. He also died at a young age and Ghalib wrote a painful elegy on his death.

Did Ghalib have a love affair? One or two? In a letter to Mirza Hatim Ali Meher, he described his affairs with a singing girl. He was condoling with him on the death of his wife and brought in his own love story. He wrote that 'he too had killed a singing girl with love, forty or forty-two years back. He still remembered her beauty and the amorous vanities and asserted that he could never forget her death.'[32] Qazi Abdul Sattar has given a romanticized version of this love affair in his novel *Ghalib*.[33] He has given the name Turk Begum to the singing girl. Ghalib wrote a mournful elegy on her death in the from of a Ghazal. The first couplet is:

---

30. *Ibid*.
31. *Yadgar-e-Ghalib*, p. 86.
32. Ale Ahmad Saroor, ed., *Aks-e-Ghalib* (Aligarh: Aligarh Muslim University, 1973), p. 111.
33. Qazi Abdul Sattar, *Ghalib* (Aligarh: Education Book House, 1986), pp. 86-96.

Dard se mere hei tujko beqarari, hai, hai:

Kiya hoi zalim teri qhaflat shoari hai, hai;

You are restless, because of my sorrow;

Alas! O, cruel one, you used to be so indifferent;

Qazi Abdul Sattar is of the opinion that Ghalib had one more love affair and that was with some singing girl of the royal court and she was loved by the king himself. His hypothesis is based on the last couplet of a Persian Ghazal of Ghalib:

Haan, Ghalib-e-Khilwat nasheen, beemi chunaan, aishe chuneen,

Jasoos-e-sultan dar makeen, matloob-e-sultan dar baghal.

O Ghalib, living in solitude, you have sometimes your fears and pleasures sometimes but the spy of the king waits for you, for you have the beloved of the king in your arms.

It is quite probable that not one but several singing and dancing girls loved the young youthful poet, the lusty Mughal. He might have been stealing pleasures and tasting forbidden fruits. He had his hopes and fears. Poor Keats all his life lived on hopes and fears—less hope and more fears. He could little think of sex or married bliss. On November 1, 1820, he wrote to his friend Brown, "I should have had her when I was in health, and I should have remained well."[34] We should also bear in mind what Murry, the great critic of Keats wrote regarding the short stature of our poet," Had Keats been six inches taller, the history of English literature in the nineteenth century might have been differenrt."[35] It is very much like saying "Had Ghalib been blessed with half a dozen kids , the history of Urdu literature in the nineteenth century might have been different." Our poets working under domestic strains of a different nature might

---

34. *The Letters of John Keats*, p. 525.
35. Middleton Murry, *Keats and Shakespeare* (London: Oxford University Press, 1958), p. 95.

have looked at Madam Muse in a different light and consequently the history of their respective literature might have been different. They never strove with life that went awry:

> Had I said that, had I done this,
>
> So might I gain so might I miss.
>
> Might she have loved me? Just as well
>
> She might have hated, who can tell! [36]

As it is, they are what they are. Conditions around them nourished their talents in the cradle of misery.

The Medical Profession

We have noted above that John Keats was apprenticed to a surgeon and he qualified as a surgeon. He was licentiate of the society of Apothecaries. Then the Muse ravished him and he could not resist her charms. We also know that Keats did not practice as a doctor and never wrote prescriptions for any patients or friends. Strangely enough, we find Ghalib writing prescriptions for his friends. How is it possible?

Medicine is a necessary part of the classical Persian system of education. It is still there in institutes like the Darul-uloom, Deoband. It is quite possible that Ghalib, while ravaging through Persian books, gathered enough knowledge of medicine. He could and he did send prescriptions to his friends through his letters. He suggested a prescription to Nawab Kalb-e-Ali Khan of Rampur which proved very effective.[37] Then, some medicines were prescribed for his friend Mirza Abdul Qasim when Ghalib stayed at Calcutta. Qasim thanked him in a poem written in Persian and called Ghalib 'Masih-e-Zaman', the physician of the world.

---

36. Robert Browning, "The Last Ride Together," 11. 39-42.
37. Ghulam Rasool Meher, *Ghalib* (Lahore: Mubarak Ali, 1941), pp. 31-32.

Our poets had gathered as much knowledge of medicine as could have helped them in earning their bread but they were cast in a different mould and had to bow down before the charms of poetry. They took to poetry because their talents found a congenial field wherein their fancy could roam freely into regions far above the ken of mortal millions.

Their knowledge of medicine could never have done so much for the 'poor wounded heart' of mankind as their poems did, do and will go on doing.

Brothers in Suffering

John Keats had two younger brothers and a sister. He being the eldest had to think of them. After his school education George worked in the counting house of Abbey for sometime. Tom also joined him there. The sister Fanny was mostly under the strict control of the guardian. Ghalib had a younger brother and a sister. What strikes us as very poignant is the death of a younger brother in both the cases.

Keats belonged to a family where consumption frequently took tolls. Some of the elder ones had died of this disease. The mother was one. The disease was incurable at that time. Young Tom had caught the infection and was already spitting blood and becoming 'spectre thin' when he was just fourteen. It was George who nursed him but by the spring of 1818 things had taken a turn. He had left the counting house and was planning to go abroad. Tom grew to be eighteen and became more serious. Keats, with his medicine, knew what fate had in store. He was struggling hard with his "Endymion" and the thought of the illness of the brother was too heavy upon him. He was left alone with the consumptive brother as George sailed to America." Of the Keats family there would now be left only a brother of eighteen, who was probably dying and a sister not yet fifteen, of whom Abbey allowed him to see very little."[38] The miseries of the world were already too much with the poet but there was

38. Walter Jackson Bate, p. 318.

George beside him. Now there were the dealings of the world and Keats must buffet all alone. It is at this time that Keats started feeling the miseries of the world pressing hard upon him:

> I have two brothers one is driven by the 'burden of society' to America the other, with an exquisite love of life, is in lingering state. My Love for my Brothers from the early loss of our parents even for earlier misfortunes has grown into an affection 'passing the Love of women'—I have been ill tempered with them, I have vexed them—but the thought of them has always stifled the impression that any woman might otherwise have made upon me. I have a sister too and may not follow them either to America or to the grave—life must be undergone.[39]

Keats had already started having a sore throat. He knew it but he was trying to make as light of his illness as he could. The autumn of 1818 brought more miseries. Throughout the months of August and September, he went out but little because Tom needed constant attention and he himself was not keeping well. It is at this time that Blackwood's brought out a sharp attack on cockney school in general and on Keats in particular. Other magazines also came out with scathing reviews of his poems and added much to the sufferings of the poet. His friend Woodhouse stood by him and wrote that 'the wealth of poetry is inexhaustible'. There was little relief but he never left his poetical ventures: by this time he was busy with his Hyperion.

There was no hope of life in Tom, he was sinking daily. Keats was always with him: he could not write, not even letters to his friends. The brother finally died on December 1, 1818. The gentle, cheerful invalid. "Nothing was left of Keat's small family life. He was altogether adrift."[40] Keats suffered alone and had strengthened himself against the onslaughts of fate.

---

39. *The Letters of John Keats*, p.151, *Shama har rang mein jalti hei sahar hone tak*—the poor candle must willy nilly burn till the day dawns, wrote Ghalib.
40. Walter Jackson Bate, p.386.

Ghalib's brother Mirza Yusuf lived in a separate house in Delhi with his wife and children. He lost his wits when he was thirty and Mirza Ghalib was much worried on this account. Mirza Yusuf got pension from the government equal to what Ghalib got. When the Englishmen invaded Delhi in 1857, they started a reign of terror. The wife and children of Yusuf escaped to Jaipur. The poor invalid was left alone with a couple of old servants. Soldiers entered his house and took away everything but left the inmates alive. In the letters of Ghalib written during these days, we find that Mirza Yusuf died after a five day fit of fever. Ghalib was in a pitiable plight—nobody could come or go this way or that. Army people with shoot-at-sight orders were there every where. There was no cloth for coffin, nobody to give a bath to the deceased, no one to make a grave and none to help in the funeral. Two or more persons could neither stand nor walk together. The neighbors came to his rescue and some soldiers of Maharajah of Patiala helped carry the dead body wrapped in a bed-sheet from his house.[41]

Mirza Yusuf died at the age of sixty. His first thirty years were normal and happy but the next thirty were extremely painful, particularly for the brother. During the 1857 turmoil, his wife and children fled to Jaipur for life but they had no means of sustenance there. The pension of Ghalib had also been stopped and he had no coppers on him to help his niece and nephews and sister-in-law. Ghalib was always worried for his innocent relatives and could never send any money to them. "The niece might well be saying my father died and my uncle followed him to his grave."Ghalib wrote.[42]

The Homeless Soul

Ghalib lived in Delhi for over fifty years and had never a house of his own. He passed all his life in rented houses. For long he was a tenant in the house of Miyan Kale Saheb but then he paid no rent or

41. Gulaam Rasool Meher, p. 36 and Sheik Mohammad Ikram, pp.124-125.
42. Malik Ram, *Fasana-e-Ghalib*, p.47.

Kale Sahib didn't ask for any rent. When he was fed up of one house, he quickly shifted to the other, rent, or no rent: but his creditors were always at his heels. He mostly lived in Qasim Jan street or near the gate of Habash Khan. The house in which he died was near the house of Hakim Mahmood Khan in the Lal Kuan area of old Delhi. It is a matter of shame for Ghalib lovers and Urdu wallahs of India that the house in which Ghalib lived carries no memory of the great poet. Mohammed Ayub wrote in *The Hindustan Times* dated 13.9.89 that many foreigners come to see his ancestors house, 2298 Qasim Jan street in old Delhi. But they are disappointed to see Ghalib's house in a dilapidated condition.

For many years the house was used as a coal and fire-wood depot. Nowadays it is being used as a store selling building-material. It is, indeed, painful to note that nothing is being done about the place. The government has been announcing again and again that it will be taken over by the authorities and developed as a national monument. Surveys have been conducted but nothing has come out of the official exercises. Mr. Ayub appeals," we request the authorities to give immediate attention towards building a befitting memorial for Mirza Ghalib at the site where his crumbling house stands today. If no immediate action is taken Ghalib's house will be no more."[43] it is to be noted that the government has established Ghalib Academy in Basti Hazrat Nizamuddin and a Ghalib Institute in Mata Sundry lane, New Delhi. These two institutes publish and propagate the works of Mirza Ghalib and encourage research through seminars and symposia.

The story is a bit similar in the case of the younger poet who also had no house of his own. After the second marriage of his mother he had to shift to London where he lived in the Hampstead Garden as a tenant of his friend Brown. His Biographers point out that he was not in a position to pay his rents. He too had kind friends who never insisted on the payment of rent. Keats like Ghalib died in a rented house in Rome. The happy aspect in the western

---

43. The Hindustan Times, 13.9.1989.

story is that the Municipal authorities acquired both the places and developed them into Memorials of their poet. In Hampsteal we have Keats Memorial House where there is a huge collection of literature about Keats and a journal is also being brought out from the same place.[44] In Rome, the building in which Keats breathed his last is now a great memorial worthy of John Keats, the poet who lived, suffered and died there.[45]

Searching for a Job

Of Keats we know that he was a qualified doctor and could take up some job or start his own practice anywhere. We also know that he didn't earn any money through his knowledge of medicine. There is no record to show that he was offered any job by any individual or hospital. That is , throughout his life he did not earn his livelihood except by the power of his pen and that was not much.

Of Ghalib we know that he never worked for his bread. He lived on the family pension. We also know that he was not trained for any trade or profession as Keats was. He gathered much knowledge and information through his vast study of classical Arabic and Persian and contemporary Urdu literature but that did not qualify him for any profession. He could at the most work as a teacher in some 'madarsa'. The English people had started running their own institutions in Delhi as they had done in Calcutta and Madras. Delhi College was recently established and teachers were wanted for that. It was in 1842 that Ghalib was called to attend an interview for the job of a Persian teacher. Mr. Thompson, the Secretary, Government of India, was conducting the interview. It was attended by Momin Khan 'Momin ', Maulyi Imam Bukhsh and Ghalib himself. Ghalib went in his 'palki' to see Mr. Thompson. The secretary was informed of the arrival of Mirza Ghalib. Ghalib got down off his 'palki' and waited for the Secretary to come and receive him. When it got

---

44. For details see preface to *The John Keats Memorial volume* (London : John Lane, the Bodley Head ,1921), p. v.

45. Walter Jackson Bate, p. 672.

quite late and the Secretary came to know the cause of delay, he smiled and went to Mirza Ghalib. He told Ghalib that he would definitely be received at the gate when he came to attend the Durbar of the Governor; now he came for a job and there was no need of any reception. Ghalib politely answered that he wanted service in order to enhance his prestige and not that present one that he had should be brought low. The Secretary pointed out that he was bound by rules and regulations. Ghalib expressed his inability to enter service and came back.[46]

He would never bow down, break he would.

Ghalib did not earn any money even from his books. There were several editions and prints in his own life time. Strangely enough, he had to purchase his own books since he had to send certain copies to his friends and well-wishers.[47] Keats was a luckier person in this respect. He had his friends in the publishing industry who took the risk of publishing his books despite all the adverse comments. When Keats had to sail to Italy for better climatic conditions, he was advanced a fairly handsome sum by his publishers. The English reading public could afford and the publishers could provide them with a happy reading material. The situation in India was different. There was a political upheaval and chaotic conditions prevailed in this society. England was a free country and people enjoyed better living conditions.

And they Died to live...

Keats had a very short span of life: not more than twenty-seven years and his last days were spent not in his London but in Italy. He was sent there on medical advice since Rome was supposed to be a warmer and better place which would do some good to him. Whenever Keats vomited blood, the doctor came and drew still more blood from his arm. As a result he had become very weak and could not travel without helpful company. Joseph Severn, his painter friend,

46. *Yadgar-e-Ghalib*, p. 26.

47. *Ale Ahmad Saroor*, p. 131.

was with him during the journey to Italy and all the time in the sick man's bedroom. There were letters from Mrs. Brawne and from his beloved wishing him recovery but the disease was mortal. The landlady, Signora Angeletti, guessed the nature of Keats illness and informed the police. It was a law in Rome that everything in a room occupied by a consumptive must be burnt after his death. There was a search and the innocent Severn played a trick on the landlady. The police could find no evidence of consumption.

Medicine was doing no good to Keats. Letters were coming to him but he could not read." Keats would no longer read the letters sent to him. ."He has made me put by 2 unopened,"wrote Severn," They tear him to pieces."One was a letter from Fanny Brawne and another was from his sister. Beside him was a small box in which he kept his special possession. "He made me put the letters into his box unread." Later he asked Severn to bury them with him."[48]

By what telepathy, or coincidence, Ghalib imagined a similar situation, we cannot say. The lover in the Urdu poet is hopeful of getting a letter from the beloved. The letter does not come; the pangs of separation and his own sufferings have brought him to the brink of death. And now the letter comes. It is too late. The lover breathes his last and the letter lay opened on his dying breast. Along with the letter comes death:

Name ke saath aagaye paigam-e-marq,

Reh gaya khat meri chhati par khula;

The English people do not have any tradition regarding numerological presentation of an event, of death or birth etc. They have another interesting feature and that is suggesting epitaphs for their tombstones. Keats had one of his own:" Here lies one whose name was write in water." Severn had given him a description of the cemetery and Keats liked and loved it. He could feel the daisies growing over him.

---

48. Walter Jackson Bate, p.690.

Keats and Severn lived in an apartment of two small but pleasant rooms in the plaza di Spagna in Rome. These now famous rooms, together with two others, contain the library of the Keats-Shelley Memorial to which five or six thousand visitors come each year.[49]

Keats's sufferings, I feel , mirror the vast and poignant sufferings of Mirza Ghalib. The Urdu poet had a longer span of life than Keats whose life's was cut snort by the hereditary ailment. During his last moments, Keats used to hold in his hands a little present that Fanny Brawne had given him, it was a small oval white carnelian. He was greatly pained at the pain that Severn might be experiencing because of his illness and imminent death. Severn, a faithful friend, patiently and quietly tended him and immortalized himself by serving Keats at his last moments. It was on Friday, February 23, 1821 that Keats sank into death.

Turning to the death of Ghalib, we note of his last years of prolonged suffering and with all those ailments which old age is subject to. He had some ulcers and stomach disturbance from time to time and was debilitated so much that he could not move about. He had his faithful servants and his wife with him all the time . A number of faithful friends frequently visited him. Then, letters were pouring in from all over the country as an 'ustaad' to so many poets; he had the arduous task of correcting and improving their poetic ventures. These poet-friends knew that a correction from Ghalib or just a word from him carried weight and even during the most sicklied last days of his life, he was not spared by his disciples and friends.

Muslims have a tradition of calculating the year of birth or death in numbers through the 'abjad' method.[50] Ghalib used to make calculations regarding the year of his death. His last years were painful to him not because he was ill but also because he was

49. Walter Jackson Bate, p.672.

50. There are certain Arabic words the letters of which are assigned numbers like 1,2,3....10,20,30etc. The letters comprising the name of a person etc.,are taken up and the numerical value added up to calculate a particular occasion.

indebted. So he wished for death almost all the time and calculated the year of his death but the date always proved false. Once there was a plague in Delhi which took a heavy toll. Ghalib wrote to a friend that there was no plague at all since it could not do away with a man of seventy and a woman of seventy.[51] Towards the last days he was mostly in a state of coma. Haali, his dear disciple, visited him on February 14, 1969. Nawab Alauddin of Loharu came to him and asked how he was . Ghalib replied, "Don't ask me how I am. In a day or so better ask my neighbours."[52] Next day on February 15, 1869 Ghalib breathed his last. The poor poet was indebted for an amount of eight hundred rupees. His widow had no source of income. The British officers wanted her presence in the court . This insult she would never bear though starve she must. She died exactly after one year on the same day.

Elegies were written on the death of Keats and Ghalib. The best one on the death of Keats is *Adonis* wherein a fellow poet Shelley pays rich tribute to another poet. The best one on the Ghalib is *Marsia-e-Ghalib* written by Haali.

Adonis is a long philosophical poem enriched with Greek and Roman myths and platonic philosophy. Shelley mourns in the most musical way the early death of his poet friend who would have lived longer, would have created more wondrous works had the criticasters and reviewers spared him. Haali brings out the poetic, human and humanitarian qualities of Mirza Ghalib in his elegy. Ghalib had lived a full life, had given the best of fruits of his mind and heart, of his privations and sufferings, of his failures and aspirations to the world in the perfect form of Ghazal. Keats in a short span of life also gave the best of his wounded heart and suffering soul in the form of Odes and some longer poems.

Before we proceed further in our study of their works, it is in the fitness of things to have a glimpse of the cities they lived in. The cities and the social environ they got therein had much to do with their poetic lives and works.

---

53. *Yadgar-e-Ghalib*, p. 89.

52. *Ibid*.

The Delhi of Ghalib

The Mughal suzerainty had made Delhi the most beautiful city in the world. Forts, parks, gardens, grand buildings, 'havelis' and palaces had enhanced the beauty of the city. After Akbar, the great Mughal, the material prosperity of the Empire continued for three more generations. Jahangir and Shah Jahan brought more fame and prosperity but then onwards certain signs of weakness became evident. The imperial power declined. The early years of eighteenth century were quite shattering to the Mughal power. In 1739, Nadir Shah occupied and ransacked the imperial city of Delhi. The country had hardly recovered from this blow when Ahmad Shah Abdali came down in 1761 to repeat what Nadir Shah had done. After this onslaught the Mughal dynasty continued for nearly a century but the royal power was confined to the city of Delhi only. The far flung provinces of the empire declared their independence. Now one after the other they were being captured and subdued by the British forces.

Quqan Baig Khan, a bright soldier of Samarkand came to India in the middle of eighteenth century. First, he served in the Punjab, and then he entered the service of Shah Alam, the second, in Delhi. He was with the Maharaja of Jaipur for some time and finally he settled at Agra. His two sons Abdullah khan and Nasrullah Baig Khan chose army as their career. Nasrullah Baig Khan rose to be the governor of Agra Fort. Abdullah Baig Khan went to Hyderabad, then came to Alwar and served under Maharao Makhtawar Singh and was killed in some conflict. This was the time when British overran states big and small and expanded their possessions. Nasrullah Baig Khan, the uncle of Mirza Ghalib, surrendered the Agra Fort to Lord Lake, the British commander-in-chief, when he reached Agra in 1803. Ghalib was a child of six at that time. Ghalib spent his early years at Agra, Akbarabad and attended neither a school nor a college but got good education at his own home particularly with the help of a Persian scholar Abdul Samad. Ghalib shifted to Delhi after his marriage in about 1812-13.

Ghalib received only a meagre pension and had to support his family along with four or five servants and a host of friends who soon started frequenting him. Delhi was a center of Urdu literature as much as it was a center of political activity. The political activity had almost come to a stand-still and Bahadur Shah Zafar, the Mughal king, had been confined to the four walls of the Red Fort. There were poetic gatherings and meetings of poets and intelligentsia in the court of Bahadur Shah Zafar. Suddenly there was the political upsurge which started from Meerut and engulfed the whole Northern India in general and Delhi in particular. During the 1857 revolt, Ghalib was there in Delhi, had to keep himself confined to his house for fear of the British soldiers who killed every Muslim, robbed every house and ransacked every place. Ghalib presents a picture of Delhi of these days which makes a painful reading. It is the painful sight of Delhi which added intensity, vitality and poignancy to the poetry of Ghalib. If Keats has the feel of trees and flowers and birds of Hampstead, Ghalib has the painful sights of Delhi to add that power to his poetic composition which made him not only the great poet but the great humanist that he was.

Delhi was no more that rich, graceful and beautiful city even before 1857 revolt as it used to be, rather during 1857 and four decades to come it was a seat of desolation, despair and dearth. Describing the misery of 1857 he wrote on December 5,1857 that "no Muslim was left alive in the city ; the poor, the rich, the craftsmen and workers all were put to death."[53] How Ghalib escaped unhurt? There were certain families of physicians employed by Raja Narendra Singh of Patiala; his soldiers, for he helped the British, kept a guard in the area and thus Ghalib could escape. The poor poet Ghalib had nothing to do with the political happenings of the day. He was absolutely innocent of what went on in the Fort or outside. Certain informers incited the authorities and Ghalib was also called by the British commander but he was acquitted. The pension that he got from the British government was stopped and it was practically impossible for Ghalib to make both ends meet. There are frequent references to the misery of the people and the city itself. Writing in

---

53. Ale Ahamad Saroor, p. 57.

a letter on January 9,1858, he pointed out that "the beauty of the city depended on several things – the Red Fort, Chandni Chowk the gatherings in the market near Jama Masjid, walks on the Yamuna bridge and the Annual Fair of the Florists, all these things were gone."[54] Ghalib had been living in the city for the last fifty one years. Now it was not a city, it was a military camp. Very painfully he counts the execution of eminent Muslims, Nawabs and land-lords, who were the grace and glory of Delhi. Most of the markets, grand buildings, gardens and parks were razed to the ground. Every market was a city in itself and there was nothing now but death and dust. There was no Urdu, no Urdu Bazaar, no city, no fort and no life. It continued for long and then by and by Muslims were also allowed to come and inhabit the city but not without identity cards. Ghalib lived and suffered during all these days.

The social environ of the poet has much to do with the poetic creation of the man. The poet cannot escape political and social upheaval and consciously or unconsciously he expresses what he finds around him. Ghalib, being a representative poet of his time, from time to time presents picture of the society wherein he lived, suffered and enjoyed and drank deep the dregs of life. His letter presents a realistic picture of the times but then his Ghazals also contain some glimpse of times. It has already been noted that the political upheavals of his times made his life miserable and added sharpness to his pen which brought out thoughtful, serious, provoking and even revolting pictures of the mystery of life and death. It is necessary to see the social life of Delhi, its customs and traditions, its culture and economy as well as its religion before we proceed further in our study.

There were four prominent institutions in Ghalib's Delhi, namely religious, educational, Khanqahs and a group of free thinkers. The religious and educational institutions and 'khanqahs' played a very important role in the social establishment. Qazi, Mufti and Mohatasib preached and propagated religion and promulgated the royal orders

---

54. Ale Ahmad Saroor, p. 162.

also. The educational institutions were headed by Maulanas and imparted religious and secular education. The "khanqahs" [55] were seats of Sufi saints who preached purity without attaching much importance to rituals? There the emphasis was on the purity of the inner life. Superficially speaking, these institutions had one aim and that is good of the people. The mosque was a symbol of religion, 'madarsa' or school of education and 'khanqah' was that of 'tasawwuf'. Besides these institutions, there was a group of free thinkers. They had a symbol of their own and it was the ale house or 'maikadah'. By his own nature Ghalib was a man of this group. These people didn't like the rigid rules of religion or education or of the 'khanqah'. Ghalib has presented pictures of Delhi city through the symbols of 'maikadah,' 'masjid', 'madarsa' and 'khahqah'. The streets of Delhi presented pictures of execution, bloodshed, massacre, convicts being taken to prison houses and punishment being awarded to them.

The popular vehicle for the gentry during these days was a palanquin which was carried by four servants. Ladies of upper classes travelled in these palanquins. Ghalib had a 'palki' of his own and was carried in it by his servants. The gentry had entertainments like drinking, playing chess and gambling. People frequented ale houses or gambling dens. The rich people of the city wasted their wealth and Ghalib too frequented these places. Once he was arrested while gambling at his own house.

The Fair of the Florists was a popular feature of life in Delhi. Ghalib has frequently used flower and its colours in his poems. Houses of Delhi, lanes and, bylanes, gardens and parks find an appropriate place in the cultural life of Delhi and Ghalib presents a picture of his own city. Architecture, engraving and painting had already reached a perfection. In the days of Ghalib, these arts were

---

55. Seats of religious heads where the followers also assembled and lived to discuss spiritual matters and entered into devotional, communal singing. These places were frequented by the devotees also.

there. Painting, a fine art, was being encouraged by even the middle class people. The art galleries, 'nigarkhane', had started coming up where even the women used to go and get themselves painted.

Courtesans and dancing girls also had a flourishing business. The Nawabs and the princess and other members of the upper class frequented these places. Ghalib too fell in love with a dancing girl. Beggars and dancing girls recited his verses and made a living. Delhi was a necessary part of Ghalib's life and thought. And so was London a part of the life of Keats.

The London of Keats

When Keats was born, revolutionary ideas were brewing in France and soon a sudden political change was there which shook the foundations of feudal aristocracy all over Europe. The French Revolution started with the fall of Bastille on July 4, 1789 and heralded the dawn of a golden age for mankind. The revolutionary ideas of liberty, equality and fraternity found a favorable response in the British romantic poets, particularly in Wordsworth, Coleridge, Shelley and Byron. Shelley moved strongly in fovour of abstract ideas and denounced age–old customs, conventions and institutions. He condemned kingship and priesthood because kings and priests were symbols of tyranny and injustice. He would not tolerate anything in the way of love and life. Wordsworth and Coleridge were greatly enthused by the happenings in France.

Later on Wordsworth was a 'lost leader' but Coleridge continued his zeal for liberty and so did Byron. Of Keats, it has been pointed out that he kept himself enclosed in a world of beauty and romance and kept quite aloof from political upheavals on the continent.

In his early days Keats was very close to Leigh Hunt who had strong political leanings. It is only for a couple of years that Keats thought of politics and political liberty but soon he came to his true domain, the world of beauty and since then he didn't look back and did never repent for his ventures into the realms of gold. Attempts are being made to trace political suggestions in his longer poem

The Fall of Hyperion which is presented in the form of a dream. The basic theme of the poem is

> That of suffering and its effect on the poetic imagination. He brings out poet's value to humanity. Keats could not complete the poem because of ill-health and there is no promise of any political theory.

It is better not to involve Keats in the chaos of political theories: but we cannot take him out of London. T. Fairman Ordish pointed out that Keats was

> A Londoner born and bred, like Geoffrey Chaucer, Edmund Spenser, like Ben Jonson, like Milton. Further, if the relations of these poets to time and place be considered, it will appear that Chaucer and Jonson belong to one category, and Spenser, Milton, and Keats to another. The former may be described, in the simple or obvious sense of the term, as realists; the latter as idealists, in the sense that their poetic energy was in the nature of reaction from their environment. In the term of De Quincy's great differentiation, the former belong to the literature of knowledge, the latter to the literature of power.[56]

Chaucer and Jonson never went out of the city of London. Spenser, Milton and Keats, living in the city, went out of the city, went beyond it, breathed a better air and endowed the atmosphere with a better light.

Keats's association with London is intimate and there is an air of locality in the career of the poet. He had exchange of visits, communion with books, with friends and with Homer himself when he appeared to him in Chapman's English. In about 1815, Keats returned from his rural circle to the centre of London where he lodged in the poultry to qualify himself as an Apothecary. Here it is the London of Edmund Kean, the great actor, who put the great Shakespeare before our poet at Drury Lane theatre. At this time

---

56. T. Fairman Ordish, "The Fulfillment of Keats," in the *John Keats Memorial Volume* .pp. 150-51.

Keats used to pass by Bread Street, Cheapside and the site of the Mermaid Tavern and other places enshrined in the volumes of Shakespeare and Milton.

Shakespeare came to him through the acted drama in the London theatre. The acting of Kean thrilled Keats and gave him new insights into the great Elizabethan playwright:

> The acting of Edmud Kean at Drury Lane "was like reading Shakespeare by flashes of lightning," said Coleridge; and he and other such speakers and writers as Hazlitt, Lamb, De Quincey, stimulated and directed an enthusiasm which took possession of all London and echoed far beyond it. History was repeating itself. Once again the doors of the playhouse opened a land of enchantment to a struggling and afflicted humanity, as in the days of Marlowe and the earlier triumphs of Shakespeare when soldiers and sailors, from the wars in the low countries and the Armada battles, mingled the eager audience. The long drawn out struggle with Napoleon was over: Trafalgar lay in the past; Waterloo had been fought and won; and soldiers and sailors were coming back to an amorphous and unorganized London, where the difficulties of living were almost as great as on the battlefield. But there was the same undying English spirit; the same dumb idealism which found expression in the theatre. In the midst of it all was John Keats ,alone with his dreams, in his lodging in the poultry; or at the theatre, in another world created by the supreme master of drama; or at the Apothecaries' Hall, within a few feet of remnants of the old Black friars playhouse , which may have echoed to the living voice of Shakespeare himself:[57]

There might have been an inner struggle in Keats to go to Shakespeare or to go to medicine and we know that it was Shakespeare who won. Ordish rightly pointed out that ' millions of human beings in his position at that moment would have taken that way almost unthinkingly, without hesitation, and they would have

57. T. Fairman Ordish, p. 153.

been right, it is the glory of Keats that he had the courage to take the other way of dim uncertainty illumined only by his own hope , which inspite of all that befell him therein, led him to his assured place "among the English poets."[58]

Keats made a heroic decision and came to Hampstead strengthened by his own spirit and hope. Here he had rich literary culture enlivened by his studies and his meetings with Shelley, Haydon, a famous painter, and perhaps Wordsworth himself. To him Hampstead, with its trees, romantic sights and sounds, flowers and birds, was a valley of health. He settled at Well Walk and devoted himself to the luxury of versification. Edmund Gosse wrote, "All of Keats that is vivid and intelligent, all that is truly characteristic of his genius and his vitality, is centered around Hampstead."[59]

Had Keats established himself as an Apothecary in the city of London, he would have ended a doctor, say, a very good doctor and a famous one but unknown to us; that is, unknown to the future generations. "Keats saved his genius from extinction when he set his face towards Hampstead and the world of the ideal which it symbolized."[60.] There amid the trees and the fields Keats had visions of Beauty and wraiths of poets like Chaucer, Spenser, Marlowe, Shakespeare and Milton. He wrote some of the best poems there and left for future generations a memory which they will cherish. Now Hampstead is the home of Keats where there is a Memorial with a library and a Journal is also being frequently brought out to commemorate him. Hampstead to him was what the Red Fort was to Ghalib in Delhi. It was the seat of love and romance and of inspiration to the young poet. "Its fields, its lanes, its trees, its heath were the scenery of one of the most glorious achievements in English poetry and literature; its natural beauty even now are touched by the light of the ideal thus thrown upon them; and the human interest of the story of Keats is centered here for ever."[61]

---

58. *Ibid.*
59. Quoted by T. Fairman Ordish, p. 154.60. *Ibid.*,p.155.
60. *Ibid.*. p. 155.
61. T. Fairman Ordish, p. 155.

He visited different places like Carisbrooke, Isle of Wight and Margate. Keats stayed at Oxford with his friend Bailey, paid a visit to Stratford-on-Avon and inscribed his name on Shakespeare's walls. At a later date he visited Scotland and went to see the cottage of Burns. After every excursion he was back to Hampstead, the home of his soul, the nest of his Nightingale and the place of seasonable fruitful poetic flowering. Hampstead was his fulfillment. His visit to Italy was as hopeful as it was hopeless. There were promises of a happy marriage after his healthy return but that was not to be.

With this detailed analysis of the lives and social environ of our poets, we may proceed further to a study of their poetical works.

3

THE POETICAL WORKS

The Poetical Works of Keats

Keats took to versifying when he was above eighteen. He never knew that the talents were there in him. In was Cowden Clarke, his school-mate, who introduced him to Spenser, the poets' poet. He got the first volume of *The Faery Queen* and romped through it like 'a young horse turned into a spring meadow.' The immediate result was a poem of four stanzas written after the matter and manner of Spenser and entitled "Imitation of Spenser." It is nothing more than an imitation and there are echoes not only from Spenser but also from Milton and his eighteenth century imitators. *The Faery Queen* awakened his genius and his poem was as successful as any first attempt might be. The immaturity shows that the attempt is like a springboard. It was in the early months of 1814.

He wrote four more poems before the year was out. It was his association with Leigh Hunt who brought out The Examiner that Keats dabbled in political events for sometime. Of Leigh Hunt Robert Gittings write," A man who knew established modern poets such as Wordsworth and those not yet established such as Shelley, brought reality and health into Keats's vague idealization of the poetic function. At last he could talk poetry with a poet."[1] Keats's next poem and a few more were in the tradition of Hunt.

"On Peace" is an irregular Shakespearean sonnet written with a patriotic fervour. Soon we find Keats with poets. "To Lord Byron"(December 1814) and "To Chatterton" (early 1815) indicate that he was deserting the medical profession and had started soaring into different regions. The patriotic element is evident in "To Hope" but his "Ode to Apollo" puts him on the right path. It shows his reverence for the Greek god of music and poetry. His reverence for the classical poetry, for Shakespeare, Spenser, Milton, Gray etc., is clearly suggested. It was possibly in March 1816 that he wrote a short poem:

> Give me women, wine and snuff
> Until I cry out, 'hold, enough:'
> You may do so sans objection
> Till the day of resurrection;
> For, bless my beard, they ay shall be
> My beloved Trinity.[2]

" Ode to Apollo" points to the fact that 'Keats was a Greek' and this short poem points to his early love of beauty and sensuousness. The seeds took root, bore fruits within the next three-four years.

Of his early poems the best one is his sonnet "On First Looking into Chapman's Homer" composed in October 1816. It was in the company of Clarke that he read *Iliad* and was carried away by the art of the mighty master of antiquity. Homer revealed to the young poet the real world of poetry. The two friends had read some famous passages from the *Iliad* and some from the *Odyssey*. Words, phrases

---

1. Robert Gittings, *John Keats* (Harmondsworth: Penguin Books, 1971), p. 138.
2. Miriam Allott, ed., *Keats*: *The Complete Poems* (London: Longman, 1970), pp. 28-29. All subsequent references are from the same edition.

and images from the pages of Homer translated by Chapman, charmed him. The effect was instantaneous and he composed his famous sonnet, sealed and dispatched it to his friend. Keats expressed his wonder and delight in a language that has started showing sings of perfection:

> Oft of one wide expanse had I been told
>
> That deep-browed Homer ruled as his demesne;
>
> Yet did I never breathe its pure serene
>
> Till I heard Chapman speaks out loud and bold.

(p.61)

His first collection of poems came out in 1817. It contained *Sleep and Poetry* and *I Stood Tip-Toe. Sleep and Poetry* was his first serious attempt to explain his poetic ambition. The poem represents his substantial achievement in writing longer poems up to this time . He points out that he was not yet a glorious denizen of the wide world of poesy and shows determination to pass through the kingdom of Flora and Pan and come to " the agonies, the strife of human hearts." He boldly talks of

> The great end
>
> of poesy, that it should be a friend
>
> To soothe the cares and lift the thoughts of man.

(p.80)

I stood Tip-Toe is rich in beauty of nature, classical allusions, sensuousness and compound words. The mythology of classical Greece appealed to him most and he brought out the element of sensuous beauty wherever he could.

> What Psyche felt, and Love when their full lips
>
> First touched; what amorous and fondling nips
>
> They gave each other's cheeks... (p.92)

Endymion (1818) is the first ambitious work of the young poet. It is a long narrative poem and tells the story of Endymion, the shepherd prince of Mount Latmos, with whom the moon goddess

Cynthia falls in love. She lures him through 'cloudy phantasms' and bears away to eternal life with her. The poem is an allegory and represents the poet's search for ideal beauty. Keats called it a 'poetic Romance' and proposed to write about 4000 lines but he left it incomplete. He drew material from different sources of Greek mythology and focussed his attention on poetic nature and its conception of ideal happiness. The poem shows signs of immaturity and the descriptive passages are weak but the "Hymn to Sorrow" and the "Ode to Bacchus" is remarkably poetic achievements. The opening lines of the poem have achieved a distinct popularity and have become a creed with the fans of Keats:

A thing of beauty is a joy forever:
Its loveliness increases; it will never
Pass into nothingness... (p.120)

The poem got scathing comments from a number of reviewers and Keats was much in gloom for sometime but his own 'domestic criticism' pulled him out of the mire and he came out with manliness which strengthened him into his poetic career. He wrote some minor poems and sonnets and then soon came to his proper field.

The year 1819 saw the flowering of his genius. It is the year of his great Odes. They are his complete poems and the brightest gem of English literature. They are distinguished by a poignancy of feeling, a rich strain of meditation and splendour of imagery. There is genuine display of deepest thoughts and feelings. Then, there is a rare fusion of sadness and joy in the Odes. They were mostly written on the spur of the moment but reveal that a wealth of accumulated wisdom and feeling went to the making of the poems. *Ode to Psyche* is a lovely poem and shows Keats's interest in Greek myths; he rather moulds myths to his poetic requirements. Psyche is a goddess to Keats though she was not considered as such in Greek mythology. He, as a worshipper of beauty presents her and her winged Love, Cupid in the most amorous posture:

Their arms embraced, and their pinions too;
Their lips touched not, but had not bade adieu,

As if disjoined by soft –handed slumber,
And ready still past kisses to outnumber
At tender eye-dawn of aurorean love. (p.516)

There is a happy mood all about the poem and Keats took pains to make it a beautiful work of art . Of this Ode, he wrote that it is "the only one with which I have taken even moderate pains. I have for the most part dashed off my lines in a hurry. This I have done leisurely—I think it reads the more richly for it and will I hope encourage me to write other things in even a more peaceable and healthy spirit.'[3]

The song of nightingale which the poet heard sitting under a plum tree in the Hampstead garden inspired the *Ode to a Nightingale.* It presents the pathetic side of human life—its fever and fret, loss of youth and beauty. The world of man is a miserable place "where men sit and hear each other groan." The viewless wings of poesy promised an escape but it turned out to be of a very short duration. This poem is considered among the greatest of his odes. It represents the fleeting experience of the poet—an intense imaginative experience in which sorrow fused into joy and world of time merges into the world of eternity. His flight into the world of nightingale is a remarkable piece of imaginative creation. Then, there are flashes of beauty and romance reaching a unique perfection in biblical and medieval association:

The same that oft-time hath
Charmed magic casements, opening on the foam
Of perilous seas in fairy lands forlorn. (p.530)

The return back to the world of reality is as painful as the flight into the world of nightingale was joyful.

The *Ode to a Nightingale* is concerned with the misery and sufferings of life. Impermanence of life and its joys and beauty is its

---

3. Maurice Buxton Forman, ed., *The Letters of John Keats* (London: Oxford University Press, 1952), p.338.

major concern. In his *Ode on a Grecian Urn*, Keats take up a different thread — the permanence of art and joy that it provides to man generations after generation, In the *Nightingale*, the world of beauty does not last and the human passions are also fleeting. In the *Grecian Urn*, the world of beauty and the human passions have been fixed and made permanent. In the *Nightingale*, beauty fades and dies, youth grows pale, love becomes cold. Here, art imparts permanence to beauty and human passions:

Fair youth beneath the trees, thou canst not leave
Thy song, nor ever can those trees be bare;
Bold lover, never, never canst thou kiss,
Though winning near the goal-yet do not grieve:
She cannot fade, though thou hast not thy bliss,
Forever wilt thou love and she be fair: (p.525)

The last two lines of the poem have raised a lot of pleasant dust and yet the message remains for all who can perceive it. It was long back, in 1817, that Keats had observed the value of a work of art. In a letter addressed to his brothers, he noted that "the excellence of every Art is its intensity, capable of making all disagreeables evaporate, from their being in close relationship with Beauty and Truth."[4] The work of Art, the Grecian Urn, comes as a noble ideal and provides to man a shelter from the mutability and transitoriness of life. Human emotions and joys are short-lived but Art can enshrine them with an ideal Beauty that never fades.

In his *Ode on Melancholy*, Keats is again concerned with the mighty issues of human life—melancholy, joy, beauty and sorrow. Every thing is fleeting. Joy comes and brings sorrow in its trail; there is no escape for man. There is a necessary relationship between joy and sorrow. Melancholy is associated with beauty, joy, pleasure and delight; there is no unalloyed pleasure anywhere:

---

4. *The Letters of John Keats*, p.70.

> She dwells with beauty—Beauty that must die;
> And joy, whose hand is ever at his lips
> Bidding adieu; and aching pleasure nigh,
> Turning to poison while the bee-mouth sips.
>
> (p.540)

Ode on Indolence is a record of a fleeting mood of languorous laziness. The languorous enjoyment of nature's loveliness is exquisite but it is transitory. The poet gives himself up to the passing joy of the moment. There is a deep strain of laziness and he feels indifferent to the best of things of life. He explained this mood to his brother George, "neither Poetry, nor Ambition, nor Love have any alertness of countenance as they pass by me: they seem rather like three figures on a Greek vase—a man and two women whom no one but myself could distinguish in their disguisement."[5] Poetry, Ambition and Love are just shadows and Keats does not feel attracted to them:

> They faded, and, forsooth: I wanted wings.
> Oh, folly: what is Love ? And where is it?
> And, for that poor Ambition- it springs
> From man's little heart's short fever-fit.
> For Poesy: No, she has not a joy-
> At least for me – so sweet as drowsy noons,
> And evenings steeped in honeyed indolence. (p.543)

The *Ode to Autumn* has a different mood. There is no questioning spirit of the poet of the earlier Odes: there is a mood of serenity about the poem. It is objective and descriptive in nature and reveals the serene tranquil mood of the poet. The poem is faultless in its art and workmanship. Keats, the perfect poet, comes before us through his pictorial power, economy of expression, classical restraint, sense of proportion and his grave and solemn music. We

---

5. *The Letters of John Keats*, p. 314.

get a graphic description of nature during autumn. The first stanza describes its gifts of ripe fruits and new crops of flowers. The second stanza presents certain images of autumn through living personifications of a rich farmer, a reaper, a gleaner and a wine–grower. The third stanza describes the music of autumn — the plaintive singing of gnats, the bleating of lambs , the chirp of crickets, the soft treble of the redbreast and the twitter of the gathering swallows in the sky.

In 1820, Taylor and Hessey published *Lamia, Isabella, The Eve of St. Agnes and other poems. Isabella; or , the Pot of Basil* is based on a story from Boccaccio's *Decameron*. It tells of a tragic tale of love. The lover is killed by the rich jealous brothers of the faithful beloved. *Lamia* is the story of a serpent – woman who entraps Lycius, a mortal human being. The theme is the destructiveness of love and the contrast between the ideal and the real. The poem is considered the most perfect of his narratives. *The Eve of St. Agnes* tells a story of love triumphing over all obstacles. Keats took up a popular superstition and wove a tale of richly decorative verse. Madeline, a beautiful maid, went fasting to bed and fell asleep in the 'lap of legends old.' Porphyro, the lover, gained access to her chamber, awakened her by means of music and won a peerless bride whom he took to his land. Besides, there were some sonnets and poems which have come to occupy an important place in English literature.

Keats tackled the legend of Hyperion twice and left it unfinished both the times. In the first version — *Hyperion,* the story is told in a simple narrative; in the second – *Hyperion, a vision,* it is in the form of an allegorical vision presented to the poet. He left the first one as he found that the story and the details with which it opened resembled in some measure those of *Paradise Lost*. The poem has been called an ' imposing fragment' written after the epic style of Milton. It has great poetic qualities and some rich suggestions:

> For 'tis the eternal law
>
> That first in beauty should be first in might.
>
> (p.428)

Keats reconstructed the poem. It is no more in the form of books, now it is in the form of cantos. The major concern here is the theme of suffering and its effect on the poetic imagination. Keats makes out a distinction between the poet and the dreamer. The poem is considered a mature attempt to express his conviction about human life. It is also incomplete but there is a promise of poetic maturity in the poem. Keats has come to understand the calling and the significance of the calling of a poet and says that "a poet is a sage; /a humanist, physician to all men." (p.760). In 1820, he had to sail to Italy and there the muse picked him up to carry to higher regions. Considering the brief span of life of our poet, we note that the achievement is a mighty affair. He touched the chords of human life and prepared a balm out of his own sufferings for the aching heart, the suffering soul and wearied mind of mankind. Having qualified himself as an apothecary, he turned all his energies to versifying and achieved immortality. What did he think of poetry? What useful purpose does a poet serve?

Keats on Poet and Poetry

The poetic talent in Keats was inborn but the realization came quite late. There was an awakening and it was not sudden. During his apprenticeship to Dr. Hammond and even a bit earlier, he came into contact with works of literature like *The Faerie Queene* and he felt that he was not made for medicine. He started thinking of poetry and the role of a poet in society. Thus in a verse letter written to his brother George in august 1816, he talked of the "living pleasures of the bard" and the happy future of a poet:

> "What, though I leave this dull, earthly mould,
> "Yet, shall my spirit, lofty converse hold
> "With after times – the Patriot shall feel
> "My stern alarum, and unsheathe his steel:
> "Or in the senate, thunder out my numbers,
> "To startle Princes from their easy slumbers.
> "The sage will mingle with each moral theme

"My happy thoughts, sententious: he will teem
"With lofty periods, when my verses fire him,
"And then I'll stoop from Heaven, to inspire him.
"Lays have I left, of such a dear delight,
"That Maids will sing them on their bridal night.[6]
...."

He knew it alright that the poet when he is dead and gone becomes dear to mankind and lives for ever. This is almost a temptation and he could not resist it. He succumbed to the temptation, wished to be bard and left lays which are still 'a dear delight 'to his admiring readers.

Soon he was reading Shakespeare and noted that every time one picks up Shakespeare one finds new meaning in him. While reading Shakespeare , he wrote to his friend Reynolds," I find that I cannot exist without poetry – without eternal poetry – half the day will not do – the whole of it –"[7]

Keats realized it quite early that poetry is not a part-time affair. It cannot be taken up half-heartedly. It needs the whole man, the whole of his energies, and the whole of his attention. One who takes up poetry must renounce other concerns. In May 1817, he wrote to his friend Hunt," These last two days, however, I have felt more confident – I have asked myself so often why I should be a Poet more than other Men, seeing how great a thing it is, — how great things are to be gained by it – what a great thing to be in the Mouth of fame –"[8] Another friend Benjamin Robert Haydon noted that Keats had in him the talents of versifying. He inspired him," God bless you my dear Keats go on, don't despair , collect incident, study characters, read Shakespeare and trust in Providence – and you will do – you must , you shall—"[9] And the same year, that is,

6. *The Letters of John Keats*, p. 5.
7. *Ibid.*, p. 21.
8. *Ibid.*, p. 25.
9. *Ibid.*, p. 27.

1817, he is bold enough to fancy Shakespeare as the presidor over his poetical efforts.

The adverse reviews of his 1817 volume of poems did not dampen his spirits. "This is a mere matter of the moment – I think I shall be among the English poets after my death," Keats wrote to his brother George.[10] There is confidence in the young man. He studies the lot of English poets and the ill-treatment that they got at the hands of their compatriots. Later on in June 1819, he wrote to Miss Jaffery, "One of the great reasons that the English have produced the finest writers in the world is, that the English world has ill-treated them during their lives and fostered them after their deaths. They have in general been trampled aside into the bye paths of life and seen the festering of society ."[11]

The temptation of fame was there for sometime, but it was a youthful fancy. When the critical comments came out, there was something more – the urge, the inevitable: nothing but poetry, fame, or no fame; reviews, favorable or unfavorable, write he must. He will write not for money, not for people, not to please any one: write he must because he cannot do without writing. He must write independently. To John Taylor he wrote in 1819,"I feel every confidence that if I choose I may be a popular writer; that I will never be; but for all that I will get a livelihood – I equally dislike the favour of the public with the love of a woman – they are both cloying treacle to the wings of independence."[12]

His poetic ambition first came out in bold statements in his long poem *Sleep and Poetry*. He expresses his desire to dedicate his life to poesy." First the realm I'll pass /of Flora and old Pan; " he seems to give himself up to the luxury of literature but then he wants to take up to higher destinies of a poet. The poet must feel the agony of life and give expression to it to soothe the ailing heart of man. So he decides:

---

10. *Ibid.*, p. 231.
11. *Ibid.* 345.
12. *The Letters of John Keats*, p. 372.

Yes, I must pass them for a nobler life,
Where I may find the agonies, the strife
Of human hearts – (p.74)

Keats condemned the 18th century poetic tradition because of its lack of human interest. A poet is not expected to be a handicraftsman: he is expected to tell 'the most heart easing things' to the people. He knows that poetry has a definite role to play in the society and points out

The great end
of poesy, that it should be a friend
To soothe the cares and lift the thoughts of man.
(p.80)

What are the qualifications of a poet? And does Keats possess what goes to make a great poet? The young poet had a couple of friends with him who could talk of literature. His brothers also could appreciate poetry. He had an urge in him to communicate what he felt about poet and poetry to someone who could favourably respond: there was an atmosphere around him and he could write to his brothers:

> I had not a dispute but a disquisition with Dilke on various subjects; several things dovetailed in my mind, and at once it struck me what quality went to form a Man of Achievement especially in literature and which Shakespeare possessed so enormously – I mean *Negative Capability*, that is when man is capable of being in uncertainties, mysteries, doubts, without any irritable reaching after fact and reason – Coleridge, for instance, would let go by a fine isolated verisimilitude caught from the penetralium of mystery, from being incapable of remaining content with half knowledge. This pursued through volumes would perhaps take us no further than this, that with a great poet the sense of beauty overcomes every other consideration, or rather obliterates all consideration.[13]

13. *The Letters of John Keats*, p. 71.

It is Negative Capability which goes to make a poet great. By Negative Capability Keats means the 'impersonality and objectivity 'of a writer. The poet or writer negates his personality in order to enable him to express any and every personality. There is no irritable reaching after fact or reason. The mind is to be a 'thoroughfare for all thoughts.' It should be 'passive and receptive.' Now Keats comes before us with a confidence. He knows and he seems to possess what makes a man a poet. He explains Poetical Character to his friend Richard Woodhouse:

> As to the Poetical Character itself (I mean that sort of which, if I am any thing, I am a member); that sort distinguished from the Wordsworthian or egotistical sublime; which is a thing per se and stands alone) it is not itself—it has no self—it is every thing and nothing—it has no character—it enjoys light and shade; it lives in gusto, be it foul or fair, high or low, rich or poor, mean or elevated—it has as much delight in conceiving an Iago as an Imogen. What shocks the virtuous philosopher delights the camelion poet. It does not harm its relish of the dark side of things any more than from its taste for the bright one; because they both end in speculation.

A poet is the most unpoetical of any thing in existence; because he has no Identity—he is continually in for—and filling some other body—the Sun, the Moon, the Sea and Men and Women who are creatures of impulse are poetical and have about them an unchangeable attribute—the poet has none; no identity—he is certainly the most unpoetical of all God's Creatures.[14]

The poet has no identity and no personality of his own. His own identity is of no consequence – what is important is the object with which the poet is concerned. Thus he has nothing to do with what is good or bad in the eyes of the people. He is like a chameleon, he changes colours. Shakespeare takes delight in presenting an evil character like Iago as much as he does in presenting a beautiful character like Imogen. That is the secret of the universality of the

14. *The Letters of John Keats*, pp. 226-27.

great Elizabethan. Keats is humbly conscious of the fact that he is a Member of the same clan. The second aspect of the poetical character pointed out by Keats is the love of beauty – 'with a great poet the sense of beauty overcomes every other consideration, or rather obliterates all consideration'. The poet finds Beauty everywhere and in every object. His love of beauty makes him Immune to all praise and blame that the people of the world may allot to him.

Keats was a conscious artist; he knew what he was about. Then, he took his job seriously; that is, he must satisfy his own conscience first and last. He thought about poetry and tried to stick to his plan, as much as the world around and his health permitted. Quite early when he started versifying , he had his own very strong ideas about poetry though he knew that he was not yet perfect in his efforts. He wrote to his publisher:

> In poetry I have a few Axioms, and you will see how far I am from their centre. 1st. I think poetry should surprise by a fine excess and not by singularity—it should strike the reader as a wording of his own highest thoughts, and appear almost a Remembrance — 2nd. Its touches of Beauty should never be half way thereby making the reader breathless instead of content: the rise, the progress, the setting of imagery should like the Sun come natural to him—shine over him in the luxury of twilight—but it is easier to think what poetry should be than to write it—and this leads me on to another axiom. That if poetry comes not as naturally as the leaves to a tree it had better not come at all.[15]

His axioms prove the old saying that 'poets are born, not made'. One cannot exert to be a poet. Poetry is there in the blood and soul and comes out at the right time like the leaves of a tree or, say, showers from the rain-clouds.

His axiom 'that poetry should come like a Remembrance' reminds us of Ghalib—*Mein ne jana goya yeh bhi mere dil mein*

---

15. *The Letters of John Keats*, p. 107.

hai.[16] Poetry is spontaneous and moreover, it is the very echo of the voice of the listener/reader.

Then Keats does not approve of any moral or dicactic preaching through poetry. Poetry should not profess any end. It should not moralise; it should be .Its very presence should be a delight and thrill: the reader should not go for meaning into it. Thus he did not like Wordsworth who would like to be a teacher first and a poet afterwards .Keats would like to be a poet first and last. "We hate poetry that has a palpable design upon us."[17]

The best of his poetic creed is revealed in his *Hyperion*, a *Vision*. Keats makes a distinction between a poet and dreamer. The poet is a 'sage, A humanist, physician to all men.' He lives and dies for the good of mankind. A dreamer has vague notions and gets confused, thereby confusing everyone around him:

> The poet and the dreamer are distinct,
>
> Diverse, sheer opposite, antipodes.
>
> The one pours out a balm upon the world,
>
> The other vexes it. (p. 670)

Keats associated poetry with the sufferings of mankind. One who suffers knows the sufferings of others. It is only through one's own sufferings that one comes to know of the sufferings of his fellow-beings. It is such a one who can be a healer of the wounds of mankind. In this respect, our poets are healers of the wounds of mankind. They provide solace and balm to the suffering hearts of their readers.

The Literary Works of Ghalib

Ghalib has a wider world, his range and output leaves Keats far behind. Keats poems have been put into one volume. We have one more volume of his letters. With the Urdu poet, the story has a variety of threads woven into a peculiar pattern. He writes in Urdu

16. 'I thought it was already there in my heart'.
17. *The Letters of John Keats*, p. 95.

and Persian and writes prose and verse with confidence. His main literary works are as under:[18]

1. *Aud-e-Hindi*
2. *Urdu-e-Mo'alla*
3. *Kuliyat-e-Nazm Farsi*
4. *Kuliyat-e-Nasr Farsi*
5. *Diwan-e-Ghalib, Urdu*
6. *Lataef-e-Ghaibi*
7. *Taigh-e-Tez*
8. *Qata-e-Burhan*
9. *Panj-Ahanq*
10. *Nama-e-Ghalib*
11. *Meher-e-Neemroz*
12. *Dastambo*
13. *Sabad cheen*

Aud-e-Hindi and *Urdu-e-Mo'ella* are collections of Urdu letters written to his friends. These were published first in 1869 in the form of books.*Aud-e-Hindi* contains, besides letters some prefaces and reviews. *Qata-e-Burhan* created a literary controversy and is purely lexical and argumentative. *Lataef-e-Ghaibi* was written under the pen-name *'Saiful Haque'* also relates to the same literary controversy which was caused by *Qata-e-Burhan*. *Panj-Ahang* contains certain specimens of Persian prose writings of Ghalib.

Kuliyat-e-Nazm Farsi is a precious collection of Persian Qasaid, Ghazals, Qataat, Masnaviyat and Rubaiyat. Ghalib wrote sixty four Qasaid in praise of his friends, patrons and Nawabs; seventeen of these are in praise of his English friends and patrons. There are three in praise of Queen Victoria, one in praise of Lord Allenborough

---

18. Ram Babu Saxena, *History of Urdu Literature*, Translated by Mirza Mohammad Askri (Lucknow: Munshi Nawal Kishore, 1929), p. 383.

and one each in praise of Sir Charles Metcalfe, James Thompson, Mr. Sterling, William Fraser, Lord Harding and Lord Canning. Ghazals are a unique treasure in Persian literature and Ghalib considered his Persian Ghazals superior to his Urdu ones. The Masnaviyat are long narrative poems resembling those of Keats.

Meher-e-Neemroz is a book of history and was written on the insistence of Hakim Ehsanullah Khan, Chief Physician to Bahadur Shah Zafar, the last Mughal emperor. The first volume contains historical details from Amir Taimur (Tamburlaine) to Humayun and it is entitled *Meher-e-Neemroz*. Ghalib wanted to write the second volume with the title *Meher-e-Neem Mah* but it was left unfinished due to the 1857 uprise. It was to contain the Mughal History from the reign of Akbar the great to that of Bahadur Shah Zafar. *Dustambo* is a record of the happenings of the revolt of the Indian people against the British Regime. It covers the period from May 11, 1857 to July 1, 1858. It is a factual representation of not all but much that happened during the most critical period in the history of India.

Sabad Cheen contains a few Qasaid, Qataat in Persian and some letters.

His letters have been collected and edited by many scholars like Maulana Imtiaz Ali Arshi, Maulvi Mahesh Prasad , Maulana Ghulam Rasool Meher, Ale Ahmad Saroor and Mirza Mohammad Askari. The best of the last and most authentic collection is by Khaliq Anjum.

Strangely enough Ghalib wrote a primer for the teaching of Persian language. The book was entitled *Qadir Namah* and it was prescribed for those who offered Persian in the Punjab University.

Gul-e-Raana is a collection of his Urdu and Persian Ghazals prepared by Ghalib himself. It was done on the request of Maulvi Sirajuddin.

His *Diwan-e-Urdu* is the greatest treasure for us. It is the greatest achievement of Ghalib in the domain of Urdu Ghazal. Since Ghalib had an inherent love for Persian and wrote the language like a native, he attached little importance to his early efforts in Urdu language. He continued writing Persian up to the end of his life but he became a bit serious about his Urdu Ghazals as he noted that there was a change in the taste of the people. Only a few knowledgeable people were left who could appreciate Persian. Now his reputation as a poet rests on his Urdu Ghazals. His letters reveal that his Diwan had been published twice before 1859. First it was published in 1842-43, with a review by Nawab Ziauddin Ahmad Khan and it contained only 1072 couplets. The second edition was brought out in 1855 and contained 1793 couplets. One complete edition was published sometimes in 1862 but there were many misprints in it and Ghalib was angry with the printer and the publisher. It was priced at six annas. Ghalib, the author of the book, got only one copy free from the publisher. He had to purchase extra copies for his friends.[19]

These days *Nuskha-e- Arshi* and *Nuskha-e-Hamidia* are very popular with the reading public. Kalidas Gupta Raza has brought out all his Urdu verses into a chronological order with the title *Diwan-e-Ghalib Kamil, Tarikhi tartib se*.[20]

My comparative study of Keats and Ghalib takes into consideration only the Urdu Diwan-e-Ghalib, say, only the Urdu Ghazals of Ghalib. The complete works of Ghalib are a huge *Magnum opus* and will be too much for Keats since the complete Ghalib stands high and apart. Keats, or even Shakespeare and Dante, will not be able to touch those heights.

The Ghazals of Ghalib have come to acquire a great popularity in the country as well as abroad. They are popular with those who know Urdu as well as with those who do not know. Dr. Abdul Rehman Bijnori started his study of Ghalib with the sentence—"There are two divinely inspired books in India—the sacred *Vedas* and the *Diwan-e-Ghalib*."[21] The praise and popularity that belongs to these

---

19. Ghulam Rasool Meher, *Ghalib* (Lahore: Mubarak Ali, 1941), pp.387-401.
20. Kalidas Gupta Raza, *Diwan-e-Ghalib, Tarikhi tartib se* (Bombay: Sarkar Publishers, 1988).
21. Dr. Abdul Rehman Bijnori, *Muhasin Kalam-e-Ghalib* (New Delhi: Anjuman Taraqqi Urdu, 1983), p.5.

Ghazals is not shared by any other literary work in the country. What is there in these poetic compositions of the Urdu poet? What is that which is not here? Life with all its ups and downs, pains and pleasures, sorrows and sufferings, love and hatred, hopes, aspirations and jealousy and frustration, and a thousand of thoughts and feelings, stand revealed in the pages of Ghalib. Here we will find the beauty of language, the richness of imagery, sincerity of emotions, the power of passion and the profundity of thought. There is a unique element of wit and humour and satire such as one will never find in any other poetical work of any language.

The early verses of Ghalib have persianised diction and the meaning seems to be buried under a heavy load of vocabulary. Soon he left it for the simplicity of expression and richness of meaning and suggestion. Ghalib avoided the beaten path and made a way of his own and invented a mode of expression which defies all efforts at imitation. His verses are remarkable for a novelty of expression and originality of thought. Then, it is his imaginative faculty that makes the ordinary look extraordinary. His early verses reveal an element treated with the powerful imagination which captures the attention of listeners and readers.

Haali pointed out that the work of a poet should not be judged on the basis of how much or little he has written. It should be judged on the basis of intrinsic worth that it has and the worth to a great extent depends on certain selected verses of the highest quality. The Urdu *Diwan* of Ghalib is full of the verses of the best quality.[22] Ghalib avoided those similes and metaphors which were popularly used by the contemporary Urdu poets. He searched heaven and earth for the most appropriate figures of speech and endowed his couplets with a rich suggestion. He avoided the popular diction and use of every day speech. He touched the common word with his magic wand and made it highly poetic:

Gham-e-hasti ka Asad kis se ho juz marg ilaaj
Shama har rang mein jalti hei sahar honey tak.

---

22. *Yadgar-e-Ghalib*, p. 106.

O Asad, none but death

Can cure the sorrows of this life;

The candle burns as it must

Until the break of dawn.[23]

Ghalib uses very simple words to convey the vital truths of life. His experiences are presented in a way that they become the story of every one. Rich humour is there even in the most religious and serious affairs:

Pakre jate hain farishton ke likhe par nahaq,

Aadmi koi hamara dam-e-tehrir bhi tha?

We stand unjustly accused on the reports

Of the angels; surely it would be better

If a man were also present

When our sins were being recorded; [24]

Ghalib comes before us a great thinker and philosopher. His observations on life and its various aspects are simply astounding. Dr. Bijnori exaggerated this aspect of Ghalib to a great extent and compared him with philosophers of the west. What I feel is that Ghalib is not concerned with dry philosophy of the ivory tower. It is every man's philosophy that we find in him. He is neither scholarly nor scholastic; he is human and humane. This aspect raises him high in the world of poetry:

Jaan di di hoi usi ki thi,

Haq to yeh hei ki haq ada na hua.

This life, granted to me by him,

I offered it back to him;

But the truth is I couldn't do

What I ought to have done for him.[25]

---

23. Translation of Urdu couplet of Ghalib is by Yusuf Husain in *Urdu Ghazals of Ghalib* (New Delhi: Ghalib Institute, 1977), p.106.
24. *Ibid.*, p. 66.

These are the simple truths of life and told in very simple language. There are some higher mystical truths also and it becomes difficult to reach up to Ghalib at times:

Hei wahi badmasti har zarrah ke khud uzrkhwah,
Jiske jalway se zameen ta aasmaan sarshar hei.
He himself is seeking an excuse
For the intoxication of each grain of dust;
He whose glorious manifestation has made drunk
The whole space from earth to sky.[26]

'Zarrah' also means creatures or all the created things, The things created by God have an intoxication, an indifference; it is because the beauty of the Creator has cast a spell on every object in the world, that is, God himself seeks an excuse for the 'masti' of his creation. At such places Ghalib rises higher into philosophical domains. Evidently the poet in Ghalib has some mighty themes to deal with. As a poet, what does he think of poetry? How a good poem is composed? What useful purpose does poetry serve? Let us see what Ghalib says.

Ghalib on Poet and Poetry

We study Ghalib not only as a poet but also as one who writes about poets and poetry and versification. While studying Keats and Ghalib together we have to note that the people of west have a long tradition of literary criticism emanating from Aristotle. Keats is not bound to Aristotle or to any other English literary critic for his ideas about poetry or his studies of Spenser, Shakespeare and Milton. In Urdu literature there is a different tradition: here the art of versification is taught by a mentor or 'Ustaad'. The disciple in turn may become a 'Ustaad' and start correcting the efforts of his own disciples. Ghalib has to be studied as a mentor who corrected the verses of a large number of disciples including Bahadur Shah Zafar, the Nawab of

25. English rendering by Yusuf Husain is not up to the mark. Here I had to do it myself.
26. Yusuf Husain, *Urdu Ghazals of Ghalib*, p. 187,

Rampur, Altaf Husain Haali, Munshi Har Gopal Tufta, Munshi Shiv Narayan Nigam,Mir Mehdi Husain, Nawab Alauddin Khan, etc. His Letters addressed to those persons contain his observations on the use of language, appropriateness of words, aptness of metaphors and other literary devices. We find that he was very particular about the use of words and proved a hard task-master to his students.

This particular aspect of Ghalib has no counterpart in the English poet. Keats had no problem of correcting or being corrected. It may be pointed out that there are many English poets like Tennyson and Swinburne who got much of their poetical learning from Keats and he was a great source of inspiration to them. Keats could suggest as he did to Shelley how to use language:[27]

> You I am sure will forgive me for sincerely remarking that you might curb your magnanimity and be more of an artist, and 'load every rift' of your subject with ore. The thought of such discipline must fall like cold chains upon you, who perhaps never sat with your wings furled for six Months together.

We know that Keats loaded every rift with ore and so did Ghalib. Ghalib while correcting the verses of his disciples always encouraged them to use the right word and apt metaphor.

Ghalib has pointed it out at several places that he learned the art of versifying from none but God. Haali has quoted Ghalib saying 'I am not a student of anyone but God.'[28] Then, in one of his Persian couplets he noted:

Ma naboodeem badeen martaba razi Ghalib
Sheir khud khwahish Aan kard ki garded fan-e-ma.

We were not agreeable O Ghalib
To accept this position for ourselves;
Poesy itself voiced the desire
To become our art.[29]

---

27. *The Letters of John Keats*, p. 507.
28. *Yadgar-e-Ghalib*, p. 13.
29, Yusuf Husain, *Persian Ghazals of Ghalib* (New Delhi, Ghalib Institute 1980), 98.

Ghalib knew that there was poetry in his blood and if we believe Haali, he started composing verses at an early age of eight or nine.[30] Like Keats he was a conscious artist and had a conscience of his own: He must follow what the conscience dictates. Nay, he must follow what poetry dictates. And what does he think of poetry?

Poetry cannot be composed under duress. Bahadur Shah Zafar, his patron, asked him to bring his Ghazals as presents but Ghalib did it only when he felt that he had really composed a good Ghazal and he must go to the royal court. He could compose only when the 'mood' was on.

Explaining the requisites of poetic composition, he wrote to Chaudhry Abdul Ghafoor Saroor," the composition of a poem is not possible through the bodily organs. It needs a heart, a mind, a taste and an urge."[31]

Ghalib knew that there was the divine power inspiring him in his efforts and he explained it in a number of couplets:

Aate hain ghaib se yeh mazamin khayal mein

Ghalib sarir-e-khamah nawai sarosh hei.

These ideas come to me from the unknown

O Ghalib, the sound produced by the scratching of my pen

Is the voice of an angel.

At another place, Ghalib says:

Pata hoon daad us se kutch apne kalaam ki

Roohul qudus agarchi mera hamzabann nahin.

I get appreciation

Of my poetry from Gabriel;

Although, of course, he does not speak

The same language that I do.[32]

---

30. *Yadgar-e-Ghalib*, p. 97.
31. Ale Ahmad Saroor, ed., *Aks-e-Ghalib* (Aligarh: Aligarh Muslim University, 1973), p. 251.
32. Yusuf Husain, *Urdu Ghazals of Ghalib*, p. 134.

It is the wounded heart within and the world of beauty all around him that inspired the poet to compose his Ghazals.

Wahi ek baat hei jo yan nafas , wan nikhat-e-qul hei
Chaman ka jalwah bais hei meri rangeen nawai ka.
It is the same thing, here breath
And there the scent of roses;
The splendour of the flower-bed
Is the cause of my colourful songs.[33]

The word that Ghalib uses is 'Chaman ka Jalwah'. That is, the beauty of the flower-garden. 'Chaman' is a symbol for Ghalib, and it stands for the world of Beauty around him.

Husn-e-Faroqh-e-shama-e-sukhan door hei Asad,
Pahe dil-e-gudakhta paida kare koi.
The glorious beauty of the candle
Of poesy is far away;
First one must consume oneself
By melting the heart, O Asad.[34]

It is not easy to touch the candle of poesy. One must have a wounded, a bleeding heart first. The poet in Ghalib has an eye for the Beautiful and a wounded heart to feel the sorrows and sufferings of others. This entitles him to the task of a poet.

The Letters of Ghalib

Are the letters of Ghalib poetry? The immediate object of poetry is the "communication of pleasure" wrote Coleridge in his *Biographia Literaria*.[35] The letters of Ghalib provide an immediate pleasure. Coleridge made a distinction between poetry and poem. Poem has

---

33. Yusuf Husain, *Urdu Ghazals of Ghalib*, p.35.
34. *Ibid*., p. 196.
35. Coleridge, *Biographia Literaria*, quoted by D. K. Chopra in Literary Criticism (Meerut: Loyal Book Depot, 1974), p. 363.

meter while it is not necessary for poetry. On this ground, he noted that the writings of Plato and Bishop Taylor are poetry.[36] I found the letters of Ghalib poetry on the same ground. We cannot read them as poems but they give us that pleasure and truth which one expects from poetry. It is in the fitness of things to have a look on the letters of Ghalib since they have come to occupy a very prominent place in the history of Urdu literature.

Ghalib used to write letters to his friends and patrons in Persian language. By the year 1850 there comes a change, he started writing letters in Urdu. He was required to write a history of the Mughal dynasty and for that he had to collect material from many persons; he wrote them in Urdu which they could easily grasp.[37] We may note that there is already a letter dated December 1848 addressed to Munshi Jawahar Singh Jauhar.[38.] It was the increasing popularity of Urdu and declining use of Persian that forced Ghalib to adopt Urdu as a medium of communication.

In 1858, there was already a good collection of letters with his friends which they wanted to get published. Ghalib discouraged them saying that his letters were casually written and that the intimate relations of friends should not be brought to public notice.[39] His friends persisted and Chaudhry Abdul Ghafoor brought out some letters under the title *Moher-e-Ghalib* in 1816 and the poet appreciated its preface.[40] *Aud-e-Hindi* came out in 1868. It was first published from Meerut. Some disciples of Ghalib wanted to bring out an edition from Delhi. They brought one entitled *Urdu-e-Moalla*. Ghulam Rasool Meher brought out a two-volume edition of his letters. More and more letters of Ghalib are still being discovered and new editions are coming out. A useful collection was brought out by the Urdu Department of Aligarh Muslim University, Aligarh in 1973.[41]

---

36. *Ibid.*, p. 365.
37. *Yadgar-e-Ghalib*, p. 156.
38. Ghulam Rasool Meher, *Ghalib,* pp. 402-03
39. *Aks-e-Ghalib*, p. 63.
40. Ghulam Rasool Meher, p. 405.
41. Ale Ahmad Saroor edited his letters as *Aks-e-Gahlib.*

The letters of Ghalib are remarkable on two counts: first, for their manner and secondly for the matter. Ghalib discarded the old method of salutation but he always kept in view the position and status of the addressee. Letter-writing became an art in his hands. His expression is simply unique. He introduced new standards of writing and brought the art to such perfection that nobody has been able to imitate it. Commenting on his letters Haali wrote, "Ghalib discarded the old stereo-typed method of salutation and left out all those traditional modes which had become indispensable for the letter writing. He starts his letters with familiar words like 'Miyan', 'Barkhurdar', and 'Bhai Saheb' and sometimes with 'Maharaj' or with any other appropriate word. Then he comes to the main points. Some times he starts his letters even without a salutation."[42] The presentation is equally unique. It is like two persons talking together face to face. It is this informality and directness of communication which makes the letters of Ghalib a precious treasure in Urdu literature. Writing to Hatim Ali Baig, he says,"Mirza Saheb, I have invented a way of writing wherein communication is conversation. Talk through the tongue of your pen from a thousand miles and enjoy the company of your friend even in being separated from him."[43] To Mirza Tufta, he wrote, "Brother, there is no correspondence between you and me. It is just talking."[44]

The letters of Ghalib are dialogues and have a dramatic quality of their own. The written word is a meeting between two friends and has all the qualities of a face to face conversation. Ghalib writes a letter to Mir Mehdi describing the visit of Miran Saheb. See how Ghalib presents the whole scene:[45]

> O Miran Saheb, Asalam Alekum. Hazrat Abab. Say may I reply to the letter of Mir Mehdi today? Sir, when did I prevent you? But in every letter I write, I send him blessings on your behalf;

42. *Yadgar-e-Ghalib*, pp. 157-58.
43. Mirza Mohammad Askari, *Adabi Khatut-e-Ghalib* (Karachi: Mubarak Book Depot, 1970), p. 17.
44. *Ibid*.
45. *Yadgar-e-Ghalib*, p. 158.

> why should you take the trouble? Nay, Miran Saheb, his letter has been lying with me for long and he must be getting angry. A reply I must send. Sir, he is like your son; how can he get angry with you? Brother, tell me why do you prevent from writing to him? Subhan Allah: you yourself do not write to him and blame me for preventing you. I see, you do not stop me; tell me why you do not want that I should write to him. What should I say? The truth is that when your letter comes it is read and listened to and enjoyed. Now since I am not there, I do not want that your letter should be there.....

There is no ceremony, no formality in the letters of Ghalib. There is a direct contact between the writer and the addressee. The simplicity, informality and directness of expression endear his letters to the reading public. Then, his very heart and soul can be seen exposed and revealed in broad colours:[46]

> Sir, Do you ever think of your friend who is known as Ghalib? What does he drink or eat? And how does he live? His old pension stopped for the last twenty-one months and I the poor fool expecting a windfall ! The pension case is lying with the officers in the Punjab. Those people – neither do they give money nor do they send any reply; neither are they kind nor unkind. O. K. Leave it and now note that since 1856, as intimated by the Vizier, I have been expecting an allowance from the royal government. Shameful for me to insist. If a traitor, I'd have been condemned, shot dead or hanged till death.

The letters of Ghalib present quite a good picture of the socio-political history of the days, particularly that of the life in Delhi during and after the 1857 uprising. Since letters are a confidential affair and are not written under any constraint, they give a truthful picture of the events around Ghalib and his own privations and sufferings. The poverty and misery that Ghalib faced during the turmoil is faithfully reflected in his letters.

---

46. *Aks-e-Ghalib*, p. 195.

About the 1857 uprising Ralph Russell of the London University wrote that "It was, at any rate in Delhi and the present-day U.P. areas a popular revolt, a plebian revolt, led by the rebel sepoys, who did what other historical forces, including the British had done before them, and legitimized their action by securing the formal approval of the Mughal king.[47]

Ghalib has presented actual details of the revolt. There is some evidence to show that Ghalib wrote some letters to Bahadur Shah Zafar regarding the political situation of the times but these letters were destroyed. The letters that we possess indicate that Ghalib was not involved in the struggle. He kept himself confined to his own house where he was looked after by the soldiers of the Maharaja of Patiala. It seems that he had no sympathy with the revolutionaries because he felt that the Mughal suzerainty had its day. The old order must change. The British order was definitely better than the declining regime of the Mughals.[48]

Ghalib gives some factual and very painful details of his dear city of Delhi. A friend wrote to Ghalib describing Delhi as a great city where people of various arts and crafts lived. Writing on February 16, 1862, he pointed out,"O, my life: This is not the Delhi wherein you were born, nor the one where you were educated, nor that one where you used to come to me in the mansion of Shoban Baig to get education, nor is it the Delhi where I have been living for the past fifty-one years; this is a camp. Muslims of trade, or servants of officers; rest all Hindus.[49] Then he counts the eminent persons of the city and of the neighbourhood who were put to sword and tearfully tells about the grand buildings which were razed to the ground. Explaining his own position, he writes in a letter of December 5, 1857:

47. Ralph Russell, "*Ghalib and the a Revolt of 1857*" in Dr. Yusuf Husain Khan, ed., *International Ghalib Seminar* (New Delhi: All India Ghalib Centenary Committee, 1969-70)
48. Pavan K. Verma, *Ghalib: the Man, the Times* (New Delhi: Penguin Books, 1989),pp. 37-39.
49. *Aks-e-Ghalib*, pp. 22-23.

> The city I live in, its name is Delhi; and the mohalla is known as the mohalla of Ballimaran but of this life I have no friend here. By Allah, you can't find a Muslim here – poor, or rich or craftsman, none; If there are some, they are from outside. Now ask me how I did survive here. Dear sir, I have been living as a tenant in the house of Late Hakim Mohammad Hasan Khan for nine-ten years and here the houses are closely situated and they are of the physicians who are in the service of Raja Narendra Singh of Patiala. The Raja had been assured by the Britishers that at the time of attacking Delhi, these houses would be spared. So after the conquest of Delhi, soldiers of Patiala are on guard here. Other wise who am I? And what is this city? Rich and poor all ran for life. Those who stayed were thrown out. Jagirdars, pensioners, the rich, the craftsman no one is here.[50]

Ghalib is very exact in presenting the ruthless destruction of Delhi. With a logical sequence he describes the destructions in his letter to Anwaruddaullah written some times in 1860 in the following words:

> Five forces one after the other assaulted this city. The first one by the revolutionaries which carried with it the faith of the people. The second one by the British soldiers which destroyed life and property, name and fame, earth and heaven and all the signs of life. The third was the attack by famine which caused the death of thousands by starvation. The fourth was that of cholera which felled many a hungry and well-fed and lastly came fever which carried away all the energy: only a few died but most of the victims were deprived of vitality.[51]

The letters of Ghalib throw revealing light on his religion and humanism. That he was a 'shia' or a 'sunni' should not detain us. That he believed in Hazrat Ali more than in Prophet Mohammed does not concern our study. What concerns us most is that he was not a fundamentalist. He was a friend of friends, brother of brothers

---

50. *Ibid*, pp. 59-60.
51. *Aks-e-Ghalib*, pp. 204-05.

and a lover of mankind. Humanism—that was his religion. The Hindus, Muslims and Christians were among his friends. During the days of 1857 turmoil, we have already noted some Sikh soldiers of Maharaja of Patiala kept guard at his house. During his early age he used to fly kites against Maharaja Balwant Singh of Bharatpur and in his later life he had some devoted disciples like Munshi Har Gopal Tufta, Munshi Sheo Narain and others who did their best to alleviate his sufferings. Tufta used to send him money and material from Agra. Mahesh Dass arranged for wine. Hira Singh, Shiv Ji Ram and Balmukund were always with him not to let him feel any loneliness during those days when no Muslim could be seen in the city .[52] Tufta was as good as a son to him. He had a number of English friends and well-wishers. In matters of religion he was above petty consideration of caste and creed. He believed in the value of human relationship and stuck to noble ideals.

He was kind and considerate to his friends and to the poor ones he gave away his precious belongings also. He knew he could not do much for them though he had a keen desire to do the best. He explained his position to Maulana Alai:

> I did not get commendation of my work as much as I deserved. I wrote and I alone understood it. Piety and liberty, and the quality of sacrifice and generosity which the Creator had endowed me with found no expression. I don't have physical power to take a stick in hand and a knapsack at my back to go to see the world. Some times I'd go to Shiraaz and sometimes stay in Egypt and then in Najaf. Nor do I possess resources to be a host to the whole world. If not the whole world, I should leave no one naked or hungry in the city wherein I live.[53]

Ghalib knows the art of laughing at himself. He can condemn himself. He had an 'objective disinterestedness' which makes a poet great. He could see himself from afar and thereby hate or love himself. In his days of penury and misery, he could be quite objective

---

52 Sheikh Mohammad Ikram, p. 133.

53. *Aks-e-Ghalib*, p. 38.

and analyze Ghalib, the indebted who was haunted by creditors and discarded by his contemporaries. The bitterness in him gets the upper hand and see how he presents a picture of himself:

> I have become a figure of fun to myself. Sadness and humiliation please me. That is, I take myself to be someone else. When I feel pain, I say Lo one more shoe at the head of Ghalib. How did he boast 'I'm a great poet; a great Persian scholar. There is none to match me far and wide'. Now say what you can to your creditors [54].

We note that Ghalib tells us a lot about poet and poetry, and about himself and the socio-political situation around him in his letters. His letters enable us to appreciate his art and thought in a better light. Let us see what useful information the letters of Keats provide us with.

The Letters of Keats

The letters of Keats also make a very fascinating and useful study. The appreciation of his poems and an understanding of the man that Keats was definitely increase when we keep a close eye on his letters. They definitely provide us a better insight into the heart and mind of the poet. Keats wrote letters to his brothers, sister and friends including his publishers. He had an idea to enjoy the writings at a later date. He wrote to his sister Fanny Keats, "You will preserve all my letters and I will secure yours—and thus in the course of time we shall each of us have a good Bundle—which, hereafter, when things may have strangely altered and God knows what happened, we may read over together and look with pleasure on times past—that now are to come."[56] The passage of time made his letters literary masterpieces and a great source of pleasure and profit for the readers, critics and admirers of Keats. We got a lot of biographical details about the family of Keats, useful comments

---

54. *Ibid.*, p.49.
55. See P.
56. *The Letters of John Keats*, p. 39.

about poetry and the character of a poet, miseries and misfortunes of life, and above all, his relationship with Fanny Brawne, the beloved of our poet.

The letters of Keats are intensely personal. He had to write to his brothers and sister as they lived apart because of the loss of their parents. To his friend Bailey, he explains it, "My Love for my brothers from the early loss of our parents and even for earlier misfortunes has grown into an affection 'passing the love of women'.[57] The cruel fate keeps them apart and "life must be undergone."[58] George got married and Tom was ill. Sister Fanny was with the guardians and Keats being the eldest member had to strengthen himself and his kin. Writing about the ill-health of Tom, Keats tells George and Georgiana Keats:

> Ours are ties which independent of their own sentiment are sent to us by providence to prevent the deleterious effects of one great, solitary grief. I have Fanny and I have you – three people whose Happiness to me is sacred – and it does annul that selfish sorrow which I should otherwise fall into, living as I do with poor Tom who looks upon me as his only comfort—the tears will come into your eyes—let them—and embrace each other – thank heaven for what happiness you have and after thinking a moment or two that you suffer in common with all mankind hold it not a Sin to regain your cheerfulness—[59]

As a friend of friends, Keats is remarkable. He had kind and generous friends and he could depend upon them.

It may be safely affirmed that his friends awakened the poetic talents in him. Friends like Cowden Clarke, Leigh Hunt and Brown led him into spacious fields of literature and then he was in his own. Friends like Woodhouse and Isabella Jones provided a lot of help and inspiration to the poet. They helped him in his studies and Isabella Jones suggested that the legend of St. Agnes might be a

57. *The Letters of John Keats*, p. 151.
58. *Ibid.*,
59. *Ibid.*, p. 229

good theme for a poem. Then, talking of his friends, we can never forget Joseph Severn, the painter who accompanied him to Rome and in whose arms our young poet breathed his last.

While discussing Keats's ideas on the poet and poetry, I have quoted extensively from his letters. It simply proves that Keats revealed the other side of his genius, that is, the critical faculty, in his letters. The oft-quoted letter is the one in which he discusses the quality which goes to make a man of genius, i.e., 'Negative Capability'.[60] It is the faculty of a poet, the faculty that makes a poet objective and see things in themselves as they are without any involvement of the personal likes and dislikes of the poet himself. His observations on the creative process are also there in his letters.[61]

Keats's thoughtful observations on life as presented in his letters from time to time make him a thinker. He knows there is misery and misfortune in life. He projected his attitude to misfortunes in a letter to Bailey, "The first thing that strikes me on hearing a misfortunes having befallen another is this. 'well it cannot be helped—he will have the pleasure of trying the resources of his spirit'-[62] He was highly philosophical for his years when he wrote to Hamilton Reynolds that "sorrow is wisdom" and very analytical in his observations when he compared human life to a large Mansion of Many Apartmants,[63] and pointed out that "the world is full of misery and Heartbreak, pain, sickness and oppression."[64] His conclusion is as valid as it is truthful, "the truth is there is something real in the world ".[65] The clouds of misery haunt him since he finds his life overwhelmed by one sorrow after another:

> This is the world—thus we cannot expect to give way many hours to pleasure—Circumstances are like clouds continually gathering and bursting—while we are laughing the seed of some

---

60. see p. 90.
61. see p. 92.
62. The letters of Keats, p. 68.
63. *Ibid.*, p. 142.
64. *Ibid.*, p. 143.
65. *Ibid.*, p. 144.

> trouble is put into the wide arable land of events—while we are laughing it sprouts it grows and suddenly bears a poison fruits which we must pluck—Even so we have leisure to reason on the misfortunes of our friends; our own touch us too nearly for words.Very few men have arrived at a complete disinterestedness of Mind: very few have been influenced by a pure desire of the benefits of others—in the greater part of the Benefactors of Humanity some meretricious motive has sullied their greatness—some melodramatic scenery has fascinated them.[66]

Keats does not feel contented with the idea that the world is' a vale of tears'; He would better call it "the Value of Soul making"[67] because sufferings and sorrows work as a mentor for mankind. He writes to George and Georgiana, "I will call the *world* a school instituted for the purpose of teaching little children to read—I will call the *human heart* and *hornbook* used in that school – and I will call *the child able to read*, the soul made from that school and its *hornbook*. Do you not see how necessary a world of pains and troubles is to school an intelligence and make it a soul?"[68]

The qualities of Keats as a poet come to us through his observations in his letters. He was fortunate enough to have certain friends who could talk poetry and discuss the process of poetic creation. His love of beauty is the most remarkable quality that impresses the readers of his poems. In his letters he frequently writes about beauty. He wrote to Bailey, "I am certain of nothing but of the holiness of the heart's affection and the truth of imaginations—what the imaginations seizes as Beauty must be truth—whether it existed before or not-for I have the same Idea of all our Passions as of Love they are all in their sublime, creative of essential Beauty."[69] He knew that he loved the principle of Beauty in all things and this alone would make him one of the greatest persons in the world. Thus he wrote to his beloved, "If I should die," said I to myself, "I

66. *Ibid*, pp. 314-15
67. *The Letters of Keats*, p. 335.
68. *Ibid*.
69. *Ibid*., p. 67.

have left no immortal work behind me—nothing to make my friends proud of my memory—but I have loved the principle of Beauty in all things and if I had time I would have made myself *remembered*,"[70] We remember him because he loved the principle of Beauty in all things and on the basis of this Love produced great works of art and beauty which will ever charm his readers. That he believed in sensations is clearly brought out by his sentence, "O for a life of Sensations rather than of Thoughts!"[71]. His sensations brought him nearer to the reality of things and he could arrive at the essence of things through his sensuous perception.

Keats's letters to his beloved contain another aspect – the loving heart- of the poet. Critics like Matthew Arnold found these letters unnecessary but most of the critics and admirers of the young poet find the creed of the poet well enunciated here. His love letters are as personal and confidential as love letters generally are but they are more than that. Keats points out his own misery and sometimes feels free to discuss poetry and his poetic creed. They are most loving, softest, sincerest and the most intimate outpourings of his soul." I would never see any thing but pleasure in your eyes, love on your lips, and happiness in your steps."[72] There is a genuine display of sincere passions and the truth of life is told in simple but powerful words, "I have never known any unalloyed happiness for many days together: the death or sickness of some one has always spoilt my hours—"[73] now when love was there, illness clipped his wings. "To be happy with you seems such impossibility."[74]

The two poets went to the past to add extra vigour, vitality and freshness to their poetical works.

---

70. *Ibid.*, p. 468.
71. *Ibid.*, p. 67.
72. *The Letters of Keats*, p. 356.
73. *Ibid.*, p.352.
74. *Ibid.*, p.503.

4

THEIR PASSION FOR THE PAST

Keats and Ghalib looked to the past, mostly lived in the past and made the past present in their works.

Past for Keats was different from the past as it appeared to Ghalib. They had different traditions and differed in their attitudes to the past. For Keats it was the best of classical Greek literature, the Greek culture and civilization and the best of English literary tradition. For Ghalib it was the best of Persian literature of the past, of his own ancestors and the best of the Mughal suzerainty that was no more there.

Keats lived very much in the 'Realms of Gold' and at times made the realms a reality for all of us to see and feel. We can see it in the Grecian Urn and the utterances of Greek gods and goddesses in his Hyperions. Ghalib failed to create that reality of the past in some concrete from but form time to time he gives us a glimpse into that:

Wuh bada-e-shabana ki sarmastian kahan,

Uthiyey bas ab ki lazzatt-e-khwab-e-sahar gayee;

Where are those drinking bouts of night?

Now get up! The delight

Of morning sleep has gone.[1]

He did create it in a different way. He imbibed the very spirit of the best of classical tradition and poets like Zahoori and Bedil spoke through him.

I cannot say that past was an escape to them, no; it was an inspiration. For Keats it was definitely a great solace, a comfort and a fruitful source of inspiration. For Ghalib, when it came to literature, it was an inspiration but there was no comfort for him. It became almost a challenge, and he must equal them, if not exceed them and as the critics of Ghalib agree, he well equalled them. When it came to the past glory of the Mughals, it was a matter of painful reminiscences. The Mughal sun was setting and the glimpse was that of the setting sun only. The Sun was on its death-bed and Ghalib witnessed its Death.

Keats and the Past

How did it happen that Keats who was being trained for the medical profession turned to the past?—from the plasters, ointments and phials direct into the kingdom of poesy: If you threw a stone said a Bengali writer, in the streets of Calcutta, it would surely fall on the head of a poet. And I add, if you threw a stone in the streets of Mughal capital city, that is ,Delhi, it would surely fall on the head of a poet and if you did it in the London of Keats, it would definitely fall on the head of a poet. Note what the so- called killer of Keats wrote.

> Of all the manias of this mad age, the most incurable, as well as the most common, seems to be no other than the Metrimonie. The just celebrity of Robert Burns and Miss Baillie has had the melancholy effect of turning the heads of we know not how many farm servants and unmarried ladies; our very footmen compose tragedies, and there is scarcely a superannuated

---

1. Yusuf Husain, tr., *Urdu Ghazals of Ghalib* (New Delhi: Ghalib Institute, 1977) p. 231.

governess in the island that does not leave a roll of lyrics behind her band-box.[2]

Poetry was in the air . One did breathe it. And so it was in Delhi in general and in the royal court of Bahadur Shah Zafar in particular. The Mughal Emperor was himself a poet of distinction and had a good coterie of poets around him. Keats and Ghalib could and did breathe poetry in the metropolitan cities wherein they lived.

Keats was not like a dairy-maid or a governess. **Metromanie** was a common disease and may be Keats was infected but there were mightier factors responsible for the malady in him. His reading habits and association with early friends gave him a direction and when he was on the path, he could easily walk alone and the friends were always there with him. Cowden Clarke, son of Dr. James Clarke, a close friend of young poet introduced him to Homer. While studying together at the school of *Dr. Clarke*, they had read many books including Pope's translation of Homer but it was in September 1816 that they again read Homer together. This time the translation was by Chapman, an Elizabethan poet, playwright and translator whose complete translation of Homer was published in 1616. It was a memorable night for Cowden Clarke when they sat down to read some memorable passages that they had read long before in Pope's translation. Clarke quotes two passages and then concludes:

> One scene I could not fail to introduce to him – the
> shipwreck of Ulysses, in the fifth book of the
> "Odysseis," and I had the reward of one of his delighted
> stares, upon reading the following lines:
> Then forth he came, his both knees falt'ring, both
> His strong hands hanging down, and all with froth
> His cheeks and nostrils flowing, voice and breath

---

2. "Review of Keats's poems of 1817 and Endymion" in the Blackwood's Magazine in John O. Hayden, ed., *Romantic Bards and British Reviewers* (London: Routledge & Kegan Paul, 1971), p. 317.

Spent to all use, and down he sank to death.

The sea had soak'd his heart through....[3]

By the time Keats had read some Spenser and but little of Shakespeare but he had not read anything so mighty and penetrating as this poetry of Homer was. He was 'transported' in the original sense in which Longinus used the word in his treatise *On the Sublime* and the immediate result was the famous sonnet "On first looking into Chapman's Homer," his first complete and perfect attempt at writing a verse.

The mighty harmonies of Homer made a Greek of Keats. The Greek master was a major formative influence which strengthened the young English poet in spirit and vigour. Homer led him into the land of wonder and romance of Greek art, literature, architecture and culture. Keats had his 'delighted stares' but at the same time he had an original quality in him as not to be branded as an 'imitator of Homer'. There was the world of beauty and wonder and he could go to this world again and again and try to create a world of beauty and wonder in his own way. The sonnet reveals how Keats was carried away by the grand master. It has rightly become a work of art and will be read again and again:

Much have I travelled in the realms of gold,
And many goodly states and kingdoms seen;
Round many western islands have I been
Which bards in fealty to Apollo hold.
Oft of one wide expense had I been told
That deep – browed Homer ruled as his demesne;
Yet did I never breathe its pure serene
Till I heard Chapman speak out loud and bold.
Then felt I like some watcher of the skies

---

3. Quoted by Walter Jakson Bate, *John Keats* (New York: Oxford University press, 1966) p.85

when a new planet swims into his ken;
Or like stout Cortez when with eagle eyes
He stared at the Pacific, and all his men
Looked at each other with a wild surmise-
Silent, upon a peak in Darien,[4]

Even before he entered the domain of Homer, he had already been to Apollo, 'the Greek god of archery, prophecy, medicine, poetry and music and protector of the Muses, and always represented as the highest type of masculine beauty and grace.' A year earlier Keats had written an Ode to him and praised him for inspiring poets like Homer, Virgil, Milton, Shakespeare, Spenser and Tasso. The concluding lines reveal his reverence for the god in a true devotional tone:

But when thou joinest with the Nine,
And all the powers of song combine,
We listen here on earth
The dying tones that fill the air
And charm the ear of evening fair,
From thee, great God of Bards, receive their heavenly birth.

(P. 17)

His friend Clarke further tells us about his reading material. "'The books, however, that were his recurrent sources of attraction were Tooke's *Pantheon*, Lempriere's *Classical Dictionary* which he appeared to *learn*, and Spence's *Polymetis*. This was the source where he acquired his intimacy with the Greek mythgology.[5] "It was Lempriere's dictionary which attracted him most: this dictionary is better known as Bibliotheca Classica and has frequently been enlarged and revised and is still in use. By the time Keats comes to

---

4. Miriam Allott, ed., *The Complete Poems* (London: Longman, 1970), p.61-2.
5. Quoted by Miriam Allott, *Keats: The Complete Poems*, p 116.

undertake a long poetical adventure, that is, long narrative poem in the form of *Endymion*, he is not only fairly well acquainted with the Greek myths but he can also shape them to his heart's desire. The poem begins with (now the oft-quoted line) 'A thing of beauty is a joy forever' and presents the story of the moon-goddess falling in love with a mortal. The story contains myths enriched with the 'power of imagination' of Keats. Keats had now added Ovid's *Metamorphosis* to his reading list. *Endymion* suggests our poet's search for the ideal beauty. It presents Keats's conception of poetic nature and search of ideal happiness. That is, through the Greek myths Keats goes to the ideals of poetic conception. The poem is rich in thought all emanating from his meditations into the Greek legends:

> He ne'er is crowned
>
> With immortality who fears to follow
>
> Where airy voices lead;........ (p. 172)

Haydon, the painter friend of Keats, fought for eight years for the official recognition of the Parthenon sculptures that Lord Elgin had brought from Athens. Keats visited the museum and frequently went to see the Elgin Marbles. The impact is tremendous and the output is unique. The marbles put him, it seems, under the load of Immortality and he was soon composing immortal works beginning with the sonnet "On seeing the Elgin Marbles" which he concluded with:

> So do these wonders a most dizzy pain,
>
> That mingles Grecian grandeur with the rude
>
> wasting of gold time , with a billowy main,
>
> A sun, a shadow of a magnitude. (p.105)

Then there is a sonnet addressed to Haydon wherein these stones have become 'these mighty things'. Thus Keats enriched himself with all that is mighty and beautiful in the ancient Greek lore. He started composing Hyperion in the autumn of 1818 but abandoned it in April 1819 realising that it had started sounding of Miltonic notes and this Keats could not do well with. Milton is all right and Keats had all respect for the creator of Satan but he would not imitate the fallen Lucifer in his fallen Saturn. He had started weaving a myth out of the myths of old and there seems nothing wrong with myth-making power of our poet but his attempt had started smelling of Milton and he had to abandon it. He took up the same legend again in July1819 and would treat of it in an epic way. He made the Greek gods and goddesses speak and behave as they would have done under the Greek skies on the mount Olympus. He left the work unfinished as he had done the earlier one. *The Fall of Hyperion* the second attempt, is another mighty effort with mighty promises and how and where Keats would have led his gods and goddesses one cannot say, but one cannot fail to see the nobility of diction and richness of thought in the poem. He wanted to express the mission of the poet, the nature of poetry and that he did quite successfully. The basic concern is the theme of suffering and its effect on the poetic imagination. The poem is considered to be Keats's most mature attempt to delineate his convictions about human life. Miriam Allott has pointed out that "Modern Critics have generally recognized the strengthened promise of poetic maturity both in the new material and in the adaption of passages from the earlier version."[6] The height of poetic imagination, according to Keats, can be reached only by those who suffer:

> 'None can usurp this height,' returned that shade,
> 'But those to whom the miseries of the world
> Are misery, and will not let them rest.' (p.667)

I find Keats reaches his mission and the perfection of his thought only through the Greek myths and legends and wherever he fails to see his mission well reflected there, he creates myths of his own but based on the Greek fabric. The poem remains a fragment like the earlier attempt and reminds us of Ghalib:

> *Hazaron khwahishen aisi ki har khwahish pe dum nikle*
> *Bahut nikale mere armaan lekin phir bhi kam nikle.*
> There are thousands of desires
> And upon each one would I die;

---

6. *The Complete Poems,* p. 657.

Many of my longings have been fulfilled

Yet still a few remain.[7]

The best gem that Keats dived out of the Aegean Sea is the *Ode on a Grecian Urn* composed in May 1819. The Urn is Greek in every respect—in design, in execution, in decoration and in the thought—content. "The sylvan historian" tells a tale of love, of ever fresh love. Sights and sounds are Greek and time cannot wither nor stale them. The rituals of Greek life are graphically presented on the Urn. The Greek vase has become a messenger for all the times to come, for generation after generation. The message contained in the concluding couplet is a mystery, or an illumination, an enlightenment; whatever it is, it is there for everyone to see and receive from it as much as he can easily assimilate. 'Beauty is truth and truth Beauty' is the Greek ideal of perfection. The basic ingredients of education with the Greeks were 'music and gymnastics' and the two contained every activity of human life to raise it to perfection. So Beauty and Truth contain within themselves every thing that you would like to know of life: more is not needed.

Before coming to the Urn, he had been to Psyche and raised her to the status of a Goddess as even the Greeks had not done. He wrote his **Ode to Psyche** in April 1919 and pointed out that the poem is:

> The first and the only one with which I have taken even moderate pains- I have for the most part dash'd off my lines in a hurry—this I have done leisurely – I think it reads the more richly for it and will I hope encourage me to write other things in even a more peacable and healthy spirit. You must recollect that Psyche was not embodied as a Goddess before the time of Apulieus the Platonist who lived after the Augustan Age, and consequently the Goddess was never worshipped or sacrificed to with any of the ancient fervor—and perhaps never thought of in the old religion—I am more orthodox than to let a heathen Goddess be so neglected—[8]

---

7. Yusuf Husain, tr., *Urdu Ghazals of Ghalib*, p. 263.
8. Maurice Buxton Forman, ed., *The Letters of John Keats* (London: Oxford University Press, 1952) p.338-39.

Keats being a true Greek in spirit, could not neglect any Goddess. He would give an appropriate fealty to her. He saw the winged Psyche and the winged boy couched side by side:

> They lay, calm – breathing on the bedded grass:
> Their arms embraced and their pinions too;
> Their lips touch'd not, but had not bid adieu, (p. 516)

Such a Goddess should not go without a proper Temple and offering, and Keats, the worshipper of Beauty, must build a temple for her:

> A rosy sanctuary will I dress
> With the wreathed trellis of a working brain
> With buds, and bells and stars without a name,
> With all the gardener Fancy e'er could feign
> Who breeding flowers will never breed the same:
> And there shall be for thee all soft delight
> that shadowy thought can win,
> A bright torch, and a casement ope at night,
> To let the warm love in; (p. 520-21)

The *Ode to Nightingale* further shows the Greek in Keats. The bird is not the one which he saw and heard singing in the garden tree of his friend Brown. That one was just an immediate source of inspiration: the fact is that the bird had been with him for long. The story of Philomel is a popular part of Greek lore. There are variations in treatment—we have the medieval and the biblical touches but the Greek character of the poem is not diminished. It runs through ' the blushful Hippocrene', and 'by Bacchus and his Pards', by the 'Queen-moon' and her 'starry fays'. The reader will feel that the poem is composed by one who is well acquainted with the Greek forests, farms, flowers and valley glades and with the Greek skies also. The poet freely wandered over there. Then the choice of words , the use of personifications and the myth-making device reveal the Greek nature of our poet.

Keats looked to the past from one more angle also. As he imbibed in him a spirit of the Greek literature and culture so he did imbibe a spirit of the Middle Ages with all the chivalry and romance associated with the times. The adventures of the Middle Ages with all the lords and ladies, knights and knight-at-arms, fairies and elves and their tales attract him. He beautifully captured the spirit of the times in a couple of poems. Keats is one of those who revelled in the past in preference to the present as distance lends a charm and enchantment to the view. Among the romantics who went to the Middle Ages are Scott, Coleridge and Keats himself.

The long narrative poem *The Eve of St. Agnes* is a fresh piece from the legends of the middle Ages. Here the legend is that of St. Agnes:

> They told her how , upon St. Agnes' Eve
> Young virgins might have visions of delight,
> And soft adorings from their love receive
> Upon the honeyed middle of the night,
> If ceremonies due they did aright;
> As, supperless to their bed they must retire,
> Nor look behind, nor sideways but require
> Of heaven with upward eyes for all that they desire.
>
> (p. 456-57)

Madeline and Porphyro belong to two hostile families. Porphyro got access into her chamber through the help of her old nurse. On her lute he sang the popular ditty 'La belle dame sans merci' which awakened her and then he eloped with her while the hungry wolves, her brothers etc., were fast asleep after a riotous feast. The subject was suggested to Keats by Mrs. Isabella Jones but by this time – Jan.—Feb. 1819, he had developed close associations with Fanny Brawne and therefrom comes the romantic celebration of erotic fantasy.

The passion of love and its intensity find an exquisite expression through the superstition of the Middle Ages. Roger Sharrock pointed out that this poem presents the consummate passion of love. He says that:

> the poems in which he writes about his youthful love,
> first love whether satisfied or frustrated, happy or
> tragic are *Isabella, The Eve of St. Agnes* and *Lamia*.......
> In the first two of these poems he is creating the facts
> and discoveries of first love out of his imagination.
> The kind of self indulgence so richly and beautifully
> carried in these poems is far removed from the
> Impersonality of the poet of negative capability;....[9]

In *The Eve of St. Agnes* he created an atmosphere out of his personal emotion and presented the lover and the beloved as he would wish them to be. This is the atmosphere Keats loved and liked to live in. He succeeded in creating such an atmosphere because he felt he lived in such a world of love and beauty which, indeed had its own terrors and fears. The legend provided him with an illustration of a happy and realised romantic love. The curious beauty of the words, their natural selection and sweet and elfin music are in close harmony with the romantic and wild scenery, with Porphyro riding across the moor with his beloved:

> They glide, like phantoms, into the wide hall;
> Like phantoms, to the iron porch they glide;
> Where lay the porter, in uneasy sprawl,
> With a huge empty flagon by his side.
> The wakeful bloodhound rose and shook his hide,
> But his sagacious eye an inmate owns.
> By one, and one, the bolts full easy slide;
> The chains lie silent on the footworn stones;
> The key turns, and the door upon its hinges groams.

(p. 478-79)

---

9. Roger Sharrok, "Keats and the young lovers" in Judith 'O Neill, ed., *Critics on Keats* (London: George Allen and Unwin, 1967) p. 53.

There is another poem from the legends of Romance though it has a different note—"La Belle Dame Sans Merci". This is also medieval in setting the atmosphere but the situation is very unhappy and miserable. The medieval accessories are here—the knight-at-arms, the cruel mysterious lady, the elfin grot and the spell and enchantment and the general supernatural atmosphere. It is one of Keats's great achievements and possesses a superb beauty unexcelled in such a short piece. *The Eve of St. Agnes* is overloaded with excessive details while this one is a simple and short piece with all the charm and romance of the Middle Ages. It is in the simple style of a ballad and tells a story with a medieval setting. The knight-at-arms was found loitering lonely and palely on the cold hill side by the poet. He told the poet a tale of love and wonder where a beautiful lady fell in love with him, lulled him to sleep and then disappeared:

> And there she lulled me to sleep,
> And there I dreamed—Ah: woe betide –
> The latest dream I ever dreamt
> On the cold hill-side.
> I saw pale kings, and princes too,
> Pale warriors, death-pale were they all;
> They cried- 'La belle dame sans merci
> Thee hath in thrall! ' (p. 505)

References from the Greek lore are spread over all the poetical works and letters of Keats. The young poet imbibed the Greek spirit because he could identify himself with the best and the most beautiful that he found around him. Strangely enough he never knew any Greek language and never read any Greek work in the original though we read in his letters that he had a keen desire to read the Greek masterpieces in the original. The work-a-day world gave him no time. But then, just with the help of translations and references he performed wonders in this field.

The very temperament of Keats was Greek: he had an inborn, instinctive love of the Greek way of life. His passionate pursuit of beauty is in the true Greek way. The keen delight in the sight of a beautiful object shows a kinship with the Greek mind. Beauty for Keats, as it was for the Greeks, is not just physical, intellectual or spiritual; it represents the fullest development of all that makes for human perfection. Objects of beauty thrilled him to sensations of rare intensity and the product was equally an object of distinction like the Grecian Urn or the song of the nightingale. Along with it, his mode of expression also developed certain classical traits. He is a Greek in his manner of personifying the powers of nature. The attitude of the ancient Greeks in the presence of nature was one of child - like wonder and delight; they deified those powers.They felts the presence of Proteus and Triton and Neptune in the sea; of dryads in the trees; of nymphs and fairies in the woods and of naiads in the brooks. And so did Keats. His instinctive delight in the presence of nature easily led him to the beautiful mythology of the Greeks. What the Greeks felt, Keats also felt. We know how he put the crown of Apollo on his head and then realised that he was not worthy of the crown of the God. He wrote an "Ode to Apollo" as a sort of apology:

> Where, where slept thine ire,
> When life a blank idiot I put on thy wreath,
> Thy laurel, thy Glory
> The light of thy story? (p. 15)

But then he knew that there was something of the true worshipper of the god of music, arts and poetry in him and some day he might be crowned with the laurel wreath of Apollo. Like a fool, we may say, he rushed in where angels fear to tread and Apollo clapped him on the shoulders knowing that one fine day he would be crowned with Immortality.

" I think I shall be among the English poets after my death"—is an oft-quoted statement of Keats. When he wrote this sentence he was thinking of the greatest of English poets like Shakespeare and Milton.

Of the past English poets, Shakespeare was the foremost in his mind. He in a way, lived with the Elizabethan dramatist. A seven volume edition of Shakespeare was always with him and the more he read Shakespeare, the more new meaning he discovered in him. He imbibed the qualities of his 'Presiding genius' to such an extent that he became one with him. He had his weaknesses, disease and death at his heels. Matthew Arnold rightly pointed out, "No one else in English poetry, save Shakespeare, has in expression quite the fascinating felicity of Keats, his perfection of lovingness. 'I think', he said humbly, ' I shall be among the English poets after my death.' He is; he is with Shakespeare."[10]

John Keats, when he was alive, mostly lived in the past. He made the past present in his poetical efforts. After his death he became a part of the past and a presence for the future generations. His passion for the past made him a part of that which is immortal in literature.

Ghalib and the Past

Keats had a long tradition of his own English Literature to depend on and derive from. Moreover, he had a rich heritage in the form of Latin and Greek literatures, through English translations. Ghalib had his own Urdu literature before him but it was very scanty – just a couple of poets and Mir, the best of all. He had inherited the fabulous Persian and the aromatic Arabic literature. Moreover unlike Keats, he had a direct acquaintance with the best of Persian and Arabic. There neither were translations nor did he need any.

There is one more interesting aspect of this facet of the literary heritage of Ghalib. The grandfather of Ghalib came to India during the reign of Mughal King Shah Alam II and his language was Turkish. Ghalib was brought up in a Persian atmosphere at Agra where Persian was the language of the elite as well as a medium of instruction. The changes in the political, literary and social circles had developed a new language, i.e. Urdu and it became the mother tongue of Ghalib. We do not know whether Ghalib derived anything from Turkish but he definitely did from the Persian tradition and the Arabic one. As a

10. Quoted by Judith O'Neill in *Critics on Keats*, p. 14.

result, Ghalib was always proud of his Turkish origin and used to call himself a "Turkish Hindu". Moreover he was well aware of the fact that his ancestors had been great wielders of the sword. Swordsman ship, horsemanship and archery were in the line but not in his veins although the family pride in the military profession was there. The glory was gone and it was a severe shock to him. It was not only passing away of the glory and grandeur of his ancestors which greatly aggrieved him, it was also the painful sight of the fading grandeur of the Mughal suzerainty that was a greater shock. It sent him a-day-dreaming which produced the most poignant thoughts, feelings, and endowed his poetic creations with a haunting melody as

Daure hei phir har gul-o-lala par khayal,
Sad qulsitaan nigah ka saman kiye hue.
Ji dhoondta hei phir wohi fursat ke rat din
Beithei rahen tasawware janan kiye hue

Again my imagination runs
Towards roses and tulips, and encompasses
A hundred flower-beds for the spectacle
My soul seeks the same leisure
That it enjoyed before, when for days and nights
I used to sit and contemplate the beloved.[11]

The beloved is not just a particular girl of flesh and blood; it is the luxury, the grandeur and glory of the past, the beauty that was and is no more and nor shall it come back. This is one aspect of the picture of the past in Ghalib.

This aspect of the past in Ghalib doesn't have much to do with the present comparative study. Keats, as much as we know through his biographers and his own voluminous letters, never took pride in what the family was or what it had been. And yet modern researches into the life and character of Keats are quite interesting.

---

11. Yusuf Husain, tr., *Urdu Ghazals of Ghalib*, pp. 216-17.

There are several accounts as to the family of Keats and ancestral professions. One recorded and firmly well believed in is by Robert Gittings in his study of Keats. He believes that Thomas Keats, the father of our poet, was one from Reading. " Many families of Keate, Keates or Keats in the West country originated from the Berkshire Keatses, and their armigerous members bore the arms of the Berkshire family, three wild cats passant in pale sable(College of Arms)".[12] Equally interesting is the martial appearance of the boy. His early years belied him, none could have seen the future poet in him. There was no mark of the Muse: as there was none in the boy Ghalib. Gittings writes about 'Keats's militant and violent temperament at school.'[13] He quotes Holmes, a school fellow of Keats.

"'He was a boy whom anyone from his extraordinary vivacity and personal beauty might easily have fancied would become great— but rather in some military capacity than in literature.'"[14] And we know Ghalib had not only a military background but quite a robust and martial appearance also.

Let us go to the travels of Ghalib into the 'realms of gold' and see what, 'goodly states and kingdoms' did he explore. Keats has his best of wanderings into the royal demesne of 'deep-browed Homer'. Ghalib had equally great worlds before him in the works of Firdausi, Sheikh Sa'di, and Rumi-masters of the ancient Persian literature. The *Shahnama* of Abul Qasim ibn Hasan Firdausi tells of the heroic tales in the form of 'masnavis' of divine love and sufi gnosis. The masnavi form is flexible and lends itself to amatory, elegic or didactic themes. Fayyaz Mahmud wrote, "Mirza Ghalib played many tunes on this instrument, some of his mathnavis taking rank with the product of the greatest masters of the form in Persia."[15]

---

12. Robert Gittings, *John Keats* (Harmondsworth: Penguin books), 1968, pp. 638-39.
13. *Ibid*, p. 45.
14. *Ibid*.
15. Fayyaz Mahmud, *Ghalib: A Critical Introduction* (Lahore: University of the Punjab), 1969, p. 125.

Besides, Ghalib might have gone through many a work of ancient masters like Umar Khayyam, Hafiz of Shiraz and Al-Maari whom he mentions at several places.

The major occupation of Ghalib was neither with the classical Arab poets nor with the classical Persian: it was with the Persian poets of the Mughal court who flourished in India during the reign of Akbar, the Great Mughal Emperor. Ghalib admired, appreciated and to some extent followed those Persian poets who were either born in India or came to India from abroad, flourished and died here. Amir Khusro, the sweet singer of India, is at the top in this list. He sang of love, the perennial strain of Ghazal, and did not mix up other considerations with the feelings of amor. He had a wider field and used various modes and mores to give full expression to the inexhaustible fountain of wit, wisdom, love, fellow-feeling and humanism but it was the love theme which attracted Ghalib. Here are a few couplets of Amir Khusro rendered into English by Fayyaz Mahmud:

Your face shines with freshness and bloom. I pray that
It may become even lovelier to kill me.
Your heart is made of granite. Let it become harder
To make an end of me.
Since Khusro has become accustomed to a wet shirt- front,
Because of his two streaming eyes
Let the ever welling tears keep his shirt-front
Dripping for ever:[16]

Moral and philosophical issues soon got mixed up with the theme of love and the mixture was a pleasant one. It happened particularly with the poets of the Mughal court.

In the 16th and 17th centuries the Mughal court attracted talents from all over the Muslim world. Poets, painters, architects and designers, musicians and missionaries flocked to the royal court.

16. Fayyaz Mahmud, pp. 146-47.

"The poets and painters had a special welcome and so some of the best Persian poetry ever written, was the work of poets, who did all their work in the Indo-Pak sub-continent." [17] Urfi, Naziri and Zahoori are some of those whose works appealed to Ghalib. There is something more than just 'love' in a typical Ghazal of Urfi. He tries to express his entire emotional experience with all its physical, intellectual and spiritual facets: the deeper probing into the soul are not yet there as they are with Ghalib. He says:

> Although men of discernment (men with gnosis) know the secrets of the mysteries, do not touch on any delicate issue, because Men of Law (the Pharisees) would declare you an unbeliever (without a moment's hesitation).[18]

Ghalib, we will note, studied and thought and developed a stronger strain in his Ghazals.

Naziri was a contemporary of Urfi but excelled him In his tone, meaningfulness and depth of emotions and intellectual aspirations. Sayyid Fayyaz Mahmoud quotes the Ghazal with the first couplet.

We are all made of the same clay, but there are degrees between us, like those between the decanter and the wine-glass. We are different from each other, without doubt, as far as colour and fragrance are concerned, but in reality we have grown out of one seed.[19]

And points out that Naziri deals with eternal issues and imbues his subject with intense feeling. He continues:

> There is no wailing or gnashing of teeth, but with dignity and poise, he acknowledges man's insignificance against the vastness of Creation. He is aware of the divine spark in man and has pride in man's intrinsic worth. His conviction that we play a key role in the drama of life and his great courage in facing the unknown, are the bass notes of his Ghazal, whose impression is that of a point of light fighting immense darkness, and not of a skirmish in the lists of love. The ghazal as a form

17. Fayyaz Mahmud, p. 147.
18. *Ibid*, p. 148.
19. *Ibid.*, pp. 149-50.

> has travelled far, when it could give a passionate utterance to such fundamental problems.[20]

Of all the Persian poets it was Abdul Qadir Bedil who most influenced the early Ghalib. It was to him that Ghalib looked for inspiration. In many a couplet he praised Bedil and eulogised his way of writing. Bedil flourished in the Muslim period (1644-1720), just a century before Ghalib when the Persian Ghazal had reached almost a perfection dealing with an immense variety of themes – "Faith and doubt, assertion of self and helplessness against the tyranny of love, man's insignificance against man's vital role in God's creative processes, a sense of futility and an ironical rebellion against the stern dictates of time, nostalgic love for the Infinite and echoless laughter in the emptiness of space; these were some of the problems which beset the mind of the poets of the Muslim world."[21] Bedil had these very themes and presented his observations in an intricate language with far-fetched metaphors; and more often than not his meanings were shrouded in mystery and obscurity. This aspect carried away the early Ghalib who asserted that 'it was a miracle to compose Urdu verse after the style of Bedil.'[22]

Bedil is Known for his intricate language, and a penchant for far-fetched images. He is full of recondite fancies also. In this respect he quite often resembles the English Metaphysical poets. Here is one of his couplets:

> In the poem of life, which from the beginning to end is continuous rhythm, the thought of this unreal existence is like the faltering of metre in a verse.[23]

We also find that the mystical and the intellectual note intermingle in Bedil. Ghalib inherited much of the imagery and intricacy of style from Bedil as is evident from the following couplets:

---

20. *Ibid.*, pp. 151-52.
21. *Ibid.*, p. 152.
22. *Tarz-e-Bedil main rekhta likhna/ Asadullah khan qiyamat hei.*
23. Fayyaz Mahmud, pp. 152-153.

1. *Shumare-e-subh marghoob-e-mushkil pasand aya*
   Tamasha-e-bayek kaf burden-i- sad dil pasand aya.
2. *Ba faiz-e-bedil inaumidi-e-javed asan hei*
   Kashaish ko hamara uqda-e-mushkil pasand aya.
3. *Hawa-e-sair-e-gul aaina-e-be mehri-e-qatil*
   Ki andaz-e-ba khoon ghaltidan-e-bismil pasand aya.[24]

1. The counting of the rosary's beads has become pleasing exploits for (my) Idol, who loves difficult exploits—a pleasant show is indeed that of stealing a hundred hearts by a single hand.
2. By the grace of Heartlessness, eternal despair is easy—the unloosing likes our difficult knots.
3. The desire to contemplate the rose is the mirror of the pitilessness of the killer—who likes the spectale of the butchered bird palpitating in its own blood.

The language and the metaphors are all in the style of Bedil. The compound word in the first couplet ' bayek-kaf-burden-i-sad-dil' i.e. ravish a hundred hearts with one hand is typically Bedilian ; the elaborate expression is entirely Persian. The early poetry of Ghalib is extensively Bedilian. The result was that early efforts of Ghalib were laughed at and condemned. Ghalib was proud of his studies into the Persian language and literature and always talked highly of Persian masters.

There were not many Urdu poets before him as the literature had just crossed over infancy to youth but Ghazal had come to its own and there were masters like Sauda and Mir Taqi Mir. Of all these Ghalib acknowledged the mastery of Mir in composing the Ghazals. At a number of places he has expressed his appreciation of the Ghazals of the great master.

---

24. Translated by Prof. Alessandre Bausani in "Ghalib and Bedil's Style", International Ghalib Seminar Vol.I, edited by Dr. Yusuf Husain Khan (New Delhi: All India Ghalib Centenary Committee, 1969-70), pp. 65-66.

Rekhta ke tumhe ustad nahin ho Ghalib,
Kahte hein agley zamane mein koi Mir bhi tha.
Apna yeh ageedah hei baqaul-e-Nasikh,
Aap be behrah hei jo mo 'taqide-e-Mir nahin.

Ghalib, thou art not
The only master of Urdu;
They say in former times
There was a man called Mir.[25]

Ghalib my conviction
Is like Nasikh's that
"One who doubts the greatness of Mir
Is himself an Ignoramus".[26]

Ghalib acknowledged greatness wherever he found it and exhibited a keen sense of appreciation where it was due. The poetry of Mir has poignancy and subtlety unsuppressed by any poet in Urdu. Moreover he has a lucidity and simplicity of expression of his own. Sayyid Fayyaz Mahmud wrote about him:

> Mir's poetry offers a unique blend of keenly felt emotion, faith in the powers that be, and strong protest against the inequities of fate. The sharp stab of emotion, nobody else has been able to convey as well as he, and the finesse of his suggestiveness is all his own. He was neither a mystic nor an intellectual, yet there is no supineness in his plaints. As for pathos, which is free from sentiment and pain which stops short of being tragic, no Urdu poet has expressed it so felicitously and with such inevitability as Mir.[27]

Certain couplets of his contemporary poets and predecessors were also much appreciated by Ghalib:

---

25. Yusuf Husain, *Urdu Ghazals of Ghalib*, p. 67.
26. *Ibid.*, p. 115.
27. Fayyaz Mahmud, pp. 159-60.

Dikhlaiye lejake tujhe Misr ka bazaar

Khwahan nahin lekin koi wan jins-e-garan ka. **Sauda.**

Qaem aur tujh se talab bose ki, kiyonkar manoon,

Hei to nadaan magar itna bhi nadan nahin. **Qaem.**

Tum mere pas hotey ho goya

Jab koi dusra nahin hota. **Momin Khan.**

These couplets have been rendered into English by Professor Alessandre Bausani:

1. "Having brought thee to the bazzar of Egypt thou must be displayed (to be sold); but there, there is no buyer for so precious merchandise." (The allusion is to the small price paid by the Egyptian merchants for the beautiful Joseph).
2. "Why should I believe that Qa'im requested a kiss from thee? He is, I admit, a simpleton but not so incapable of learning (as not to have understood that a kiss is not requested but taken).
3. "It is if thou werest with me, whenever nobody else is with me."[28]

It has been pointed out that Ghalib was so much enamored of the couplet of Momin that he was willing to give away his Diwan in return of this one. There is a strange drama in all these verses. The first two are in the form of a dialogue. The dialogue is not only highly poetic, it is dramatic also. The third verse is not a dialogue, it is a situation of quiet contemplation, the situation of loneliness raised to the best of situations, that is, the companionship of the Beloved. It could have been surpassed only by Ghalib and he did it and with a poignancy of his own:

My soul seeks the same leisure

That it enjoyed before, when for days and nights

I used to sit and contemplate the beloved.[29]

---

28. Alessandre Bausani, p. 64.
29. Yusuf Husain, *Urdu Ghazals of Ghalib*, p. 217.

The two poets went to the past in search of the models of perfection and they were able to find models of their own choice and liking. They went to the grand masters of the past and the past fed them and nourished them. Then they went to the past to seek support for their native personal talents. It is only when the plant is firmly rooted to the ground that it can best flourish and spread its branches far and wide. That is what Keats and Ghalib did. They could grow well because they knew what tradition was; they could maintain their freedom also; they could stand on their own feet and spread the wings of their imagination where it could best flourish.

In his early efforts Ghalib was a 'Bedilian', that is , his ghazals were full of intricate linguistic combinations and far-fetched similes and metaphors after the style of Bedil. The result was that the essential poetic quality was lost in the elaborate expression. Ghalib was soon conscious of it. His friends also brought this fact home to him and when he sat down to compile the first collection of his ghazals for press, he eliminated quite a number of his couplets which were too 'Bedilian'. Exactly after fifty years of his death the manuscript, now popularly known as Nuskha-e-Hamidia was discovered in the Hamidia library of Bhopal.[30] It shows that Ghalib, on the advice of his friends deleted many of his ghazals from his first printed Diwan but the Nuskha-e-Hamidia contains all that was almost lost to the readers and critics of Ghalib. Critics have discovered signs of immaturity and plenty of 'Bedilianism' in the early ghazals of Ghalib.

In his letter addressed to Maulavi Abdul Razzaq Shakir, Ghalib pointed out that 'From the age of fifteen to twenty- five he wrote purely on imaginary themes and it became a voluminous Diwan within ten years. When he came to discretion, he rejected it and deleted page after page. He kept only 10-15 couplets out of it.[31] .

---

30. Mufti Mohamad Anwarul Haq, *Diwan-e-Ghalib Jadeed, Alma'roof Ba Nuskha-e-Hamidia* (Lucknow: Uttar Pradesh Urdu Akademi, 1982), pp. 3-6.

31. Mirza Mohammad Askari, ed., *Adabi Khatut-e-Ghalib*, p. 122.

On the basis of his close acquaintance with the past Masters, Ghalib could take to a destination of his own. He bowed down before only a few of them, paid due reverence where it was necessary but always maintained his freedom and distinction. The simplicity and lucidity, charm and meaningfulness is not the result of his imitating any Grand Master: it is a development, a growth and a perfection achieved by him through Nature and Art.[32]

Ghalib imitated none for he felt there was none before him whom he could imitate. He indeed, confessed that he never used a structure the authority of which he could not find in the works of the past Masters. Ghalib had an unfailing memory and stored the best of classics in his mind which in turn put forth a work of art, unimitated and inimitable.

Far from the London of his day, Keats went to the ages gone by—the Greek realms of Gold and the Elizabethan world of wonders created by the dramatist Shakespeare. He paid fealty to Apollo, the Greek God of Poetry and could, in quite an innocent way, put the Laurel crown of the god on his head. Then, it was Shakespeare who charmed him most. A single word, or a phrase from Shakespeare would send him to aesthetic ecstasy as the ones from the *Tempest*:

> Keats writes to his friend John Hamilton Reynolds: Whenever you write say a word or two on some passage in Shakespeare that may have come new to you; which must be continually happening notwithstanding that we read the same play forty times—for instance, the following, from the Tempest, never struck me so forcibly as at present,
>
> "Urchins"
>
> Shall, for that vast of night that they may work,
>
> All exercise on thee—"
>
> How can I help bringing to your mind the line—.
>
> In the dark background and abysm of time.

32. Longinus, the great romantic critic long back noted that both Nature and Art go to produce a sublime work of art. See D.K. Chopra, ed. *Literary Criticism: An Anthology* (Meerut: Loyal Book Depot, 1974), p. 132.

I find that I can not exist without poetry—[33] No critic ever found that Shakespeare was too much with him or for that reason he himself never felt that he was imitating the inimitable. But the spirit of Shakespeare was with him and he cultivated in him those qualities which go to make a great poet and which were coming up in him also. What is the quality that goes to form a man of Achievement? He found it was 'Negative Capability' which Shakespeare possessed so enormously.[34] His painter friend Benjamin Robert Haydon had notions of a good Genius presiding over him. Keats too felt the presence of some genius presiding over his efforts.

" Is it too daring to Fancy Shakespeare this Presidor?"

Wrote Keats to Haydon.[35]

The influence of Milton on Keats was much like that of Bedil on Ghalib. Ghalib had to be told that he was becoming too much of 'Bedilian' while Keats could judge himself quite early and could come to his own true self. Milton had Latinised our English but Keats did not allow Latinism to overtake him. Early Ghalib is too Persianised while Keats is not Latinised. He is sometimes childish and youthful as much as a novice cannot avoid being. While he came to write *The Fall of Hyperion*, he had already noted it to his dismay that his earlier attempt was much in the line of Milton. He wrote to his friend Reynolds," I have given up *Hyperion*—There were too many Miltonic inversions in it—Miltonic verse cannot be written but in an artful or rather artist's humour. I wish to give myself up to other sensations. English ought to be kept up."[36] And so Keats took English in simple sensuous way since he loved phrases 'like a lover.' There was a time when Urdu poetry (Rekhta) was almost an insult to Ghalib and he advised his readers to 'overlook his Urdu verse since it did not contain the true quality of Ghalib'[37] and a time came when he was proud of his Urdu verse:

---

33. The Letters of John Keats, p. 21.
34. *Vide supra*.
35. The Lletters of John Keats, p. 29.
36. *Ibid*, p. 384.
37. Haali, *Yadgar-e-Ghalib*, p. 106.

Jo yeh kahe ki Rekhtah kiyonke ho rashk-e-Farsi

Gufta-e-Ghalib use ekbar do suna ki yoon.

To one who says "How can

Urdu be by Persian envied?"

Just once recite a verse of Ghalib

So he can see that 'tis like this.[38]

That is, Ghalib found his true genius In Urdu (and his true popularity, too), and not in his Persian endeavors (although in his Persian works he is equally great). He went to the past but became Great not because of his imitation of the past, he became great in spite of the past.

O thou who art fascinated by the eloquence

Of the ancient masters of poetry,

Be not a scorner of Ghalib,

Who is part of thine own time.[39]

Keats became great not that he imitated the ancient masters: paying due respects to the past he became great in his own way by following the ' sensations' of his heart. He maintained his individuality, his distinction and that made him great. When he came to write the second *Hyperion*, he wrote English as it ought to be written. The poem was considered as his 'most mature attempt'. It has been recognized as the strengthened promise of poetic maturity but fate was not kind to him and the deteriorating health did not permit him to complete the poem. His earlier works, particularly Odes, had already been blessed with immortality by Apollo.

---

38. Yusuf Husain, *Urdu Ghazals of Ghalib*, p. 111.
39. Yusuf Husain, *Persian Ghazals of Ghalib* (New Delhi: Ghalib Institute, 1980), p. 67.

5
THEIR THEMES

Ghalib: The Theme of Love

Urdu poets are notoriously popular for being poets of love. Urdu poetry is commonly condemned for dealing with 'Aashiq-Mashooq' and their petty follies, foibles, delusions and day-dreaming and all that goes on in the 'trade of love'. I cannot deny the fact that the major concern of Urdu poets is love but then what life is without love. In English literature it began with the father of English poetry, that is, Chaucer, whose *opus* bears testimony to the fact. *Amor Vincit Omnia*, that is,'love conquers all' cannot be forgotten by any reader of Chaucer. The theme travels meanderingly through the ages to 'The Love Song of J.A Prufrock' of T.S.Eliot to the modern poets like Ted Hughes and Geoffrey Hill and many a one love—begone songsters. "It is better to have loved and lost than never to have loved at all." Wrote Tennyson, who was basically a love—poet in the tradition of Keats. Love, in its Proteun shape, plays hide and seek with the mortal millions and more so with the poets of all languages and literatures, of all nations and of all ages. It may be love divine or love profane or just simple love of youthful man and woman. It may be romantic love, passionate love or love with a lot of guile and bile. It may be mystic love or it may be mortal, quite on the mundane plane. With love go life and all multifaceted, multidimensional mystery that life is surrounded with. Love was, is and shall be the only theme worth thinking about when one thinks of literature.

Ghalib was assigned the task of writing a history of the Timurs.[1] The court recorders used to send him page after page written in Urdu. His task was to transliterate it into Persian. His friends thought that Ghalib must be a great historian also. Presupposing that Ghalib was a scholar in terms of history, his friends sought clarifications on certain points related to history. Ghalib told them that he was absolutely ignorant of history, and explained his main concern through a Persian couplet.[2]

Ma qissa-e-Sikander-o-Dara nakhwandaheem

Az ma bajuz hikayat-e-meher-o-wafa mapurs.

I do not know the story of Alexander nor that of Daraius. Ask me not anything but the legends of love and loyalty.

Thus he is essentially concerned with love and the faithfulness of the lovers to one another and his *opus* is a testimony to the truth of his statement.

Dr. S.M. Ikram pointed out that "Love is a popular topic with the writers of Ghazal and Ghalib is no exception to it. It may be asserted that Love and Life are the two important themes of the poetry of Ghalib."

In his early poems Ghalib wrote of Love purely on imaginary lines. He presented imaginary, that is, just fanciful images and pictures and situations of love. He does not claim to have any experience of love-life with all its petty passions or mighty motions like jealously, rivalry, heartache or pangs of separations. We can get an idea of this aspect with the help of a few couplets of his early period.

---

1. The Mughals derived their pedigree from Timur, popularly known as Tamburlaine in the West.
2. Altaf Husain Haali, *Yadgar-e-Ghalib* (Lucknow: U P Urdu Academy, 1982), p. 54.

1. *Dar pe rahne ko kaha aur keh ke kaisa phir gaya*
   Jitne arse mein mera lipta hua bister khula.
2. *Bosa nahin na dijiye dushnaam hi sahi*
   Akhir zaban to rakhte ho tum gar dahan nahin
3. *Phir bekhudai mein bhool gaya rah-e-koo-e-yar*
   Jata wagarna ek din apni khabar ko mein.
4. *Waan gaya bhi mein to unki galiyon ka kaya jawab*
   Yaad thin jitani duayen sarf-e-durban ho gayeen.
5. *Ulajhate ho tum agar dekhte ho aaina*
   Jo tumse shahar mein hon ek do to kyonkar ho.
6. *Shabko kisi ke khwab mein aya hai wuh kahin*
   Dukhte hain aaj us but-e-nazuk badan ke paon.
7. *Maine kaha ki bazm-e-naaz chahiye ghair se tihi*
   Sun ke sitam zarif ne mujhko utha diya ki yoon.
8. *kiya khoob tumne ghair ko bosa nahin diya*
   Bas chup raho hamare bhi munh mein zaban hai.
9. *Gada samajh ke wuh chup tha meri jo shamat aae*
   Utha aur uth ki qadam mein ne pasbaan ke liye.

   1. She allowed me to stay at the door –
      Yet ere I reached there
      She changed her mind again
      And sent me off – with bedding still unopened. (p. 72)
   2. If you will not give a kiss
      So be it. Abuse me then,

3. Dr. SM. Ikram, "Ghalib ki Ishqia shairi", in *Ahwal-o-Naqd-e-Ghalib*, ed., Mohmad Hayat Khan Sayyal (Lahore: Nazar sons, 1967),p. 392.

4. The English rendering is by Yusuf Husain Khan in his *Urdu Ghazals of Ghalib* (New Delhi: Ghalib Institute, 1977), page No. is given immediately after the couplet or ghazal.

At least you have tongue,
Even if you have no mouth. (p. 132)

3. Again in self forget-fulness
I have lost the way to the street
Of the friend; else one day
I would go there to get news of me. (p. 139)

4. Even if I go there, what reply
Shall I give to her scolding,
Whatever words of blessing I recall
Were spent on the door –keeper. (p. 143)

5. Thou art vexed at the sight
Of thine own image in the mirror;
If there should be two more like thee
In the city, then how will it be? (p. 156)

6. Perhaps last night
She appeared in someone's dream;
Today that delicate – bodied one
Has aching feet. (p. 153)

7. At her assembly I rashly said
"No stranger should be present (here)".
With her usual tyrannous and subtle wit
She showed me the way out, like this. (p. 111)

8. Excellent: Did'st thou not give
A kiss to that other fellow?
Please keep silent— we too
Have a tongue in our mouth. (p. 167)

9. He was silent, mistaking me
To be beggar, but as ill-luck
Would have it, I got up
And touched the feet of her gate–keeper. (p. 237)

There are some quaint and funny situations dealing with the lover beloved relationship. The poet is not satisfied with the presentations of the contemporary poets. He must add something 'out of the way' to be distinguished from the others. The flickering mood of the beloved is presented in the couplet 1 where the lover was permitted to stay at the door of the beloved and he started unrolling his bedding, but in the meantime the naughty beloved changed her mind and ate her words. The visit to the beloved is presented in couplet 4 where the unhappy lover was detained at the door. He requested the door keeper in choicest words of blessing and endearment to permit him enter in. Now if he stood face to face with the beloved and listened to all her abuses and curses, what words of blessing he will use? He had already exhausted his vocabulary on the door-keeper. Then in couplet 8, there is another very interesting situation. She has been to some rival and was kissed but she says she was not. The lover says that he too has a tongue in his mouth, meaning thereby that he can prove it and more interestingly, that he can prove it by kissing her cheeks : it will be a kiss of the cheek that has already been kissed. The situation in couplet 6 is another unique affair where the beloved visits a rival in the dream and feels ache in her feet in the day. Another unique situation is there in couplet 9 where the lover is mistaken to be a beggar by the gate- keeper. It is the matter of great humiliation to the hapless lover. He falls on his feet and seeks admittance. The beloved in all these couplets is one from the pages of Urdu poetry past and contemporary but the lover is not one like one found any where. He faces fantastic situations and is like the traditional lover of Urdu poetry much humiliated. All these presentations as Ghalib confessed are purely fanciful. Much thought or practical experience did not go to the making of these.

Then, Ghalib was married at an early age, he shifted to Delhi, visited singing and dancing girls, fell in love with a one or two of them and there was a change. And the change was there both in head and heart, in thought and feeling and in linguistic presentation and imaginative reconstruction. He was now well exposed to the cotemporary trends of poetry as he became a frequent visitor to the court of poet – king Bahadur Shah Zafar where poetic gatherings were a regular feature. Now he was exposed to the keen arrows of eye lashes, to the pangs of separation as well as to the happy union, kisses and embracements. Most of the situations still seem to be imaginary and fanciful but there is a genuine touch of feeling and emotion now. There is a sincerity of passion and force of expression. Genuine occasion and expression do not come just from the texts, old or new. It has much to do with the confrontation of the situation and there were occasions for him now in the court, outside the court and, indeed, some happy-un-happy situations at home. His amorous alliance/s with some courtesan gave him a new depth in the affairs of love. Such is the case of the 'domni' (the dancing girl) whose early death caused Ghalib write one of the best poems of the agony of love. Here are some of the couplets:

1. *Dard se mere hei tujh ko beqarari hai,hai*
   Kiya hai zalim teri ghaflat shoaari hai, hai.
2. *Tere dil mein gar na tha aashoob-e-gham ka hausla*
   Toone phir kiyon ki thi meri gham gusari hai,hai.
3. *Kiyon meri ghamkhwargi ka tujh ko aaya tha khayal*
   Dushmani apni thi teri dostdari hai,hai.
4. *Umar bhar ka toone paiman-e-wafa bandha to kiya*
   Umr ko bhi to nahin hai paaedari hai, hai.
5. *Zahar lagati hei mujhe aab-o-hawa-e-zindagi,*
   Yaani tujh se thi ise nasaazgari hai, hai.
6. *Gul fashani hai naz-e-jalwah ko kiya ho gaya*
   Khak par hoti hei teri lalakari hai, hai.
7. *Sharm-e-ruswai se ja chhupna naqaab-e-khak mein*
   Khatm hei ulfat ki tujh pe pardadari hai, hai.
8. *Khak mein namoos-e-paiman-e-muhabbat mil gayi*
   Uth gayi duniya se rah-e-rasm-o-yari hai, hai.
9. *Ishq ne pakra na tha Ghalib abhi wahshat ka rang*
   Rah gaya tha dil mein jo kuch khauf khwari hai, hai.

1. It seems my sorrow
Makes thee restless
O, cruel one, what has happened
To thy indifference? Alas, alas!

2. If thou had'st not the courage
To bear grief's terror,
Why did'st thou console
My lamenting heart? Alas, alas!

3. Why did the thought of sympathizing
With me occur to thee ?
Thus my friendship has
Become thine own enemy. Alas, alas!

4. if thou had'st given a pledge
Of life long love, what of it?
Life itself
Has no permanence. Alas, alas!

5. To me the water and air
Of life are like poison
Since these did not
Agree with thee, Alas, alas!

6. What happened to the rose scattering
Of thy brilliant coquetry?
Now there are tulips
lying on thy grave. Alas, alas!

7. To guard thyself from calumny
Thou has hidden thyself
Behind a veil of earth; thou art unmatched
In keeping the secrets of love. Alas, alas!

8. The honouring of love's pledge

Is now beneath the dust;
Gone forever are the ways
And laws of friendship. Alas, alas!

9. O Ghalib, love had not
Yet caught the colour of madness;
In the heart was a longing for infamy
Which remains unfulfilled. Alas, alas! (pp.168-69)

Kalidas Gupta Raza who has made a chronological compilation of the poems of Ghalib, says that the poem was composed sometimes in 1821 when Ghalib was reaching towards maturity of body and mind, thought and feeling as well as that of lucidity of expression. The poem a is a poignant lamentation on the death of the beloved, the beloved who was faithful, smothered her love and doing so went to the grave quietly. She did not reveal the secret of her love to any one, just suffered quietly the pangs of unfulfilled love.

What type of beloved did Ghalib have? Urdu poets do not necessarily have beloved of flesh and blood. In most of the cases it is, I mean, all their love-business-call it love-prattle, just imaginary. There is a strong tradition to have a beloved, endow her with all cruelty and charms, make her favour the rival and let the poet-lover suffer the stings of jealousy and pangs of separation. Ghalib followed the traditional but endowed his beloved with the grace and qualities quite different from those of the traditional one. There is nothing of the courtesan or the vulgar in her. She is a pious lady residing in a palatial residence with a keeper and gate. Nobody is allowed to go to her without permission. She is always in her veils and has a sense of self respect. She is an ideal beloved. If the poet –lover has lost his heart to her, so has done many a hapless youth. An Ideal and beyond reach; so is the beloved in the ghazals of Ghalib . The following couplets reveal only a part of her piety:

1. *Dhool dhappa us sarapa naaz ka shiwa nahin,*
Ham he kar baithe the Ghalib pesh dasti ek din.

2. *Sharm ek adaa-e-naaz hei apne hi se sahi*
Hein kitne be hijab ki hein yoon hijab mein.

1. Thumping and slapping are not
   The habit of that graceful one;
   O Ghalib, it was we
   Who started this one day. (p. 111)
2. Coyness, even with oneself
   Is but a form of dalliance;
   How many unveiled ones
   Go about covered by a veil? (p. 137)

The graceful beloved has nothing to do with squabbling, the least possible violent act. It is the poet- lover who started thumping and slapping. Then she is very coy: even if there is no veil, her coyness itself is a veil to her.

It does not mean that the beloved of Ghalib is all through soft-spoken, delicate and gentle. She drinks alright, gets irritated and more often than not snubs the poet lover. But this aspect is an inalienable part of the female coquetry; that is, she must attract attention. And she uses her own ways and wiles and a ready wit:

1. *Sar udane ke jo wade ko mukarrar chaha*
   Hans ke bole ki tere sar ki qasam hai hum ko.
2. *Tum unke wa'de ka zikar unse kiyon karo Ghalib*
   Yeh kiya ki tum kaho aur wuh kahein ki yad nahin.
3. *Dekhye laati hei us shokh ki nakhowat kiya rang*
   Uski har baat pe hum 'nam-e-khuda' kahte hein.
4. *Yeh fitna aadmi ki khana veerani ko kiya kam hei*
   Hue tum dost jiske dushman uska aasman kiyon ho.
5. *Yehi hei aazmana to satana kisko kahate hein*
   Udoo ke ho liye jab tum to mera imtihan kiyon ho.

   1. When I wanted her to confirm
      The promise of my execution,
      smilingly she said,
      "We swear by thy head". (p.150)

2. Ghalib why should'st thou recall
her promise to her? How would'st
Thou feel, if she retorts
"We don't remember it at all" (p..145)

3. Let us see what colour the pride
Of the saucy one will adopt;
For every word she speaks, we say
"May God preserve thee" (p. 132)

4. The mischief of thy friendship is enough
To utterly destroy one's home;
To him whose friend thou art,
Why should the sky be enemy? (p. 160)

5. If this is merely testing,
Then what is vexing?
When thou dost belong to the enemy,
Why should'st thou demand my trial? (p.161)

The beloved has a sharp wit and cannot be won over. "We swear by thy head" is ambiguous: it may mean ' by your head, we'll behead you' as well as 'by your head, we'll not behead you'. Her very name stands for destruction, as couplet 4 indicates. True to the tradition, the beloved favours the rival to tease the poet-lover. Ghalib is true lover, a man of faith and fidelity. He is devoted to her in spite of all odds and ends. No mischief from the beloved or from the cruel heavens can make him forget the beloved. He stands for a Bond, be it the bond of enmity if friendship is not possible.

1. *Qata' kijiye na taa'llaq hum se*
Kutch nahin hei to adawat hi sahi.

2. *Wabasta us se hein ki muhhabat hi kiyon na ho*
Kijiye humare sath adawat hi kiyon na ho.

3. *Hum koi tark-e-wafa karte hein*
Na sahi ishq, musibat hi sahi.

4. *Yaar se ched chali jaye Asad,*
   Gar nahin wasl to hasrat hi sahi.
5. *Us fitna khoo ke dar se ab uthte nahin Asad*
   Is mein hamare sar pe qiyamat hi kiyon na ho.

   1. Don't severe thy relations
      With us; if there be nothing else
      At least there is enmity—
      So let it be. (p.206)
   2. We are not bound by this,
      That thou must necessarily love us,
      But have some dealing with us,
      Even if it is enmity. (p.148)
   3. We shall never give up fidelity;
      If there is no love, then
      Let there be calamity—
      So let it be. (p.207)
   4. Ghalib, let there be sweet teasing
      With the friend; if there is no union,
      Then there is smothered desire—
      So let it be. (p.207)
   5. Asad will not raise himself
      From the threshold of that disturber
      Of the Peace, even if doomsday
      Were to pass right over his head. (p.149)

Romantic love has infinite possibilities. There is one emotion overtaking the lover at this time but then within no time it disappears and is replaced by another one. There is jealousy at one time and at another the poet-lover is happy that the beloved is always there with him, in his very heart and mind. He is rich in his thoughts of beloved irrespective of the difference or indifference of the tyrannous one. And at times the cruel one is kindly listening to woeful ballads of Ghalib where romantic love is eulogized and presented in a variety of mores and moods. The best of his love poems is:

1. *Muddat hoi hei yaar ko mehman kiye hue*
   Josh-e-qdah se bazm chiraghan kiye hue.
2. *Karta hoon jam' phir jigar-e-lakth lakth ko*
   Arsa hua hei da'wat-e-mizgaan kiye hue.
3. *Phir waza'-e-ehtiyat se rukne laga hei dam*
   Barsoon hue hein chak gareeban kiye hue.
4. *Phir gam-e- Nala ha-e-sharar bar hei nafs*
   Muddat hoi hei sair-e- chiraghan kiye hue.
5. *Phir purshish-e-jarahat-e-dil ko chala hei ishq*
   Samaan-e-sad hazar namakdaan kiye hue.
6. *Phir bhar raha hei khama-e-mizgaan bakhoon-e-dil*
   Saaz-e-chaman tarazi-e-damaan kiye hue.
7. *Baaham digar hue hein dil-o-deeda phir raqeeb*
   Nazzara-o-khayal ka samaan kiye hue.
8. *Dil phir tawaf-e-koo-e-malamat ko jae hei*
   Pindar ka sanam kadah veeran kiye hue.
9. *Phir shauq kar raha hei kharidaar ki talab*
   Arz-e-mata'-e-aql-o-dil-o-jaan kiye hue.
10. *Daure hei phir harek gul-o-lala par khayal*
    Sad gulsitaan nigah ka samaan kiye hue.
11. *Phir chahta hoon name-e-dildaar kholna*
    Jaan nazar-e-dil fareb-i-unwaan kiye hue.
12. *Maange hei hei phir kisi ko lab-e-baam par hawas*
    Zulf-e-siyah rukh pe pareeshan kiye hue.
13. *Chahe hei phir kisi kjo muqabil mein aarzoo*
    Surme se tez dashna-e-mizgaan kiye hue.

14. *Ek no bahar naaz ko take hei phir nigah*
Chehra farogh-e-mei se gulistaan kiye hue.
15. *Phir ji mein hei ki dar pe kisike pare rahein*
Sar zeir baar-e-mannat-e-darbaan kiye hue.
16. *Ji dhondhta hei phir wuhi fursat ke raat din*
Beithe rahen tasawwur-e-Janaan kiye hue.
17. *Ghalib hamein na chedh ki phir josh-e-ashk se*
Beithe hein ham tahiya-e-toofan kiye hue.

1. A long time has passed since the friend .
Was my guest; when by the ferment of the cup
The whole company was illuminated.
2. Again I gather the pieces of my liver;
An age has passed since the invitation
Was given to her lashes.
3. Now again, on account of over-caution
My breath is choked; it is a long time
Since I tore my front-opening.
4. Again the breath is hot with spark-exhaling sighs;
A long time ago we went to see
The spectacle of the illumination.
5. Love has come again to ask about
The condition of heart's wound, having first
Prepared a hundred-thousand salt-cellars.
6. I am again dipping the pen of eye lashes
Into heart's blood, to make an embroidered
Design of flowers on the skirt.
7. Again the heart and the eye
Have become rivals—the one for gazing
And the other for thinking about her.

8. The heart goes back
   To the street of reproach, and there
   Lays waste the idol temple of selfish pride.
9. My yearning love once more demands a customer
   To whom the wares of reason, heart and soul,
   Can be offered for the sale.
10. Again my imagination runs
    Towards roses and tulips, and encompasses
    A hundred flower-beds for the spectacle.
11. I want to open the letter of the beloved again,
    So that I may gift away my soul
    To its deceptively written address.
12. Once more there is longing to see her
    Appear on the balcony, her black tresses
    All dishevelled about her face.
13. Desire wants her to stand before me,
    Face to face, when she has sharpened
    Her dagger-like eyelashes with antimony.
14. Again the eyes yearn to gaze at a coquette
    Fresh as spring, with rose like face,
    Flushed with the splendor of wine.
15. Again my heart yearns to lie
    On her door-step, and put my head
    Under the obligation of the door-keeper
16. My soul seeks the same leisure
    That I enjoyed before, when for days and nights
    I used to sit and contemplate the beloved.
17. O Ghalib, don't disturb us!
    With gushing tears we are determined
    To produce a deluge. (pp. 215-17)

The English rendering, more often than not, does convey neither the beauty nor the meaningfulness of the original. All great works of Beauty are untranslatable but we must have the nearest best for the sake of appreciation and evaluation. And Yusuf Husain is the only help to us.

I have quoted the ghazal in full for two reasons. First, it presents Romantic love in all its beauty and splendor. There is no' parched tongue' and no 'sad satiety' as we will note in Keats. Here it is an idealized picture of the lover-beloved in their various moods and passions. It is, indeed, love unfulfilled. It is not reduced to dust and ashes: it is in its sublime form. Secondly, it presents some sublime pictures. The beloved used to be a guest of the poet- lover and there was all beauty, fragrance and drinking and illumination, merry- making and chatting all the time. For long she has not been invited; she must come again. He wants to be killed by the lashes, to drink together and see her 'purple- stained mouth'. And if the meeting is not possible, no matter. He would like to sit and think of the beloved all day and night as he used to do in the past happy days of leisure and pleasure.

' Contemplate the beloved' in couplet 16 fails to convey the idea of the Urdu ' tasawwur – e – janaan'. This compound word has as much beauty and meaningfulness as "The Bright star" of Keats.[5]

Faiz Ahmad Faiz, the famous revolutionary poet critic of Pakistan, appreciated the poem for a different reason. He noted that in most of the cases the couplets in the ghazals are in their meaning independent of one another but in this ghazal there is a unique continuity and one couplet goes well with the preceding as well as the succeeding one. Thus the ghazal is an example of an organic whole.[6] It was pointed out by John Holloway that the Odes of Keats taken together constitute an organic whole.[7]

---

5. See below.
6. Faiz ahmad Faiz,"Ghalib ki ek Urdu Ghazal" in *Aajkal* ed. By Mehdi Abbas Husaini, New Delhi: Publications Divisiion, Feb. 1974.
7. John Holloway," The Odes of Keats" in Juditho'Neill, ed. *Critics on Keats* (London: George Allen, 1967), p. 59.

Along with the idea of love go the ideas of rivalry and jealousy. As tradition would have it, poet-lover has a rival and it is presupposed that the unkind beloved showers favours on the rival and thus adds to the agony of the true lover. Consequently the lover is tormented by jealousy. We have already noted that the friend visited someone in the dream, as a result of which she felt pain in the legs. See how Ghalib presents the visit – it is a visit in some dream.The lover in Ghalib would never bear the reality of the situation. Here are a few couplets to show the element of rivalry and jealousy in Ghalib:

1. *Ziker us pariwash ka aur phir bayaan apna*
   Ban gaya raqeeb aakhir jo tha razdaan apna.
2. *Tujh se to kutch kalam nahi hei par ai nadeem*
   Mera salaam kahyo agar namabar mile.
3. *Nazar lage ne kahin uske dast-o-bazoo ko*
   Yeh log kiyon mere zakham-e-jigar ko dekhte hein.
4. *Chhora na rashk ne ki tere ghar ka naam loon*
   Har ek se poochta hoon ki jaoon kidhar ko mein.
5. *Ishq mein bedad-e-rashk-e-ghair ne mara mujhe*
   Kushta-e-dushman hoon aakhir, garchi tha bimar-e-dost.

   1. Talk of that lovely nymph,
      And our description of her beauty—
      Our former keeper-of-secrets, it seems,
      Has now become our rival. (p. 67)
   2. My boon companion, I have no complaint
      To make to thee; but if thou dost meet
      The messenger that thou did' st recommend,
      Just wish him well, on my behalf. (p. 238)
   3. Pray God that her hand and arm
      Be protected from the evil eye;
      Why do these people peer so keenly
      At the depth of my heart's wound? (p. 130)

4. For fear of envy of others,
I do not mention the name of thy house;
I ask everyone I meet
Only "where should I go?" (p. 138)

5. In love, the tyranny
Of the other's envy killed me;
Finally I have been slain by a foe,
Although first afflicted by the friend. (p. 79)

Rivalry in love is quite natural. The poet-lover will go only for the most beautiful nymph. He will have to send her a message of love. He cannot go to her; it is below dignity. The messenger heard of the beauty of the beloved in the choice words of the lover (like Ghalib). How can he resist the temptation of falling in love with her. In couplet 2 above, the messenger has not returned back to the poet-lover. He has just fallen in love with her. Ghalib asks a companion to remind the bearer of the message what task he was assigned by the hapless lover. And the whole story is presented in the form of a salutation to the messenger. There is another aspect of the element of the romance. The poet-lover does not want that the beloved be seen or heard by anyone; or that any other person should come to know of her house. When he goes to her, he just asks every passer-by "where should he go?" He even does not want that the people should see his wounds made by the tyrant one. The evil-eye of the rivals may afflict her(who made the wound). And finally, it is envy that is undoing the lover. It is, indeed the love of the friend but then it is envy of the foe which results in great misery to the lover. Ghalib presents, an analytical study of love, rivalry and jealousy; such a frank and bold presentation Urdu poetry had not yet seen.

Ata Mohammad Sho'la noted about the beloved of Ghalib "Ghalib is the first Urdu poet who diverted the attention of the Urdu-knowing people from the courtesans to the basic problems of life and tried to present the beloved as a member of civilised and cultured society."[8]

---

8. Ata Mohmmad Sho 'la, "Ghalib aur Tasawwur-e-Mehboob". *Shair,* Bombay, Ghalib Number 1969.

At times we note that Ghalib treats of love in a lighter vein, he does not seen to be quite serious. But this aspect is not there in his poems: there the poet-lover is faithful and devoted to the beloved. His concept of love has been called 'romantic' by Dr. S.M. Ikram.[9] I have already quoted in full the poem wherein he laments the death of his beloved. In a letter to Mirza Hatim Ali Beg Meher he makes a mention of his love while consoling with him on the death of his beloved.[10] In another letter addressed to the same friend, he comes before us in a different light. Meher is still depressed on account of the death of his beloved. Now Ghalib condoles with him in a different tone: "In my early youth a pious man advised me that we should not go for austerity, we should not condemn a life of evil ways. Drink, eat and make merry. But remember be a fly on the sugar-candy and not a fly on honey. So I acted upon this advice. One who does not die may lament the death of the deceased one. No shedding of tears and no elegiar tone, please! Thank God for liberation. And if you are happy in bondage, take a Munna Jaan if Chunna Jaan is gone."[11] The letter is written in a light tone and does not do justice to the thinking of Ghalib on the theme of love. In his youth, because the times were like that, he might have courtesans for pleasure or passion but Ghalib the poet knows distinction between the two as is evident from the following couplets:

1. *Har bul hawas ne husn parasti sho'ar ki*
   Ab aabroo-e-sheewa-e-ahl-e-nazar gayi.
2. *Farogh-e-sho'la-e-khas yek nafas hei*
   Hawas ko pas-e-namoos-e-wafa kya
3. *Khanazad-e-zulf hein zanjir se bhagen ge kiyon,*
   Hein giraftar-e-wafa, zindaan se ghabrain ge kiya.

---

9. Dr. S.M. Ikram, *op. cit.*
10. Prof. A.A. Saroor, ed., *Aks-e-Ghalib*, (Aligarh: Muslim University, 1973) , p. 111.
11. *Ibid.*, p . 114.

1. Every father of lust now claims
   To be a worshipper of Beauty, the honour
   Of men of true vision is gone. (p. 231)
2. The brightness of the flame
   From straw is momentary:
   Of the honour of fidelity
   Lust knows- - what? (p. 62)
3. We are the slaves of her tresses- -
   Should we then flee from chains?
   We are the captives of faithfulness- -
   Should we fear prison - - or what? (p. 58)

In couplet 1 Yusuf Husain gives the literal translation. 'Father of lust' means a man of lust. 'True vision' should be understood to mean 'true love' and the whole idea of Ghalib becomes clear. In the couplet 2 Ghalib asserts that passion or lust is momentary like the brightness of flame which springs when a piece of straw catches fire: while love is a permanent aspect of life: it is not a passing show. In couplet 3, he puts his own theory of love in the most romantic colours: the poet-lover is chained by the slender tresses of the beloved. He is a slave to fidelity: what does he care for prison chains or prison houses? There is no question of going from one beloved to the other. It will be an insult of love.

Union with the beloved is an important aspect of romantic love. All the efforts, struggles and movements of the lover are for union or 'wisal'. Ghalib does not seem to be very keen on this issue. Union with her or 'wisal' amounts to 'love's sad satiety' in the words of Keats. Moreover, it amounts to the ceasing of all activities in Ghalib, it amounts to the lessening of the 'desire' and efforts for the achievement of the ideal. The beloved is an ideal and an ideal is considered beyond grasp. Here are a few couplets of Ghalib to give us an ideal of efforts for 'wisal' and 'wisal' itself:

1. *Wuh aaye ghar mein hamare khuda ki qudrat hei*
   Kabhi hum unko kabhi apne ghar ko dekhte hein.

2. *Unke dekhe se jo aajati hei munh par raunaq*
   Wuh samajhte hein ki bimaar ka haal achcha hei.
3. *Gar tere dil mein ho khayal, wasl mein shauq ka zawal*
   Mauj muheet-e-aab mein mare hei dast-o-pa ki yoon.
4. *Neend uski hei dimagh uska hei raatein uski hein,*
   Teri zulfein jiske baazoo par pareshan ho gayeen.

   1. Her visit to our house would be
      A proof of God's omnipotence;
      Sometimes we gaze at her,
      And then look back at our house. (p. 130)
   2. By seeing her, my whole face is brightened;
      And she thinks that the sick one's condition is good.
      (p. 144)
   3. If thou thinkest in thy heart
      That in union my yearning love would lessen,
      The tidal wave of the sea, beating hands
      And feet, showed me it would be like this. (p. 111)
   4. His is the sleep, his the desire,
      And his are all the nights.
      On whose embracing arm
      Thy tresses lie dishevelled. (p. 143)

Couplet 1 is very popular but the English rendering is not upto the mark. The idea is that of wonder and astonishment at her arrival. Is it possible? Is it true? Does she really stand in my house? My poor house! Couplet 2 is equally popular and difficult to be put into any other language. The 'sick one' is the love-lorn' poet-lover who is naturally brightened when the beloved happens to look at him. Couplet 3 indicates that 'wisal' lessens desire. The wave in union with ocean tries to come out and run to the shore to strike its head against. How happy is the man who attains union with her? is the idea in couplet 4.It reminds us of many a picture in Keats.

Ghalib: The Theme of Beauty

Beloved and the concept of beauty are two distinct terms. Beauty is a wider term and comprehends all that is there in the visible and invisible universe. Beloved is just an aspect: for mortal human beings in general and for the poets in particular all Beauty is almost summed up in the beloved . Beloved is the direct and easily intelligible aspect of Beauty that manifests itself in various objects, thoughts and feelings 'Matter'. Says Dr. Bijnori, 'has no shape. It has no beauty and no ugliness. Beauty is not external, it is internal. Beauty does not lie in the mass of the matter, it lies in the eyes of the beholder. The heart of an observer of Beauty is a Flame. Matter is only a gauze around the lamp."[12] The learned critic asserts that the poet is spell-bound by the revelation of the Divine Beauty through the material objects. Beauty in itself is Divine: It was, is and shall be and needs an observer to find it out. It is everywhere – in birds, beasts, flowers, blades of grass, clouds, in the face of a maid, in the moon and the sun and the sea.

When we come to Ghalib with a view to studying his concept of Beauty, we note that he presents life as a manifestation of the Divine Beauty. There is Divine Beauty all around us in the world but it is the assigned task of the poet to see, and reveal that Beauty as much as his talents permit him. Beauty is not there in the body, nor is it there in the spirit: "Beauty is there in Beauty; the task of the poet is to create it and this is their secret."[13] Ghalib had that insight and talent which perceived beauty in its various manifestations and could give it an exquisite expression by putting together all the forces of 'nature and art'.[14]

---

12. Abdul Rehman Bijnori, *Muhasin kalam-e-Ghalib* (New Delhi: Anjuman Taraqqi-e-Urdu, 1983), p. 76.
13. *Ibid.*, p. 18.
14. Longinus, the great romantic critic, long back pointed out that the sublime art is a product of the inborn talents and much study and exercise on the part of the writer. See R.A. Scott-James, *The Making of Literature* (London: Secker& Warburg, 1953), Chapter eight.

In his early efforts, and even in latter ones, Ghalib presents Beauty on external plane. It is the beauty of the female face and character. In many a couplet of incomparable sweetness, he presents the beloved:

1. *Dekh us ke sa' id-e-seemin wa dast-e-pur nigar*
   Shakh-e-gul jalti thi masle shama, gul parwana tha.
2. *Le to loon sote mein usake paon ka bosa magar*
   Aisi baton se wuh kafir badguman ho jaega.
3. *Tere sar-o-qamat se yek qad-e-aadam*
   Qiyamat ke fitne ko kam dekhte hein.
4. *Ham se khul jao bawaqt-e-mai parasti ek din*
   Warna ham chareinge rakh ke 'uzr-e-masti ek din.
5. *Mange hai phir kisi ko lab-e-baam par hawas*
   Zulf-e-siyah rukh pe parishaan kiye hue.
6. *Mere dil main hei Ghalib shauq-e-wasl, shikwa-e-hijraan*
   Khuda wuh din kare jo us se mein yeh bhi kahoon wuh bhi.
7. *Lakhon lagao ek churana nigah ka*
   Lakhon banao ek bigarna utab mein.

1. They saw her silvery mien
   And decorated hands;
   The twig of the roses burned like a candle
   And the rose was its moth.[15]
2. I would have kissed her feet
   While she lay sleeping—
   But refrained, since from such deeds
   That infidel would have become suspicious. (p. 47)

15. This couplet is quoted from Kalidas Gupta Raza, *Diwan-e-Ghalib* (Bombay: Sakar Publishers, 1988), p. 118.

3. The commotion of the Day of Doom
Is less by the stature of one person;
Thy cypress-like stature
(Was cut out of it).[16]

4. At the time of drinking wine, one day
Be free and unrestrained with us;
Else we shall tease thee, pretending
The excuse of drunkenness, one day. (p. 112)

5. Once more there is longing to see her
Appear on the balcony, her black tresses
All dishevelled about her face. (p. 216)

6. Ghalib, in my heart is a longing
For love's union, and a complaint
About separation; would to God
That I Could tell her this, and that, too. (p. 166)

7. One stolen glance as here
And ten million blandishments;
Ten million bedecking of herself
Against one angry gesture.

All the couplets are on the physical plane; they deal with physical aspect of the beauty of the Beloved. The beautiful appearance of a woman attracts one, willy nilly. It is more so in the case of a poet who is born to love and sing of his love. Even in this presentation, Ghalib is unique. Couplet 3 presents the beloved as the commotion of the day of doom. Her cypress- like stature was shaped (cut out) of the 'Fitna-e-qiyamat'. Couplet 7 is again remarkable in revealing the beauty of the Beloved coquette. The stolen glance and the angry face have a charm of their own, far above any make up.

---

16 The translation by Yusuf Husain is not upto the mark ; it is my own rendering.

Urdu poets have generally been depreciated for not paying proper attention to the beauty of nature and English poets are supposed to be the worshippers of nature. It is pointed out that they are faithful observers of nature and put forth minute details of the varying aspects of the beauty. A close study of Shakespeare, Milton, Wordsworth and some other romantic poets proves the facts but it does not substantiate the idea that our Urdu poets are lacking in the observation and presentation of the beauty of nature. I make a mention of Haali, the famous disciple of Ghalib and another poet Nazir Akbrabadi and come to Ghalib because Urdu critics have not observed this aspect in the poems of Ghalib.

Ghalib is a poet of Beauty and found Beauty all around him and more so in the object of Nature like the stars, the sun and moon, the dew-drops, the waves of the sea, spring and autumn and flowers which he could see in plenty, in the Fort and by the bank of the river Yamuna where he had frequent walks when he first came to Delhi. The beauty of the stars was fascinating to him. Haali quotes an incident.

> Once Ghalib lay on his cot and looked towards the sky. Seeing the stars scattered in a disorderly way, he commented, "A task which is done with a prior planning mostly turns out to be awkward. Look to the stars. How unplanned they lie scattered. There is no proportion; no arrangement; no creepers and no buds. But the emperor is sovereign. Not a single one can move of its own."

His patron recovered after a long illness and Ghalib composed a few couplets on the beauty of Nature.

1. *Phir is andaaz se bahar aai*
   Ki hue meher-o-mah tamashaai.
2. *Dekho ai sakinaan-e-khitta-e-khaak*
   Is ko kehte hein aalam araai.
3. *Ki zameen ho gayi hei sar ta sar*
   Raukash-e-sathe charkh-e-minaai.

---

17. *Yadgar-e-Ghalib*, p. 65.

4. *Sabze ko jab kahin jagah na mili*
   Ban gaya roo-e-aab par kaai.
5. *Sabza-o-gul ke dekhne ke liye*
   Chashm-e-nargis ko di hei beenaai.
6. *Hai hawa mein sharaab ki taseer*
   Badah noshi hei bad paimaai

   1. Again the spring came with such a spendour
      That the sun and the moon have become its spectator.
   2. Behold, O dwellers of the earth
      This is called world –adorning.
   3. The earth has put to shame
      The surface of the enamelled sky.
   4. When the verdure could find no more place on earth
      It became the green film on the water's surface.
   5. To behold the greenery and the flowers
      The eye of the narcissus has been given sight.
   6. The air is full of intoxication;
      To move in it is like drinking wine. (pp. 265-66)

This is a ghazal and there is a continuity of thought as it was written for a particular occasion. It brings out the beauty of the spring season though in the limited way as there is no mention of various birds, beasts and scenes so popularly associated with the spring season. We should keep in mind the tradition of Urdu poetry where nature with all its flora and fauna had not yet become a topic with the poets as ghazal was almost a product of urban culture. Whatever Ghalib did carries weight from this point of view also. Moreover, we can easily find hundreds of couplets in his Urdu *Diwan* where he presents Beauty of nature in its different aspects. The whole ghazal with the concluding words of couplets 'mauj-e-sharab' is a unique lyric in praise of wine and all the joys, pleasures and thrills associated with wine. Here are some more couplets from other ghazals:

1. *Hei josh-e-gul bahar mein yaan tak ki har taraf*
Urte hue ulajhte hein murgh-e-chaman ke paon.
2. *Nahin bahar ko fursat na ho bahar to hei*
Tarawat-e-chaman-o-khoobi-e-hawa kahie.
3. *Theen banat-u-na'sh gadroon din ko parde mein nihaan*
Shab ko unke ji mein kiya aaya ki uryaan ho gayeen.
4. *Ug raha hei dar-o-deewar pe sabza Ghalib*
Ham bayabaan mein hein aur ghar mein bahar aai hei.
5. *Bhooke nahin hein sair-e-gulistaan ke ham wale*
Kiyonkar na khaaiaye ki hawa hei bahar ki.

1. The bird of the garden
Tries to fly, but everywhere
Her feet are fast entangled
In the spring ferment of flowers. (p. 153)
2. If the spring is short - lived
Still it is the spring; so recount
The freshness of the flower-bed
And the excellence of the air. (p. 261)
3. The daughters of constellation
Lay hidden in the veil of daylight;
What has caused them
To display their nakedness at night? (p. 142)
4. O Ghalib, lush grass
Is growing over the doorway and the wall
While we wander in the wilderness;
Spring has visited our house. (p. 230)
5. We are not hungry
To promenade in the garden,
But why should one not gulp it
Since it is the air of spring. (p. 266)

Every couplet presents beauty in an aspect almost unobserved by anyone before Ghalib. In couplet 3, the stars – the fairy-companions of the moon Goddess in Keats, are presented as the daughters of the constellation. They lie hidden in the veils all through the day but, see, in the night how they throw away their thin garments and reveal all their beauty and splendor to the human beings below.

Couplet 5 tells of the intoxicating charm of the air during the spring season: who will be so dead of soul and cold of heart as not to go out to feel the sensation of the genial air.

The object of beauty, wherever and whatsoever it is, creates in the seer a great feeling of delight. Moreover, there is a feeling of awe and wonder at the sight of the miraculous objects. The poet is simply wonder-struck to see how and wherefrom the objects come up and who the creator is. It is for the poet, for one who watches and receives and for one who has a heart to be charmed. And all the time there is a high mark of interrogation before him. What is the source of all this beauty all around us?

1. *Yeh pari chehra log kaise hein*
   Ghamza-o-Ishwa-o-ada kya hei.
2. *Shikan-e-zulf-e-umbreen kiyon hei*
   Nigeh-e-chashm surma sa kiya hei?
3. *Sabza-o-gul kahan se aae hein*
   Abr kiya cheez hei hawa kiya hei?
   1. Who are these fairy-faces? And what are all
      These amorous winkings, these blandishments and coquetry?
   2. Why these ambergris-perfumed, curling tresses?
      What is this antimony-anointed glance?
   3. From whence come this verdure and all these flowers?
      What is the cloud, and what the air? (p. 241)

Ghalib's love of beauty touches strange boundaries. He finds pleasure even in pain. The thorns of life frighten him not, not do the boils in the foot. The sword of the killer is not an instrument of torture to him. To be killed by such a fairy child is no death. And here he makes no distinction between life and death. Death for Beauty is death conquered; it is the very essence of life:

Muhabbat mein nahin hei farq marne aur jeene ka

Usi ko dekh kar jeete hein jis kafir pe dam nikle.

In love there is no difference

Between life and death; we live

For the sight of the same lovely infidel

For whom we give up our life. (p. 264)

In one of his early couplets he lamented that life is impossible without love and that he had no strength with him as to enjoy the miseries that follow the life of love:

Be ishq umr kat nahin sakti hei aur yaan

Taaqat ba qadr-e-lazzat-e-aazar bhi nahin.

Without love one cannot pass one's life,

But here we donot even have the power

To savour the taste of suffering. (p. 122)

It is the 'taste of suffering' which has given a new dimension to his poetry of love. Ghalib led a life of poverty, misery and deprivations and was well-acquainted with the misfortunes that may befall to the life of even the lowest. Consequently he came to see strange pleasure in the wounds that the sword of time inflicted upon him. He presented this aspect of life in many a painful couplet of beauty:

1. *Ishq se tabeeat ne zeest ka maza paya*

   Dard ki dawa paai dard-e-ladawa paya.

2. *Zakhm par chirjkein kahan tiflaan-e-be parwah namak*

   Kiya maza hota agar pathar mein bhi hota namak.

3. *Ishrat-e-qatlgah-e-ahl-e-tamanna mat poochh*

   Eid-e-nazzarah hei shamsheer ka uryaaan hona.

4. *Koi mere dil se poochhe tere teer-e-neem kash ko*

   Yeh khalish kahan se hoti jo jigar ke paar hota.

5. *Joo-e-khoon aankhon se bahne do ki hei sham-e-firaq*
   Mein yeh samjhoonga ki sham'een do farozaan ho gayeen.
6. *Ham ko sitam aziz sitamgar ko ham aziz*
   Nameherbaan nahin hei agar meherbaan nahin.

   1. From love itself
      Nature has found life's savour;
      Found the cure for pain,
      Found the pain without a remedy. (p.28)
   2. The thoughtless boys donot sprinkle
      Salt on wounds; 'twould be a blessing
      If in the stones they throw
      There should be salt. (p.104)
   3. Ask not the lover's joys
      As they reach the place of execution;
      The naked scimitar appears
      As the 'Id moon to their sight. (p. 45)
   4. Someone should ask about the pleasure
      From the half – penetrated arrow;
      If it had passed right through the liver,
      It would not prick like this. (p. 69)
   5. Let a stream of blood flow from the eyes,
      For 'tis the night of separation;
      so I shall think that there
      Two candles have been lit. (p. 142)
   6. We are fond of cruelty;
      The cruel one is fond of us;
      Although she is not kind,
      Neither is she unkind. (p. 132)

Ghalib loves love because it has given a meaning to life. Love is not only a whole time affair but it is also a matter of enduring pain. Other misfortunes pale into insignificance before the mighty pangs of it. Hence these pangs are not a matter of sorrow: they are to be appreciated and enjoyed. The arrow which pierces the heart half way gives the true pleasure of suffering. The blood flowing from the eyes has been compared with the candles by the poet thereby heightening the intensity of pain and beauty of tears. A close relationship between the lover and the beloved is maintained: one is cruel and unkind and the other derives pleasure out of this cruelty and harshness.

And now I come to the final phase of Beauty in Ghalib. As I noted earlier, beauty in the world is a manifestation of the Divine Beauty. Everything in the world is a design of the creator. It is he who appears in the flowers, in the sunset, sunrise, the moon and the face of a beautiful woman. All things flow from Him—all joys, pleasure and pain also; so they are all beautiful. Here are some couplets:

1. *Kah sake kaun ki yeh jalwagari kiski hei*
   Pardah chhora hei wuh usne ki uthae na bane.
2. *Asl-e-Shahood-o-shahid-o-mashhood ek hein*
   Hairaan hoon phir mushahida hei kis hisaab mein.
3. *Jabki tujh bin nahin koi maujood*
   Phir yeh hangama ai khuda kiya hei.
4. *Lataafat be kasaafat jalwa paida kar nahin sakti*
   Chaman zangaar hei aaina-e-baad-e-bahari ka.

   1. Who can tell
      Whose is this glorious revelation?
      He has let down a veil
      Such as none can lift. (p.257)
   2. The reality of the sight of God,
      The one who sees, and what is seen,

All in effect are one; I am amazed
Then, what is all this witnessing? (p. 137)

3. When nothing exists in the world without Thee.
Then O God, what is all this tumult for? (p. 241)

4. Purity cannot manifest itself
Without impurity;
A flower-bed is the rust
On the mirror of the spring breeze. (p. 41)

From the Persian poets Ghalib had imbibed much of the mystical tradition. The mystical poet saw the Divine Beauty in every object around him. The world as such is but a manifestation of the Divine glory. The pleasure of the Divine is to manifest itself in a variety of forms. Explaining he mystical concept of Beauty, Fayyaz Mahmood wrote:[17a]

> God is not only omnipotent and all-good, He is the source of being and beauty. He is also the friend, the Beloved and the ecstasy of thinking of him is 'the wine' and 'the intoxication.' These symbols occur in all sufi poetry and a drunk may not just be a wine bibbler and a sinner, he may really be one who looks on His face and is drunk with His Beauty. The world is nothing but a mask worn by Him and the one passionate desire of all poets who have sufistic leanings is to lift that veil and gaze on him raptly.

In the couplet 4 above, Ghalib has expresses a very powerful idea. Divinity is Purity, It is the Beauty supreme. In order to manifest itself into the world, it must assume some form. The form, whatever it be, will always be in material terms. It can never be that much beautiful as the form divine which it symbolizes. It may even be ugly, impure and sometimes painful also. Hence Beauty can be seen in the ugly and painful as they are all manifestations of the Beauty Divine.

17a. Fayyaz Mahmood, *Ghalib: A Critical Introduction* (Lahore : University of the Punjab, 1969), p. 129.

Keats: The Theme of Love

John Keats has been a popular poet with the reading public of all the ages but he was, is and shall be a favourite with the young people, both boys and girls. It has been aptly pointed out that " Keats is a poet who has always held an important place among the authors studied at school between the ages of fourteen and seventeen."[18] The reason is not far to seek : he loved , he wrote of love and presented love in a variety of moods and passions. And love is the central concern of human life everywhere and in every age. It is not too much to say that a poet is one who sings of love, of love and nothing but love. It is the only mighty passion before which all the passions pale into insignificance because it dominates other considerations.

His early efforts in this direction were mostly imaginary like those of Ghalib. For long Ghalib remained in the world of imagination as Muslim society does not allow free mixing of the sexes. It was definitely more orthodox in the days of Ghalib. His early poem "Kite" is an illustration. Keats's "Give me women, wine and snuff" is in direct contrast:[19]

Give me women, wine and snuff
Until I cry out, 'Hold enough!'
You may do so sans objection
Till the day of resurrection;
For, bless my beard, they ay shall be
My beloved Trinity.

Ghalib in his " Kite" wants to keep himself away from the fatal charms of the female tribe. So does Keats in his early poetic venture.

Fill for me a brimming bowl,
And let me in it drown my soul;

---

18. Roger Sharrock, "Keats and the Young Lovers", Judith O'Neill, *Critics on Keats*, p. 50.

19. *The Complete Poems*, pp. 28-29.

But put therein some drug, designed
To banish woman from my mind. (pp. 6-7)

The two poems of Keats simply show his two different states of mind where the youthful boy is carried away and then scared by the charms of woman's beauty. He is moving towards romance this way or that—and strangely enough, he puts before us different pictures of man-woman love. His first long poem of love with its opening lines

A thing of beauty is a joy for ever:
Its loveliness increases; it will never
Pass into nothingness, but still will keep
A bower quiet for us, and a sleep
Full of sweet dreams, and health, and quiet breathing.
(p. 120)

promises to be great but *Endymion*: *A Poetic Romance* turns out to be a big poetic extravaganza and does not bear as much fruits as the labour Involved in . Moreover, it is not the love of man and woman that keeps Keats in a mood of romance; it is the love of a mortal and an immortal: it is the love of a shepherd- prince for the Goddess of Moon. There is much borrowing and much invention and the poem is interspersed with stray thoughts of great value as

He ne'er is crowned
With immortality who fears to follow
Where airy voices lead; .... (p. 172)

But on the whole the poem does not treat of love on the human plane and should not detain us for long. It is the presence of the Indian Maid which lends grace to the melancholy mood of love when she sings of the pain of suffering and high-cloyed sorrow:

To sorrow
I bade good morrow,
And thought to leave her far away behind.
But cheerly, cheerly,

She loves me dearly,
She is so constant to me, and so kind.
I would deceive her
And so leave her,
But ah, she is so constant and so kind!
Beneath my palm trees, by the river side,
I sat a – weeping.
In the whole world wide
There was no one to ask me why I wept
And so I kept
Brimming the water-lily cups with tears
Cold as my fears. (p. 253)

The picture of sorrow presented here goes well with the sorrow and suffering with which we are already familiar in the ghazals of Ghalib.

Keats is just a young boy and he knows that he is not yet mature in his understanding and presentation of love. In the preface to *Endymion* he wrote,[20]

> The imagination of a boy is healthy, and the mature imagination of a man is healthy; but there is a space of life between, in which the soul is in a ferment, the character undecided, the ambition thick-sided: thence proceeds mawkishness, and all the thousand bitters which those men I speak of must necessarily taste in going over the following pages.

When he comes to handle the theme of love again, there is not only a healthy imagination but a mature one also. He treats of youthful love in his poems *Isabella; or, the pot of Basil, The Eve of St. Anges* and *Lamia.*

The story of Isabella is derived from Boccaccio, the great Italian writer of *Decameron* but Keats treated of it in a way of his own.

20. *The Complete Poems,* p. 119.

Isabella, the sister of rich business brothers, loves and is loved by Lorenzo, a young business man and dealer with the brothers. They used to meet and enjoy the stolen moments of the bliss of love but they were espied upon. The two brothers are covetous and greedy and yet

> How was it these same ledger-men could spy
>
> Fair Isebella in her downy nest?
>
> How could they find out in Lorenzo's eye
>
> A straying from his toil? (p. 335)

They hatch a conspiracy and ask Lorenzo to go with them early in the morning so that he may be sent to some foreign country on a certain business. They take him to the forest and put him to the sword. The sister is told that Lorenzo had taken ship for a foreign land. The poor girl believes it and waits for Lorenzo and for waiting for long her beauty starts withering. And no Lorenzo came. Then one day in a vision she saw Lorenzo standing there before her and weeping. The phantom told her how he was killed and where he lies buried. She goes there with her trusted nurse and a knife hidden in her clothes. She locates the spot, unearths the body, cuts off the head, buries the body back and comes with the head of Lorenzo which she kept in a pot of Basil and all the time watered it with her own tears. The plant grew wonderously fragrant and bright and bred suspicion in the brothers. One day when the girl was away, they stole the pot and examined it in a secret place. To their dismay they found the head of Lorenzo. Horrified they left Florence never to return again. She searched her Pot of Basil but no one could say who stole it. She withered and pined and died. It is of such a love that Ghalib frequently sang:

> *Yeh na thi hamaari qismat ki wisal-e-yaar hota*
>
> *Agar aur jeete rahate yehi intzaar hota.*
>
> It was not our fortune to enjoy
>
> Love's union with the friend;
>
> Had we lived longer, then how
>
> Anxiously must we have tarried.

Keats concludes this poem thus:

> And so she pined, and so she died forlorn
> Imploring for her basil to the last.
> No heart was there in Florence but did mourn
> In pity of her love, so overcast. (p. 351)

Keats talks of love through another tale of love wherein the lovers escape into a happy wilderness. *The Eve of St. Agnes* is based on popular myth:

> They told her how, upon st Agnes' Eve,
> Young virgins might have visions of delight,
> And soft adorings from their love receive
> Upon the honeyed middle of the night,
> If ceremonies due they did aright;
> As, superless to bed they must retire,
> And couch supine their beauties lily white,
> Nor look behind, nor sideways, but require
> Of heaven with upward eyes for all that they desire.
>
> (pp.456-457)

Madeline is under the sweet whim. The brothers along with their guests are feasting, drinking and merry-making. She too has to dance but with a very careless regard and all the time seeks an opportunity to run to her chamber and that she does unespied. In the meantine the faithful knight, her lover Porphyro enters the mansion. He startles the old nurse who helps him to his lady's chamber and hides in a closet so

> That he might see her beauty unespied ,
> And win perhaps that night a peerless bride,
> While legioned fairies paced the coverlet
> And pale enchantment held her sleepy-eyed. (pp. 463-64)

Unespied he sees her beauty divine as she enters and prepares to undress to sleep in the dreams of St. Agnes. The art of Keats as a poet of Love, of romance and beauty reaches a perfection unequalled by any other poet. The stanza describing the beauty of Madeline has become a classic of English romantic poetry:

Full on the casement shone the wintry moon,
And threw warm gules on Madeline's fair breast
As down she knelt for heaven's grace and boon;
Rose-bloom fell on her hands, together pressed,
And on her silver cross soft amethyst,
And on her hair a glory, like a saint.
She seemed a splendid angel, newly dressed,
Save wings, for Heaven, Porphyro grew faint;
She knelt, so pure a thing, so free from mortal taint. (p. 467)

She dreams and sees fair Agnes in her dream. Porphyro comes out of his closet, takes up her lute and sings an ancient ditty called 'La belle dame sans mercy'. She opened her eyes and saw her dream come true but the glory of dream was not there . He looked pallid, chill and drear. In the dream he looked immortal with his dear complaining. Now they plan to escape from the cruel mansion unto the land of freedom and love. He had a home of his own for the fair bride over the southern moors.

The story reaches its end with the union of the lover and the beloved. Madeline lives in a world of fancy surrounded by her cruel brothers and escapes into a land of fancy with her lover. Fancy is too much with Keats. It is as if pleasures were possible in a land of fancy, and not in our world of reality. Love seems to be too delicate and sensitive a being for our life of reality. At the end, they are phantoms. And it all happened 'ages long ago.'

Keats derived the story of *Lamia* from Burton's *Anatomy of Melancholy*, who quoted it from Philostratus. Lamia is a witch, a serpent woman and she is transformed by Hermes into a beautiful woman. She loves young Lycius who is spell-bound by her beauty. She was a lovely graduate of Cupid's college and uses her charms to the best advantage.

And soon his eyes had drunk her beauty up,
Leaving no drop in the bewildering cup,
And still the cup was full- (p. 627)

The young lover thought she was a fairy and must disappear soon but no, she was very much there in flesh and blood. And then he saw her and heard her:

Let the mad poets say whatever they please
Of the sweets of Fairies, Peris, Goddesses,
There is not such a treat among them all
Hunters of cavern, lake and waterfall,
As a real woman, lineal indeed
From Pyrrah's pebbles or old Adam's seed. (p. 531)

He must have her as his bride. It is Lamia who through her magic makes all the arrangements for decoration and feasting. The questioning spirit of Keats is at work because he is to discuss what love is and what destruction does it bring in its train:

Love in a hut, with water and a crust.
Is – love, forgive us! – cinders, ashes, dust;
Love in a palace is perhaps at last
More grievous torment than a hermit's fast.
That is a doubtful tale from fairy land,
Hard for the non-elect to understand. (p. 634)

Appolonius, the old teacher of Lycius, comes to the feast uninvited. He is a sage and he cannot see his disciple enthralled by a witch. Lamia does not want him in the feasting. But he is definitely there and all her charms are gone.

Do not all charms fly
At the mere touch of cold philosophy? (p. 645)

Appolonius fixes his gaze upon Lamia and denounces her as a serpent. She gives out a frightful shriek and vanishes into air. Lycius cannot bear the shock; he falls down and dies.

Isabella or the Pot of Basil is a tragic story of love. It is a pathentic tale full of high sentiments and love as a Lord of Terrible aspect. *The Eve of St. Agnes* is a story of triumphant love with a lot of romance and adventure. The story of *Lamia* is also a story of love but here Keats introduces an element of magic, and makes his story a Tragedy of love. We feel pity for the serpent- woman because she loves, as well as for her lover to whom her love brought death. This is the destructive aspect of love.

Ode to Psyche presents a very happy picture of Love but it is again not on the mortal human plane.Psyche is the 'human soul' presented as a goddess with her lover Cupid, the god of love. What is remarkable is the happy mood of the poem and the happy union:

They lay calm-breathing on the bedded grass;
Their arms embraced, and their pinions too;
Their lips touched not, but had not bade adieu,
As if disjoined by soft-handed slumber,
And ready still past kisses to outnumber
At tender eye-dawn of aurorean love. (p. 516)

Psyche was not yet raised to the Olympean hierarchy and Keats would like her to be worshipped as a Goddess. So he would make a temple for her, be her priest and do all the adorations meet. He will build a rosy sanctuary for her

And there shall be for thee all soft delight
That shadowy thought can win,
A bright torch, and a casement ope at night,
To let the warm love in! (p., 521)

In his famous *Ode to a Nightingle* he comes to the human love on a very mortal plane. Love and female beauty are treated here in a very unhappy and melancholy mood. It is the mood of the times. His younger brother Tom had recently died. The world with all its heavy weight of misfortune was on his shoulders. He must seek an escape from the world ' where men sit and hear each other groan'. There is no room for any happiness in the world.

Where Beauty cannot keep her lustrous eyes,

Or new love pine at them beyond tomorrow. (p. 527)

Ruth and her story also donot present any happy picture of love. The whole poem is a study in transiency. And when he comes to the next poem *Ode on a Grecian Urn*, it is all a study in permanence.

Love is a permanent passion: one who is in love, he can never be out of it unless indeed, he is out of life. So when Keats writes of this aspect of life or that he can not ignore love. While describing the Grecian Urn and all the legends painted on it, he comes up to a very powerful aspect of love – its eternity. There we see the lover chasing the beloved, her struggle to escape and his warm love. It is a massage for all the generations to come:

Bold lover, never, never can't thou kiss,

Though winning near the goal – yet do not grieve:

She can not fade, though thou hast not thy bliss,

For ever thou wilt love, and she be fair! (p.535)

Commenting on these lines Miriam Allott pointed out that " Love is the permanent possession of the lovers only by being unsatisfied." This love is called happy and the adjective happy is repeated by Keats several times because it is above the sensual love:

For ever warm and still to be enjoyed,

For ever panting, and for ever young-

All breathing human passion far above,

That leaves a heart high-sorrowful and cloyed,

A burning forehead, and a parching tongue. (pp. 335-36)

By this time Keats had his own experience of love happy, unhappy and sometimes pleasantly painful. Sometimes Fancy cheated him so well and sometimes it gave him no consolation. It was tne state of idolence. When he comes to evaluate life and all that life promises, he finds himself disillusioned. In his long letter addressed to George and Georgiana Keats he pointed out 'neither Poetry, nor Ambition, nor Love have any alertness of countenance as they pass by me: they seem rather like three figures on a vase—a man and two women whom no one but myself could distinguish in their disguisement."[21]

The figures appear before him and he does not seem to be charmed by one or the other. This is how he treats of them in his *Ode on Indolence*:

> They faded, and, forsooth! I wanted wings.
>
> Oh, folly! What is Love? And where is it?
>
> And, for that poor Ambition – it springs
>
> From a man's little heart's short fever-fit.
>
> For Poesy! No, she has not a joy-
>
> At least for me- (p.543)

Love becomes a Dream to be enjoyed for ever when he comes to his very personal love as it is his only solace. It is in the sonnet *Bright Star*. The passion reaches its chastened climax in the last lines where the love of man and woman is presented through purely personal imaginings:

> No- yet still steadfast, still unchangeable,
>
> Pillowed upon my fair love's ripening breast
>
> To feel for ever its soft fall and swell,
>
> Awake for ever in a sweet unrest,
>
> Still, still to hear her tender-taken breath,
>
> And so live ever- or else swoon to death. (p.738-39)

The feeling of jealousy of which there is plenty in Ghalib is first encountered in *Endymion* but we find it on a very realistic plane in his *Ode to Fanny*. This Ode is rich in those feeling of pathos, jealousy, uncertainties and misgivings which are frequently encountered in the Ghazals of Ghalib. Here Keats has his own experience of love and all its painful pleasures. Confined to his bed, he lived next door

---

21. Maurice Buxton Forman, ed. *The Letters of John Keats* (London : Oxford University Press, 1952) p.314.

to Fanny Brawne and saw her moving out with all her glamour around. He presents himself as a beggar of love, as Ghalib never is. A woman is one who can be swayed to and fro by every wind that blows.

I know it, and to know it is despair
To one who loves you, sweet Fanny,
Whose heart goes fluttering for you everywhere,
Nor when away you roam,
Dare keep its wretched home,
Love, love alone, has pains severe and many:
Then loveliest, keep me free
From torturing jealousy.
Ah, if you prize my subdued soul above
The poor, the fading, brief pride of an hour,
Let none profane my holy See of love,
Or with a rude hand break
The sacramental cake;
Let none else touch the just new-budded flower.
If not- may my eyes close,
Love, on their last repose. (pp. 441-42)

Keats does not give us pictures of some imaginary beloved. Women of flesh and blood, married and unmarried, were there around him and he was carried away by the beauty of a couple of them. Is Beauty confined to the face of woman only? Is Beauty such a narrow idea? Let us go into details to see what Beauty means to Keats.

Keats: The Theme of Beauty

When we think of Keats,' Beauty' comes to our mind. Keats and Beauty have almost become synonymous. We cannot think of Keats without thinking of Beauty. Beauty is an abstraction; it does not give out its meaning so soon to its votaries. For Keats, it is not a mystery. He sees Beauty everywhere just as a mystic sees the vision of God, of his object of worship everywhere. Keats made Beauty his object of wonder and adoration. What is his idea of Beauty? Let us seek help from the writings of the poet himself.

The oft-quoted lines from *Endymion* 'A things of Beauty is a joy for ever: Its loveliness increases; it will never / Pass into nothingness,' have become a stumbling block in the way of understanding what he means by Beauty because the readers take the line for granted and never go into details to see what Keats here means by ' thing of beauty'. Keats says that there is dearth of noble nature, the days are gloomy and the ways of human life are over—darkened but then

Some shape of beauty moves away the pall
From our dark spirits.

It is some 'shape of beauty' which removes the darkening clouds from over our life. In his characteristic way, he enumerates the objects of Beauty:

Such the sun, the moon,
Trees, old and young, sprouting a shady boon,
For simple sheep; and such are daffodils
With the green world they live in;and clear rills
That for themselves a cooling covert make
'Gainst the hot season; the mid-forest brake,
Rich with a sprinkling of fair musk rose blooms;
And such too is the grandeur of the dooms
We have imagined for the mighty dead,
All lovely tales that we have heard or read-
An endless fountain of immortal drink,
Pouring into us from the heaven's brink. (p.121)

Most of these 'things of beauty' are the objects of nature. Loveliest of all is the face of woman of which he does not speak here as it is implied in the ' lovely tales'. Tales are, indeed, beautiful because of the love of man and woman. And we know he has already composed his sonnet 'On first looking into Chapman's Homer' wherein he talks of 'the realms of gold, and many goodly states and kingdoms...' That is, a great work of poetic composition is also a thing of beauty and a joy for ever. That its loveliness increases is a literal truth, proved by the passage of time.

Endymion is the first poem in which he dealt in detail with his concept of beauty. The theme of the poem is the poet's quest for ideal beauty. Cynthia, or the moon symbolises ideal Beauty while Endymion, the shepherd stands for the human soul in search of beauty. He attains his object through human love, that is , the love of Indian maid. The poem has allegorical significance wherein Cynthia, the Indian maid and the moon become one, suggesting a unity between Nature, Humanity and the Higher Spiritual Essence. Robert Bridges, a famous poet of 20th century, interprets this poem in the following words:

The moon represents "poetry" or Ideality of desired objects, the principle of Beauty in all things. It is supersensous quality which makes all desired objects ideal: and Cynthia, as moon-goddess, crowns and personifies and this represents the ideal beauty or love of woman: and in so far as she is also actually the moon as well as the Indian lady,— who clearly represents real or sensuous passion— it follows that the love of woman is in its essence the same with all love of beauty.[22]

The poem was badly reviewed by the journals of the day like Blackwood's and Edinburgh Quarterly,[23] and Keats was also pained but he had a way of his own and wrote to his friend J.A. Hessey, "Praise or blame has but a momentary effect on the man whose love of beauty in the abstract makes him a severe critic on his own works."[24] His friends also pointed out that the thing was not up to the mark. He was asked to write a Preface. He refused as a Preface

---

22. Quoted by Dr. S Sen ed. *John Keats: Selected Poems,* (New Delhi: Unique Publishers, 1990), p. 302.
23. John O. Hayden, ed. *Romantic Bards and British Reviewers* (London: Routledge & Kegal Paul, 1971) see pp.317 onwards
24. *The Letters of John Keats*, pp. 221-222

is addressed to the public and he had no "feel of humility towards the public – or to anything in existence—but the eternal Being, the Principle of Beauty."—He asserted that " I never wrote one single line of poetry with the least shadow of public thought."[25] It is his love of Beauty and devotion to the eternal Being, the Principle of Beauty, that forces him to write. Praise or blame cannot sway a man who is swayed by the mighty Principle.

All Keats's poetry from *Endymion* to *Hyperion* has one dominant theme and that is Beauty. There is the sensuous aspect in many of his sonnets and longer poems. He seems to be quite an epicurean when we find his eyes resting on 'Light feet, dark violet eyes and parted hair, / Soft dimpled hands, white neck and creamy breast, ear open 'To catch the tuning of a voice divine.' (p. 44) In "Calidora" he had already been surrounded by 'The Sweetlipped Ladies' and the beauty of the female form goes on haunting him in *The Eve of St. Agnes*:

Anon his heart revives, her vespers done,
Of all its wreathed pearls her hair she frees;
Unclasps her warmed jewels one by one;
Loosens her fragrant bodice; by degrees
Her rich attire creeps rustling to her knees.
Half hidden, like a mermaid in see-weed,
Pensive awhile she dreams awake, and sees,
In fancy, fair St. Agnes in her bed,
But dare not look behind, or all the charm is fled. (pp. 468-69)

It is so in *Lamia* where Keats takes his readers to 'That purple-lined palace of sweet sin' and frankly confesses that there is no such a treat among Fairies, Peries, Goddesses etc., as a real 'woman'. By the time he wrote *Lamia*, he had come to experience the love of a woman. He Knew that the charm and beauty of a woman had a fatal effect on man. And truly enough, Keats presents

25. *Ibid.*, p. 129.

before us the fatal aspect of love of woman. We cannot say that he was killed by the unkindness of Fanny Brawne because it was understood that the day he came back from Italy all healthy and in cheerful spirits, the two will be tied in nuptial knots.[28] We are told of his last days.

Frequently he held in his hand a little present that Fanny Brawne had given him – a small, oval, white Carnelian. It was the only tangible thing left to remind him of their engagement; for he would still not have her letters opened.[26]

Beauty of nature is spread all through the *Ouvres* of Keats. Like Wordsworth he is not a worshipper of Nature but he is a lover of the Beauty of Nature. He admires what Nature shows and reveals. The sun and the moon with all their Greek connotations, the stars or, say, the 'starry fays', 'silver lamps' the pastoral eglantine, the musk rose, the daffodils, hills and rills, songs of birds and rustling of leaves find a prominent place in the poems of Keats. He finds Nature Beautiful, in any form and every form and at every time of the year. Spring with all its greenery, fragrance, colours and music is beautiful but Keats finds Beauty even in autumn because he has an eye for the Beautiful. His *Ode to Autumn* is a unique presentation of the season which has mostly gone unseen and unsung by even the best of poets.

His early poems are luxuriously rich in the beauty of nature. As early as 1815, he wrote a sonnet addressed to Solitude and it presents a picture of

> Nature's observatory—whence the dell,
> In flowery slopes, its river's crystal swell,
> May seem a span; let me thy vigils keep
> 'Mongst boughs pavilioned, where the deer's swift leap
> Startles the wild bee from the foxglove bell. (p. 23)

---

26. Walter Jakson Bate, *John Keats* (New York: Oxford University Press, 1966), p. 625.

Again he wrote of the beauty of nature so that he might take the theme of patriotic lore for the delight of his soul:

Oh, how I love, on a fair summer's eve,
When streams of light pour down the golden west,
And on the balmy zephyr tranquil rest
The silver clouds, far, far away to leave
The meaner thoughts, and take a sweet reprieve
From little cares; to find with easy quest,
A fragrant wild with Nature's beauty dressed,
And there into delight my soul deceive. (p. 46)

In "Sleep and Poetry" he has a plan for his poetic ventures. He knows that for a successful life in act and thought, he must first go to Nature:

First the realm I'll pass
Of Flora and old Pan: sleep in the grass,
Feed upon apples red and strawberries,
And choose each pleasure that my fancy sees;
(pp.73-74)

In the same poem Keats reveals his mission: to bring balm to the suffering mankind through an understanding of the misery of human life:

Yes, I must pass them for a nobler life,
Where I may find the agonies, the strife
Of human hearts— (p. 74)

The beauty of nature detains him for quite a long time. And it is natural for one of Keats's nature. He just cannot leave unseen the swarms of minnows 'Staying their wavy bodies' gainst the streams/ To taste the luxury of sunny beams/Tempered with coolness.'[27] Day

27. " I stood tip –toe upon a little hill", p. 89.

in and day out, any weather, any season, there is beauty in nature all around every object. 'The poetry of earth is never dead'. It only needs an eye that watches and a heart that appreciates and Keats was endowed with both. The whole of *Endymion* is 'a flowery band' to bind the reader with nature and its various manifestations. The luxuriant details of nature are there in abundance.

When he comes to compose his Odes he finds the beauty of nature all around him and around every object. The song of the nightingale is the haunting melody. It sends him to the 'embalmed darkness' in the forest where the bird sings at her 'full-throated ease.'

The beauty of nature and his appreciation of it can be seen in the choicest words:

> I cannot see what flowers are at my feet,
> Nor what soft incense hangs upon the boughs,
> But, in embalmed darkness, guess each sweet
> Wherewith the seasonable month endows
> The grass, the thicket, and the fruit-tree wild-
> White hawthorn, and the pastoral eglantine;
> Fast-fading violets covered up in leaves;
> And mid-May's eldest child,
> The coming musk rose, full of dewy wine
> The murmurous haunt of flies on summer eves.
>
> (p. 528)

He composes three stanzas about Autumn with an exquisite expression of the different aspects of Autumn. And it comes from his direct observation as we note from his letter written to Hamilton Reynolds.

How beautiful the season is now – How fine thc air.

A temperate sharpness about it. Really, without joking, chaste weather – Dian skies- I never lik'd stubble –fields so much as now– Aye better than the chilly green of the Spring. Somehow the stubble—plain looks warm – This struck me so much in my Sunday's walk that I composed upon it.[27a]

Keats gives us a graphic description of the season of autumn. The first stanza is all ripe – fruitfulness, budding and flowers for the bees. The second stanza gives an authentic picture of Autumn through personifications of a rich farmer, a reaper, a gleaner and a wine grower. The third stanza is all music—the plaintive singing of the gnats, the bleating of the lambs, the chirp of the crickets, the soft treble of the red breast and the twitter of the gathering swallows in the sky. That he could see so much of beauty in autumn and express it with all lucidity is a rare feat of imaginative creation.

The nightingale and its song are the objects of nature which have become immortal in the hands of the poet. The 'hungry generations' cannot tread the bird down. The song will ever be there to give solace and comfort to the wearied and grief stricken-mankind. The *Ode on a Grecian* Urn is rich in nature as the Urn tells ' A flowery tale more sweetly than our rhyme:...' The 'Sylvan historian' has captured the spirit of spring in the trees, their boughs and leaves, and the trodden weed.

For Keats there is beauty in ' sweet-lipped ladies', in 'beaded bubbles winking at the brim' in blushful hippocrene' in ' the conquering sun of Spring' and in the tales and legends, old and new. The works of Homer, of Spenser and Shakespeare had a fascination for him. The Greek myths cast a spell on him and Elgin Marbles invited him again and again. The mighty works of art kept him in thrall and the poet always came from them with a mighty idea , a beautiful product or a pleasant sensation. 'On first looking into Chapman's Homer' is an example. Then, he read Cary's translation of Dante's *Inferno*:

> The fifth canto of Dante pleases me more and more—
> It is that in which he meets with Paulo and
> Francesca—I had passed many days in rather a low

27a. *The Letters of John Keats,* p. 384.

State of mind and in the midst of them I dreamt of
Being in that region of Hell. The dream was one
Of the most delightful enjoyments I ever had in my
Life—I floated about the whirling atmosphere as
It is described with a beautiful figure to whose
Lips mine were joined as it seemed for an age—
And in the midst of all this cold and darkness I
Rested on them sometimes with the lightness of a
Cloud till the wind blew us gain—

It was Hayden who took Keats and Reynolds to the Elgin Marbles, a recent collection from the Parthenon. Keats frequented these mighty works of art and was greatly charmed and inspired. He might have seen several vases, urns and marble pieces of Greek art and came out with his own work –*Ode on a Grecian Urn.* His *Urn* has stood the test of time and remains a sublime work of Art. He might have seen many things and he felt that ' there is left so much room for imagination'. That is why the *Ode* is so much full of question marks."The people of the world will fill in the blanks in their own way; I have felt certain blanks while telling my tale to them", sang Seemab Akbarabadi.[29] The questioning spirit amply illustrates the sense of wonder at the presence and further innumerable possibilities of the Beauty in the objects:

What leaf- fringed legend haunts about thy shape
Of deities or mortals, or of both,
In Tempe or the dales of Arcady?
What men or gods are these? What maiden loth?
What mad pursuit? What struggle to escape?
What pipes and timbrels? What wild ecstasy?

(p. 534)

---

29. *Bharegi bad mere isko duniya lakh rangon se/ Khilayen chhor di hein meine kutch apne fasane mein.*

The last two lines have raised a lot of controversy:

'Beauty is truth, truth beauty'—that is all
Ye know on earth, and all ye need to know.

His logic is simple: What is Beautiful is Truthful. What is ugly cannot be truthful. Find truth through beauty and /or beauty through truth. It is like Mahatma Gandhi's formula: God is love, love is God. Find one and you will see that the other one is also there. Beauty is no more a sensuous, physical or a sentimental affair. It has spiritual associations; it is a concern of the soul of man for the salvation of man. Search for salvation must come from the heart of man and Keats knew it. "I am certain of nothing but of the holiness of the Heart's affections and the truth of Imagination—what the imagination seizes as Beauty must be truth –whether it existed before or not – for I have the same Idea of all our passions as of Love they are all in their sublime, creative of essential Beauty."[30] Commenting on this aspect of the beauty in Keats. Matthew Arnold observed:

> The truth is that 'the yearning passion for the Beautiful', which was with Keats, as he himself truly says, the master passion, is not a passion of the sensuous or sentimental poet. It is an intellectual and spiritual passion. It is 'connected and made one', as Keats declares that in his case it was, 'with the ambition of the intellect'. It is, as he again says' the mighty *abstract idea* of Beauty in all things.' And in his last days Keats wrote: 'If I should die, I have left no immortal work behind me—nothing to make my friends proud of my memory; *but I have loved the principle of beauty in all things*, and if I had time I would have made myself remembered.' He has made himself remembered, and remembered as no merely sensuous poet could be: and he has done it by having 'loved the principle of beauty in all things'.[31]

---

30. *The Letters of John Keats*, p. 67.
31. Matthew Arnold, *Essays in Criticism, Second Series*, quoted by Judith O'Neill, p. 13.

Keats's idea of beauty is a very comprehensive one. It is not confined to what seems good, or beautiful or pleasing; it goes beyond these boundaries even to the most painful and unpleasant aspect of life. A true poet must see life as a whole if he has a truly poetical character. Explaining what a poetical character is and particularly his own poetical character. Keats wrote to his friend Woodhouse,

> ... it is not itself—it has no self—it is every thing and nothing – It has no character—it enjoys light and shade; it lives in gusto, be it foul or fair, high or low, rich or poor, mean or elevated—It has as much delight in conceiving an Iago as an Imogen. What shocks the virtuous philosopher delights the camelion poet. It does no harm from its relish of the dark side of things any more than from its taste for the bright one...[32]

An important aspect of his concept of beauty is to put joy and sorrow together. Joy and sorrow and melancholy and happiness cannot be seen nor appreciated in isolation. There is no 'unalloyed' happiness for him and there is no fear that does not promise hope. He loves the two with the same devotion: they are one and the same for the true poetical character. In his lyric "Welcome joy and welcome sorrow" he brings out the close relationship between the two and welcomes both.

> Welcome joy and welcome sorrow,
> Lethe's weed and Hermes' feather;
> Come today and come tomorrow,
> I do love you both together!
> I love to mark sad faces in fair weather,
> And hear a merry laugh amid the thunder.
> Fair and foul I love together: (p. 387)

In this poem, it may be noted, he has presented some peculiar but beautiful pictures all taken from the real phenomena of human

32. *The Letters of John Keats*, pp. 226-27.

life—'Serpent in red roses hissing; Cleopatra regal—dressed with the aspic at her breast;....'One of the dear phrases of Keats' the sweetness of the pain' occurs in this very poem. It is because of this sweetness that pain cannot be neglected; pain is an essential part of our life. The necessary relationship between joy and sorrow is best presented in his *Ode on Melancholy*. The first stanza of the poem tells us that true melancholy is not to be found among thoughts of oblivion, death or gloom. In the second stanza we note that melancholy descends suddenly and is linked with the perception of beauty and its transience. In the last stanza, Keats associates melancholy with beauty, joy, pleasure and delight and indicates that it can be felt only by those who can experience these intensely. Here is the third stanza:

> She dwells with Beauty—Beauty that must die;
> And joy whose hand is ever at his lips
> Bidding adieu; and aching Pleasures nigh,
> Turning to poison while the bee-mouth sips.
> Aye, in the very temple of Delight
> Veiled Melancholy has her Sovran shrine,
> Though seen of none save him whose strenuous tongue
> Can burst joy's grape against his palate fine;
> His soul shall taste the sadness of her might,
> And be among her cloudy trophies hung. (pp. 540-541)

Keats was not an escapist: he accepted life as it is. And life is rich in its joys and sorrows. He does not view the one in isolation from the other, he must see beauty in its entirety. Middleton Murry, in his trend—setting study *Keats and Shakespeare*, pointed out:[33]

33. John Middleton Murry, *Keats and Shakespeare* (London: Oxford University Press 1958) p. 75.

> 'Beauty in all things.' This was Keats's great poetic intuition, and the revelation of this beauty the great human purpose to which he dedicated himself and for which he was prepared to die. It sounds simple; it is tremendous. It involves a profound acceptance of life as it is, a passing beyond all rebellion, not into the apathy of stoic resignation, but into a condition of soul to which the sum of things—'foul or fair, high or low, rich or poor'—is revealed as necessary and true and beautiful: and for the creative genius of the poet it means not only to have this vision, not only to have attained 'high reason, and love of good and ill,' but to have the purpose and the power to reveal to men that good and ill are to be loved; not only the faculty to see that the sum of things is supremely beautiful, but the faculty to show to other men that it is supremely beautiful.

One has to take a very comprehensive view of things in order to arrive at the beauty of things. And when we have the totality of things with us, we will not hate any thing. The world of agony and strife will look as beautiful as the world of joys and pleasures.

In his *Endymion* he had pointed out that he would like to roam through the beautiful world of flora and pan and then he would bid these joys farewell in order to arrive at the true beauty of the things in the world. He would go to 'a nobler life where I may find the agonies, the strife of human hearts'—Keats reaches this stage in the second *Hyperion.*

The first *Hyperion* presents the fall of Saturn in his majesty and suggests the rise of powers more beautiful than his clan. His brother Oceanus consoles him in his hour of suffering and here Keats propounds the law of Beauty which is the eternal law: they have bred more beautiful progeny like the trees of forest which breed beautiful birds:

> We are such forest-trees, and our fair boughs
>
> Have bred forth, not pale solitary doves,
>
> But eagles golden feathered, who do tower

Above us in their beauty, and must reign
In right thereof. For 'tis the eternal law
That first in beauty should be first in might; (p. 428)

Those who have replaced the fallen gods are definitely superior to them in beauty. This sums up Keats's fundamental concept of beauty which he considered above all other things. The new gods are eager to give new shape to things They want to attain more knowledge in order to give birth to art and beauty.

In the second *Hyperion* Keats laid emphasis on the theme of suffering and its effect on poetic composition. He brings out poet's value to humanity and makes a clear distinction between a dreamer and a poet: the 'poet is a sage/ A humanist, physician to all mankind.' The dreamer vexes the world by his foolish imaginings while the poet 'pours out a balm upon the world.' But who can reach such a height, the height of poetic creation. Moneta, the mother of muses, informs the poet,

'None can usurp this height,' returned that shade,
'But those to whom the miseries of the world
Are misery, and will not let them rest. . . .' (p. 667)

The second *Hyperion* is a poem rich in thought content and it is great in its promise as the poet left it incomplete.

In fine, Beauty is there everywhere; it needs an eye to behold it. It goes with joy as much as it goes with sorrow. Life with all its pains and pleasures, springs and autumns, hopes and fears – life taken in its totality is beautiful. Beauty is the only reality: it is the truth of life. Death is as beautiful as life is. Keats found that the 'Principle of Beauty' operated all through every aspect of human life. Whatever Keats wrote he did it for the eternal Being, 'the Principle of Beauty,' and never stooped from the noble height wherefrom he could see the 'agony and strife' of mankind to arrive at the conclusion that 'Sorrow is wisdom.' He wrote to his brothers Tom & George Keats on 21 Dec. 1817 that 'with a great poet the sense of Beauty overcomes every other consideration, or rather obliterates all consideration.'[34] With Keats Beauty obliterated every other consideration.

Love and Beauty are not the only aspects of life with which our poets are concerned; these, indeed, are the basic issues with them but life is more than that and they know it. Ghalib and Keats see other issues like God, religion, fate and the mystery of life and in their own way render them for us to think about. Some philosophical issues are discussed in the next chapter.

---

34. *The Letters of John Keats*, p. 71.

6

THE PHILOSOPHIC OUTLOOK

Ghalib: God and Religion

Do poets have a religion? Do they believe in our gods and religious codes just as we do? Or they are a tribe apart? Was Shakespeare a Christian? Then why did a particular sect of Christians in America condemned him as an atheist and proposed a ban on his teaching.? Was Milton of the Devil's party? Do the poets alone see 'the necessity of atheism' in this priest – infested society? Coming to our poets, we note that Keats was born of Christian parents in a Christian country and baptized in the true Christian rituals. And yet they say 'Keats was a Greek', ' Beauty was his religion' and that 'he was a worshipper of Beauty'. Our Ghalib laughed at God, His angles and Paradise which was just a 'fool's paradise' in his reckoning. They are a tribe apart! They have everything to do with you and nothing with your gods and goddesses. And they were born in this religion or that and must have their own convictions, faiths, beliefs, idols and practices.

Ghalib is Muslim because he was born in a Muslim family, not that he accepted Islam of his free choice. He believed in the Allah of the Quran but not with that piety and respect which Muslims generally have towards Allah. As regards rituals of the Muslims he was the least respectful, the most indifferent; while his wife was a devout lady offering 'Namaaz' five times a day regularly and observing all the fasts in the month of 'Ramzaan'. Khwaja Altaf Hussain Haali, his dear disciple from Panipat, has recorded an incident. It happened when Delhi was conquered by the Britishers. Ghalib among others was also captured and presented before Col. Brown, the Commanding Officer. By appearance Ghalib looked a good Muslim. "You are a Muslim?" asked the Colonel. "Yes Sir," answered Ghalib, "but only half". "What do you mean ?" asked the Colonel again. "I drink wine but I do not eat pork". The officer smiled, had some more questionings with him and then respectfully and politely bade him to go. It may be noted that intoxicating drinks and pork are prohibited in the Quran. Ghalib used to drink, let me say, like a fish but he always drank imported from England and France. He could get his requirements through his friends and sometimes got it even from Meerut if it was not available in Delhi. At home wife, a pious lady, had to keep his eating utensils apart.

His biographers never mention if he ever offered prayer or observed fasts. There are frequent references to drinking alright in his letters as well as in poems. He was fond of gambling also and gambling is again an anathema to the Muslims. He was even arrested for keeping a gambling den. There are several anecdotes regarding his no observance of fasts. "How many fasts did you observe, Mirza, this time?" asked Nawab Mustafa Khan. "Not just one, Sir".[2] He answered with a pun on the word 'one'. Here 'one' suggests (1) that Ghalib missed only one fast and that (2) he did not observe a single one. There is one more interesting incident when he was caught gambling in the month of Ramzaan in his house by his friend Maulana Azurdah. "It is said that the devil is imprisoned in this month", said the visitor. Ghalib quipped, "yes, but he is imprisoned in this very house". Evidently Ghalib seems to be

1. Altaf Husain Haali, *Yadgar-e-Ghalib* (Lucknow: Uttar Pradesh Urdu Academy, 1986), p. 36.

2. *Ibid.*

very disrespectful to God. The fact is that when he talks of God he is always in lighter mood. When he talks of prophet Mohammad and his issues, he is always serious and respectful. Haali writes that 'Mirza had absolute faith in the truth of Islam and accepted one-ness of God' as the fundamental principle of Islam.[3] There is definitely a difference between the faith of the poet and his writings. Haali concludes his observation,[4]

> Though his real religion was 'suleh kul' (peace with all), yet he was much inclined towards the 'shia faith' and believed that Hazrat Ali (the son-in-law of prophet Mohammad) was the best of all the Ummah after Prophet Mohammad himself.

Haali was present when Ghalib breathed his last. The disciple participated in the rituals and noted that the 'namaaz' was offered in the sunni way although he wanted that it should have been offered in the shia way also as Ghalib had the same love for both the sects. All the rituals were performed according to the sunni traditions.[5] In order to arrive at a clear picture of his faith, let us turn to a letter written by him to his friend Nawab Aminuddin Ahmad Khan wherein he detailed his practice and confessed that he was a sinner as he did not practice piety and drank much. His belief in Allah and the message of the Prophet is clearly brought out: [6]

> "I am a pure monotheist and a perfect believer. With my tongue I say there is no God but Allah; and in my heart 'no God but Allah'. 'No' is to make 'but Allah' more effective, is my conviction.

This letter holds key to the faith of Ghalib. He believed in one Allah, or God and would never ascribe a second or a companion to him. This is 'shirk'[7], a great sin. Like a true Muslim he believed in the Holy Quran, in Prophet Mohammad and all those prophets who

---

3. *Ibid.*, p. 67.
4. *Ibid.*, p. 68.
5. *Ibid.*, p. 90.
6. Ale Ahmad Saroor, *Aks-e-Ghalib* (Aligarh: Aligarh Muslim University, 1973), p. 28.
7. The sin of ascribing a partner to Allah.

had been before him. And then he had a great veneration for the children of Prophet Mohammad. Hazrat Ali, the son-in-law of the prophet, was next to the Prophet in his eye and on this count many of his acquaintances took him to be a Shia, of the group of Ali. He was indeed one who did not follow the rituals as Muslims generally do.

Of his religion two elements can be noted. First, he believed that this word is a manifestation of the Beauty of God. There is one power, and that is all- powerful. In this respect his ideas resemble those of the Hindu philosophers, the Neo-platonists and the sufi – saints. A few of his couplets can be quoted here for a better understanding of his mystic vision.

1. *Juz naam nahin surat-e-aalam mujhe manzoor*
   Juz waham nahin hasti-e-ashya mere aage.
2. *Hei gheib gheib jisko samajhte hein ham shahood*
   Hein khwab mein hanooz jo jage hein khwab mein.
3. *Haan khaaeyo mat fareb-e-hasti*
   Harchand kahein ki hei, nahin hai.
4. *Hasti ke mat freb mein ajaaeyo Asad*
   Aalam tmatmaam halqa-e-daam-e-khayal hei.
5. *Ham mawahhid hein hamara kesh hei tark-e-rasoom*
   Millattein jab mit gayeen ajzaa-e-eimaan ho gayeen.[8]

   1. The appearance of the world is only a name;
      The existence of things is but a fancy before me.
      (p.261)
   2 What we call witnessing is in truth
      The unfathomable mystery of the invisible;

8. English translation by Yusuf Husain Khan from *Urdu Ghazals of Ghalib* (New Delhi: Ghalib institute ,1977), page number is given immediately after the translation of the couplet.

Even when one seems awake in dreams
One is still, in fact, asleep. (p. 138)

3. Be not deceived by existence;
However they may say it is, yet 'tis not so. (p. 221)

4. O Asad, be not deceived
By this existence;
The whole universe is nothing
But a noose of the snare of thought. (p. 171)

5. We believe in the unity of God,
And our religion all ritual does eschew;
When creed and dogma cease to exist
They become part of True Faith. (p. 144)

All the couplets quoted above indicate that the world as we see it is an illusion, it is a mirage; it seems but it is not. We should not be deceived by the appearance of things. This a philosophic concept wherein the world is Naught. This is a Platonic concept also. And secondly, the couplets indicate that there is one God, one supreme power which is invisible. Ghalib believed that there are many creeds, and dogmas and people follows different paths to reach the supreme power. In his view, the true faith is beyond the ceremony of rituals. We can follow the path of true religion only if we do away with the formalities of rituals. He can in no way be called a fundamentalist; the fact is that he laughed at fundamentalism and condemned the practices of the fundamentalists of his day and his letters bear testimony to this fact.

Ghalib was generous, broad minded and of a very cosmopolitan nature. He had his friends not only among the Muslims but quite a large number among the Hindus and quite a few among the Christians also. Among his Muslim friends were mostly members of the royal family, Nawabs and other feudal lords. He did not mix up with the masses but was very sympathetic and considerate to his servants. Of his Hindu friends very close to him were Munshi Har Gopal Tufta, Munshi Shiv Naraian and Jawahar Singh. His Hindu friends helped him in his time of need when the 1857 disturbances had deprived him of every facility. They helped him getting his works printed.

We cannot forget Raja Balwan Singh with whom he used to enter into kite-flying competitions in his early youth at Agra.[9] He once wrote to him, "My dear one, I take you to be by son – I may or may not write you a letter but you are in my heart."[10] He had close acquaintance with a couple of dozen or so English men also. He made no distinction between man and man on the grounds of religion or sect. All those who came to him were welcome and dear to him. His religion in practice was the religion of 'Suleh kul'.

Ghalib: His View of Life

Does Ghalib have a philosophy of life ? Poets are poets, not philosophers. They have their own approach to the problems of life and their approach can not be called systematic, well-organised or consistent. But then, they are endowed not only with sight but with insight also. They suffer their own pangs but much more than that they suffer the pangs of others. They suffer because man suffers ; they laugh because man laughs. But their suffering or laughter is not like that of others. Their suffering and joys are presented in such a way that they become a part of every man's life. Ghalib was not a philosopher but he was deeply contemplative and he had his own views about the ways of the world. As a result most of his observations are highly philosophical in the same way as the views of Shakespeare, Tulsi Das, Kalidas and Keats are. Shakespeare says of life,

> ..... it is a tale
> Told by an idiot, full of sound and fury,
> Signifying nothing.[11]

---

9. Letter to Munshi Shiv Narain, See *Aks-e-Ghalib*, pp.119-120.

10. *Ibid*, p. 125.

11. *Macbeth Act.* V. Sc. V. 11. 26-28.

And Milton, when he finds himself blind and unable to do as much as he would, consoles himself in the following words:

They also serve who stand and wait.

Keats finds the world a place "where men sit and hear each other grown". And Ghalib comments on the misries of life in a highly philosophical way:

Raat din gardish mein hein saat aasmaan

Ho rahega kutch na kutch ghabraein kiya ?

Day and night without cessation

The seven skies are in revolution;

Something will happen so

Why be over-anxious? (p. 73)

All this is not philosophy but it is the best of philosophy for everyman. It is not the philosophy for the selected few or for those who are already learned; it is the proper food for the tenderest stomach. So it is in Ghalib in many a couplet where he talks of our everyday life in a way that is exclusively his own:

Rau nein hei raksh-e-umr kahan dekhye thame

Ne haath bag par hei na hei paa rakaab mein.

The steed of age is galloping,

Let us see where it will stop

The hand does not hold the rein

And the foot is not in the stirrup. (p. 137)

This is a very simple but this is the most profound philosophy of life. Life passes; time fleets, one can not predict what will happen tomorrow. This is not the philosophy of books and voluminous dictionaries[12] but this is everybody's concern. From this viewpoint we may observe two lines of thinking in the ghazals of Ghalib. The first note is that of melancholy, gloom and frustration and the second that of patience and resignation.

The Two Strains of Thought

The dominant note in the poetry of Ghalib is that of gloom, sadness and pessimism. There are certain factors behind it. The Mughal suzerainty was gone and with it was gone the family, prestige and pelf of many a noble people. The princes had become paupers. They depended on pension from the British rulers and it was definitely very merge. The 1857 happenings caused great sufferings and privations. Ghalib had to keep himself confined to his own house. He had been getting just rupees sixty two as pension which was very insufficient. He saw the fall of many a noble one with his own eyes. He had some of his private sorrows. His brother was mentally deranged. His wife gave birth to child after child but none survived. He adopted two children of his wife's brother. One, Aarif died and caused fresh sorrow to the poet. There were miseries and sufferings all around. In his early life he had to face the harsh criticism at the hands of his contemporary poets and poetasters. His pension was stopped after the revolt. He ran here and there but all in vain. Miseries were heaped upon miseries and the outcome was an *opus* poignant, powerful and at times quite heart-rending. The art of Ghalib lies in making the personal universal. Here are some couplets:

1. *Zindagi apni jab is shakl se guzri Ghalib*
   Ham bhi kiya yaad kareinge ki khuda rakhte the.
2. *Jise naseeb ho roz-e-siyah mera sa*
   Wuh shakhsh din na kahe raat ko to kiyonkar ho.
3. *Qaid-e hayaat-o-band-e-ghum asl mein donon ek hein*
   Maut se pahle aadmi gham se nijat paye kiyon.
4. *Manhasir marne pe ho jiski umeed*
   Naumeedi uski dekha chahiye.

---

12. "a study of the processes governing thought and conduct; theory or investigation of the principles or laws that regulate the universe and underline all knowledge and reality; included in the study are aesthetics, ethics, logic, metaphysics, etc." *Webster's New Twentieth Century Dictionary*, Second edition.

5. *Naghma ha-e-gham ko bhi ai dil ghanemat janiye*
Be sada ho jaayega yeh saaz-e-hasti ek din.

6. *Mumkin nahin ki bhool ke bhi armeedah hoon*
Mein dasht-e-gham mein aahoo-e sayyaad deedah hoon.

7. *Khazaan kiya, fasl-e-gul kehte hein kisko, koi mausam ho*
wahi ham hain, qafas hei aur maatam baal-o-par ka hei.

8. *Sanbhalne de mujhe ai naumeedi kiya qiyamat hei*
Ki damaan-e-khayaal-e-yaar chhoota jae hei mujh se.

1. O Ghalib, when life has passed
In such wretched conditions,
How can we say that with all this
We also had a God? (p. 234)

2. One like me, to whom
Dark days are fated,
May call his night the day;
Else for him, how will it be? (p. 156)

3. The prison of life and the fetters of grief
Are one and the same;
Until death, why should one hope
To be free from clutches of sorrow? (p. 146)

4. Whose whole hope is
Centered on death,
One can well imagine
His helplessness!

5. O heart, even the notes of sadness
Should be considered blessed;
The instrument of existence
Will be still and soundless one day. (p. 113)

6. It is not possible that, even by mistake,
I should find ease and comfort;
In the wilderness of grief, I am the deer
Which has espied the hunter. (p. 319)
7. What is autumn? And what is spring?
Whatever the season, we are the same;
The cage remains the same, and the same
Is the moaning for feathers and wings. (p. 206)
8. O despair, help me to hold my own;
What a catastrophe 'tis for me
That the shirt of the thought of my friend
Is slipping from my grasp. (p. 214)

Where there is life, there is suffering. As long as one is alive, one must suffer: suffering is one's lot. The idea is presented in a very lucid language and sometimes in a very metaphorical way as in couplet 6 above where the poet compares himself with a deer who has seen a hunter in the forest. There can be no respite for the poor forked creature.

There can be no better expression of the helplessness of man than the one given in couplet 5 where all hope depends on Death – Death alone will release one from the pangs of life. When a person suffers so much how he can say that he also had a God? (couplet 1). Even the notes of sadness, moaning and groaning are counted a blessing since even this moaning and groaning will no more be heard. This is everybody's fate. The sorrow of Ghalib is the sorrow not of the poet alone; it is the fate of all. Who is there in the world was ever blessed with unalloyed pleasure? Every pleasure, if there was any, had in its tail a sting sharp and painful. Hope may be a toy in the hands of children; it is not there in the world of grown- up people:

Khaak bazi-e-umeed, kaarkhaana-e-tifli.
Yaas ko do aalam pe lab be khinda-e-wa paaya.

Hope is a game of sand – castles,
A children's workshop; despondency laughs
At the two worlds with wide open lips. (p. 267)

The note of gloom and pessimism reaches its climax in the famous couplets:

1. *Rahiye ab aisi jagah chalkar jahan koi na ho*
   Ham sukhan koi naho aur ham zubaan koi na ho.
2. *Be dar-o-deewar sa ek ghar banaya chahiye*
   Koi hamsaaya na ho aur pasbaan koi na ho.
3. *Pariye gar beemar to koi na ho teemardar*
   Aur agar mar jaaeye to nauha khwaan koi na ho.

   1. I long to go away
      And live in a forsaken place
      Where no one would talk to me
      Nor would I see any who spoke my tongue.
   2. There I shall build a house
      Without door and without walls;
      There will be no neighbors,
      Nor any sentinel there.
   3. Should I fall ill
      There will be none to attend,
      And should I die
      There'd be no mourners for me.

Was Ghalib an escapist? Yes, he was but only as much as Keats was. The two tried to escape but from one sorrow they were plunged into another and from one misery they were rolled to another without respite. The only respite was in the world of imagination and that was only a make –believe, an illusion, not a reality, a very temporary respite with every thought to bring the dreamer back to the grim reality of every day life.

Does Ghalib never talk of any respite? Is there no ray of hope in him? Yes, but it is like the lightning in the sky; he would very much like a loan of happiness from his sleeping fate but the fear haunts him, 'How can I repay the debt'. (p.110) Here are a couple of couplets to strengthen and cheer up a weary man:

1. *Hasad se dil agar afsurdah hei garm-e-tamaasha ho*

   Ki chashm-e-tang shaayed Kasrat-e-nazzara se wa ho.

2. *Dekhiye paate hein usshan buton se kiya faiz*

   Ek brahmin ne kaha hei ki ye saal achcha hei.

   1. If thy heart is low with jealousy,

      Then busy thyself observing the world;

      Thus will the narrowness of thine eyes

      Open to the exuberance of the spectacle. (p. 147)

   2. Let us see what benefits the lovers receive from the idols;

      A Brahmin has predicted "This year will be good".

      (p. 244)

The first couplet is a serious one and opens the eyes of those who have a narrow vision of life. In order to be free from the petty feelings like jealousy, one must have a comprehensive view of life – life which has a rich variety of faces and facets of different kinds. The second couplet is just a joke. Till this year no lover was ever allowed any concession by the beloved. Let us see if the beloved is kind this year. The fortune- tellers have predicted that the year was to be very propitious.

Man has to resign to his fate. He is all the time haunted by misfortunes; since misery is with him all the time, let Misery be his friend. And that is what happens with Ghalib. (And we will see soon, it so happened with our young poet also.) When one grows accustomed to pain, pain loses its sting, its power to subdue the victim is also reduced. Man learns to live with pain and sorrow. Sorrow becomes the very reality of life, an essential acceptance of the reality of life. He accepts misfortune as his lot since it is ordained like this. Since it cannot be avoided, it is to be borne:

1. *Gham-e-hasti ka Asad kis se ho juz marg ilaaj*
   Shama har rang mein jalti hei sahar hone tak.
2. *Ranj se khoogar huwa insaan to mit jata hei ranj*
   Mushkilein itni pareen mujh par ki aasaan ho gayeen.
3. *Ishrat-e-qatra hei darya mein fana ho jana*
   Dard ka had se guzarna hei dawa go jana.
4. *Raat – Din gardish mein hein saat aasman*
   Ho rahega kutch na kutch ghabraein kiya;

   1. O Asad, none but death
      Can cure the sorrows of this life;
      The candle burns as it must
      Until the break of dawn. (p. 106)
   2. The man habituated to pain,
      For him pain disappears;
      So many have been my troubles
      That now they are easy to bear. (p. 144)
   3. To be annihilated in the sea
      Is the delight of every drop;
      When pain exceeds the limit
      It becomes its own remedy. (p. 58)
   4. Day and night without cessation
      The seven skies are in revolution
      Something will happen, so
      Why be over-anxious? (p. 73)

This is the state of utter despair for which there is no remedy; death is the only escape. Couplet 2 indicates a state of philosophic resignation to the sorrow of life. The same is illustrated with the help of a metaphor in the next couplet. When we know the pain is incurable, it becomes its own cure since there is no other cure; man learns to live with pain. One has to leave every thing to God, or say to chance as in couplet 4—the world is in constant motion; things take a shape of their own.

Why, then, we poor mortals, helpless creatures, should flutter and fret? Leave it to the Almighty, He is to move the machine of this mighty universe, we are just a drop in the ocean. To be one with the ocean and go back to the Super Soul is the greatest pleasure of every soul.

One very interesting aspect of the poems of Ghalib is regarding the higher density of man. Man is not just a handful of dust or clay, he has mighty ambitions, great goals and sublime aspirations. He has a sense of self respect and will not bow down before petty hurdles in the way. The world, as it is, is a petty space for his eternity-measuring steps. And here Ghalib rises higher than any other poet of the East or West:

1. *Taa't mein ta rahe na mei-o-angbeen ki laag*
   Dozakh mein dal de koi lekar bahisht ko.
2. *Gar tujhko ho yakeen-e-ijabat dua na maang.*
   Yaani bajuz ek dil-e-be mudda'a na maang.
3. *Bandangi mein bhi wuh khudbeen-o-khud aara hein ki ham*
   Ulte phir aaye dar-e-ka'ba agar wa na hua.
4. *Hei pare sarhad-e-adraak se apna masjood,*
   Qible ko ahl-e-nazar qibla numa kahte hein.
5. *Hei kahan tamanna ka dusra qadam ya rab*
   Ham ne dasht-e-imkaan ko ek naqsh-e-pa paya.

   1. So that in one's devotion
      No temptation for wine
      And honey should intrude.
      Throw Paradise to hell. (p. 155)
   2. If thou art certain of thy prayers
      Being granted—then for nothing

Should'st thou ask; pray only
For a heart free from desire. (p. 106)

3. Even in servitude we are so headstrong
And opinionated that finding,
The gate of the Ka'ba shut,
We forthwith turn back.[13] (p. 75)

4. He whom we worship is beyond
The limits of perception; the ka'ba
Is but the direction for our prayer
And not the object of our adoration. (p. 131)

5. Where is the next step of desire?
We find that the desert of potential existence
Is a mere foot print. (p. 267)

At times, the translation does not do justice to Ghalib as in couplet 3 above. The word 'headstrong' does not convey the idea of 'khudbeen'; i.e. one who has the power of self analysis; one who can see what one is. And the idea contained herein is powerful. He will not enter the ka'ba if its gate are closed. They must be open to receive him. The couplets 4 and 5 present the unlimited aspirations and suggest untiring and unending quest on the part of man.

13. This couplet has been translated by Sajjad Zaheer in one of his essays on Ghalib:

True, we are the creature of God,
But even as such we are free man with self – respect,
If the gate of Ka'ba is not opened to welcome us,
We turn our backs and come away from it.

Sajjad Zaheer, " Ghalib and progressive Urdu Literature", Dr. Yusuf Husain Khan, ed., *International Ghalib Seminar*, (New Delhi: All India Ghalib Centenary Committee, 1969-70), p. 114.

Of the higher desting of man, of the value of struggle in life, as reflected in Ghalib, Malik Ram, an eminent critic of the poet, spoke in the Centenary Seminar at Delhi:

> He does not deny obstacles in the way, but to be overcome by them or leave the effort, is not advisable on the part of man. On the contrary man should learn a lesson from it and in the light of this knowledge and experience must march onwards. You might have noted that streams in the hills are very fast moving and it is very risky to cross over them but people do not leave crossing over them. They bring big boulders, throw them into the water and use them as footstools. The stones that were stumbling blocks are used to make way here. That is what wise people do. The obstacles that they meet in the way become helpful in their march onwards.[14]

The learned critic quotes the following couplet of Ghalib:

Ahl-e-beenash ko hei toofan-e-hawadas maktab
Latma-e-mauj kam az saili-e-ustaad nahin.

For men of vision, the flood of troubles
Is but the school of experience;
The blows of the waves seem
Like the teacher's slaps on the face. (p. 128)

If man wants to make progress in life, he will have to forshake the beaten track. Man can not march onwords if he is unable to break through the shackles of conventions and traditions. Ghalib broke through many a convention and made a way of his own in the world of literature. One has to do the same in every aspect of life to make this world a better place. This is possible only when he is able to break from the crowd, the flock of sheep:

Hein ahle-khirad kis rawish-e-khaam pe naazan
Pa bastagi-e-rasm-o-rah-e-aam bahut hei.

---

14. Malik Ram, " Ghalib aur Maqam-e-Insaniyat"' Dr. Yusuf Husain Khan, ed. , *International Ghalib Seminar*, (New Delhi: Sad Salah Yadgaar-e-Ghalib Committee, 1969), Urdu Ed., p. 337.

About what special precepts
Are the people of understanding boasting?
By common customs and rituals
They are bound too much. (p. 255)

The ethical note is very prominent in Ghalib. But here and there lie scattered gems of rare didactic virtue. In life Ghalib was a man of high moral values, believed in the dignity of man, received well and was received well every where, paid proper regard to friends and foes and never stooped to low bickering. He was generous to a fault and sacrificed his own comforts for the sake of others. Neither was he greedy nor selfish nor narrow in any walk of life. Like the Greeks he saw life as a whole and summed up human qualities of love, loyalty, faith and good deeds in a number of couplets:

1. *Wafadaari bashart-e-ustawari asl-e-Eimaan hei*
   Mare butkhane mein to ka' be mein garo Brahmin ko.
2. *Baski dushwar hei har kaam ka aasan hona*
   Aadmi ko bhi mayessir nahin insaan hona.

   1. Steadfast devotion
      Is the foundation of all faith;
      If the Brahmin dies in the temple
      Bury him in the Ka'ba. (p. 158)
   2. It is most difficult
      For every task to be feasible;
      Often it is not feasible
      For man even to be human. (p. 45)

The Brahmin who dies in his temple is a true believer, a man of true faith as he lays down his life for his faith. We all are men but how many of us are human. We are men because we are *homo sapiens*. Are we human? The ethical note, the same that was struck by Gandhiji long after, the same that we still need very much not only in our country but all over the world, is here put in the simplest words for everyone to see and follow:

1. *Na suno gar bura kahe koi*
   Na kaho gar bura kare koi.
2. *Rok lo gar galat chale koi*
   Baksh do gar khata kare koi.
   1. Do not listen if someone talks ill of thee;
      Say nothing if someone harms thee.
   3. If someone goes wrong, then hold him back;
      If he commits a fault, forgive it. (p. 249)

Keats: God and Religion

John Keats was born a Christian, died a Christian and was buried like a Christian. Did he live like a Christian? And what respect did he have for the Christian faith?

In December 1816 he wrote a sonnet "Written in Disgust of Vulgar Superstition" which he did not care to publish. The sonnet is almost a negation of Christianity and it is surprising how at such an early age he lost faith and became an agnostic. Jackson Bate notes about the sonnet, "Here we glimpse for the first time—at least in any really graphic way—the youthful, almost absentminded agnosticism with which he began his adult life. "Agnosticism" is the most positive word we can justifiably use."[15] The poems and letters of Keats contain little about his religious faith and his critics have also not found much here. Moreover, this aspect does not have any bearing on his poetic faith and practice.

Keats wrote a letter in march 1819 to his sister Fanny to answer certain questions regarding the Christian faith. We do not have a copy of her letter but Keats answers every question to satisfy the curiosity of the sister. We note that Keats was fairly well acquainted with the Christian religion. In the letter he explains the 'Sacraments of our church' , communion of saints and many other terms. In the

---

15. Walter Jackson Bate, *John Keats* (New York: Oxford University Press, 1966), p. 133.

same letter he quotes Genesis 3 chapter, verse (15) "and I will put enmity between thee and the woman and between thy seed and her seed; It shall bruise thy head and thou shall bruise his heel "Interestingly enough Keats signs himself at the end as "Your affectionate Parson John—"[16] He wrote the letter in earnest, and not in jest. He knows the Christian faith though we do not find him having any faith in it.

He was engaged to Miss Fanny Brawne on December 25, 1819. The thought of marrying her as per rites and ceremonies of the Christians was almost a torture. He was forced to contemplate marriage according to the rites of the Christian Church and he had been hating Church practice for long. Robert Gittings comments,

> This was a dilemma of a higher order than any other. Fanny was an orthodox Christian believer; Keats was strongly anti – clerical. His bitterness with what he called "the pious frauds of religion" was abnormal. He loathed the Church. Every anti-clerical remark in reading or conversation drew from him a mark of approval. Yet now he was proposing to bind himself by one of the sacraments of the Church.[17]

Immediately before and after his engagement, there was almost a compromise with religion. He would come to any understanding because of the Beloved. He will live and die for the Beloved, religion or no religion. He had already written to Fanny Brawne on October 13, 1819.—

> Your note came in just here—I cannot be happier away from you. This is richer than any Argosy of pearls. Do not threat me even in jest. I have been astonished that Men could die Martyrs for Religion – I have shudders at it. I shudder no more – I could be Martyred for my Religion—Love is my Religion – I could die for you.

---

16. Maurice Buxton Forman, *The Letter of John Keats* (London: Oxford University Press, 1952), pp. 289-90.

17 Robert Gittings, *John Keats: The Living Year* (Melbourne: William Heinemann, 1954), pp. 196-97.

My creed is love and you are its only tenet.[18]

Keats stayed with Benjamin Bailey at Oxford for some weeks in 1817. Bailey was studying for Church and the two friends must have discussed certain issues regarding Christian faith. It is at this time that Keats read the Bible and Church history. He had an honesty of character and used to express his doubts and definitely exhibited a sceptical nature. Bailey pointed out that as an orphan child Keats was left to his own resources and did not get any religious education:

> In one word his religious education seems to have been greatly or wholly neglected: and he was early thrown among men, such as his friend Mr. Hunt, ... and of others of the literary society of that day. Yet he was no scoffer, and in no sense was he an infidel. When he visited me at Oxford, I had much earnest conversation with him on this subject. He well knew and always respected my feelings and principles. He promised me, and I believe he kept his promise, that he would never scoff at religion. And when he returned to London,-it was remarked to me afterwards by one of his most intimate friends,—there was a decided change in his manner regarding religion.[19]

When Keats struggled with Death in Rome, he recollected the days he spent at Oxford. Bailey had shown great veneration for Jeremy Taylor, a parson of 17th century. Now Keats wanted his books as he thought there must be such a book as could give him faith and hope. Severn the painter in whose arms Keats breathed his last, procured a copy of Taylor containing both Holy Living and Holy Dying and "Severn began to read from it to Keats every evening".[20]

That he was an agnostic, had no faith in the Christian ritual and dispensation and that he wanted some faith to die with is evident from the preceding observation. That he had scoffed at religious practices is also implied therein. Leigh Hunt, who brought about the

---

18. *The Letters of John Keats*, p. 435.

19. Quoterd by Walter Jackson Bate, p. 217.

20. *Ibid.*, p. 691.

meeting of Shelley and Keats, and introduced the two poets to the public through his journal The Examiner, was an atheist. He was quite close to Keats though senior to him by eleven years (b. October 19 1784) and brought out the first biography of Keats. Shelley we know, always proclaimed the necessity of atheism. Keats's painful family life and the friendly circle around him did not allow him to think much of the luxury of religion. And yet it was there with him a couple of times. First when he talks of the last days of Tom to George and Georgiana, "I will not enter into any parsonic comments on death, yet the common observations of the commonest people on death are as true as their proverbs. I have scarce a doubt of other—neither had Tom."[21] Secondly, he talks of immortality when he writes to Fanny Brawne of his love and death, "I long to believe in immortality. I shall never be able to bid you an entire farewell. If I am destined to be happy with you here—how short is the longest life. I wish to believe in immortality—I wish to live withn you for ever."[22] His belief in immortality seems to be more in the nature of a belief of the poet – lover.

While going through his poems I noted that he was neither frightened of nor respectful to the God of Jesus Christ as he was to Apollo,[23] the Greek God of poetry, prophecy, music, healing and light. Keats was listed as a certified apothecary in December 1816. A young lady sent him a Laurel Crown –may be it was a piece of encouragement as he had soon decided to abandon medicine for poetry. Miriam Allott quoted Woodhouse, a friend of Keats, how the aspirant put the crown on his head, "As Keats and Leigh Hunt were taking their wine together at the house of the latter the whim seized them to crown themselves with the laurel after the fashion of the elder Bards'..." "Hunt removed the wreath from his own brows... Keats however in his mad enthusiastic way vowed that he would not take off his crown for any human being: and .... wore it .... as

21. *The Letters of John Keats*, p. 245.
22. *Ibid.*, p. 501.
23. "always the most symbolically weighted of mythological names for Keats." Walter Jackson Bate, p. 228.

long as the visit lasted"[24] Keats wrote a couple of sonnets; in one of these he pointed out:

> What is there in the universal earth
>
> More lovely than a wreath from the bay tree? (p. 110)

Soon Keats realised that he was playing with the emblem of the mighty god. He wrote to his brother George, "I hope Apollo is not angered at my having made Mockery of him at Hunt's." And then in utter humiliation, regret and shamefulness, he wrote an apology to Apollo. The poem to Apollo reveals his sense of shame and guilt at his folly: "Where, where slept thine ire. When like a blank idiot I put on thy wreath" and concluded it with the following lines:

> Why was I not crushed – such a pitiful germ?
>
> O Delphic Apollo:
>
> The Pleiades were up,
>
> Watching the silent air;
>
> The seeds and roots in earth
>
> Were swelling for summer fare!
>
> The ocean, its neighbor,
>
> Was at his old labour,
>
> When who, who did dare
>
> To tie for a moment, thy plant round his brow
>
> And grin and look proudly,
>
> And blaspheme so loudly,
>
> And for that honour, to stoop to thee now?
>
> O Delphic Apollo: (pp. 111-112)

The Greek gods and goddesses were very much alive to him. He could feel their presence and make the old legends live again :

---

24. Miriam Allott, ed. *Keats: The Complete Poems* (London : longman, 1980), pp. 109-10.

he successfully did it in *Endymion* and the *second Hyperion*. The Christian lore did not provide him with any substantial thought. He took Christian myths in *The Eve of St. Agnes* and *The Eve of St. Mark* but the treatment is romantic. The Greek lore is the solid foundation on which stands the mighty structure of Keats's poetic mansion.

And what about his philosophy of life; Did he have any philosophy of life? Yes,in the same sense as Ghalib had, though not so deep and contemplative. His admirers raise him sky high in the domain of thought and ideas. Lionel Trilling wrote in his study of Keats in the light of his letters, "Keats was nothing if not a man of ideas."[25]

Exploring his poems we note that he had a desire to study "old philosophy". In On Seeing a Lock of Milton's Hair, he chanted :

> But vain is now the burning and the strife
> Pangs are in vain, until I grow high – rife
> With old philosophy,
> And with glimpses of futurity! (p. 294)

The poem was written on January 21, 1818 and on April 24, 1818 Keats wrote to Taylor that he had read little but he had a great desire to do some good to mankind through the power of his pen –

> There is but one way for me—the road lies through application, study and thought. I will pursue it to that end purpose retiring for some years. I have been hovering for some time between an exquisite sense of the luxurious and a love for philosophy—were I calculated for the former I should be glad—but as I am not I shall turn all my soul to the latter.[26]

Through Bailey Keats came to know of Hazlitt and his works particularly the *Principles of Human Action* and he was enthused

---

25. Lionell Triling, " The Poet as Hero: Keats in his Letters", quoted by Judith O'Neill, ed., *Critics on Keats*, (London: George Allen and Unwin, 1967) p. 18.

26. The *Letters of John Keats*, pp. 133-34.

by the idea of 'disinterestedness of human mind'. It is this 'disinterestedness' that developed into a kind of poetic philosophy in Keats. His own study of the 'Poetical Character' and the art of Shakespeare led him to the 'Negative Capability' concept.[27] He formulated a theory of poetry where the poet is the most unpoetical being and has a power to present facts and objects disinterestedly. He is yet to formulate his ideas about human life.

Keats: His View of Life

His ideas of life and its manifold aspects, ilts miseries and human sufferings are there in letters as well as in his poems. Man to him is, in Shakespeare's phrase 'a poor forked creature' and there is no possibility of any unalloyed happiness for him. He explains human happiness with the help of a metaphor, " for instance suppose a rose to have sensation, it blooms on a beautiful morning it enjoys itself – but there comes a cold wind, a hot sun – they are as native to the world as itself: no more man can be happy in spite, the worldly elements will prey upon his nature—"[28] The world is 'a vale of tears'. He does not hold this view for long although he found nothing but tears all around him. The world that he confronted was a miserable sight and he would very much like to forget it, to dissolve and fade into a dream-world. He gives us a glimpse of the real world in his *Ode to a Nightingale*:

> Here where men sit and hear each other groan;
> Where palsy shakes a few, sad last gray hair,
> Where youth grows pale, and spectre-thin, and dies
> where but to think is to be full of sorrow
>   And leaden-eyed despair;
>   Where Beauty cannot keep her lustrous eyes,
>   Or new love pine at them beyond tomorrow. (pp. 526-27)

---

27. See Chapter III.

28. *The Letters of John Keats*, p. 334.

Keats had to face such a world. He was a bold person and had seen much of suffering. He was not there to bow down and accept the world as 'a vale of tears'. He had to struggle hard and must think in manly terms. The world soon became to him "The vale of Soul making" and then he explains his views in unambiguous term:

> I will call the *world* a school instituted for the purpose of teaching little children to read—I will call the *human heart* the *hornbook* used in that school—and I will call the *child able to read, the soul* made from that *school* and its *hornbook*. Do you not see how necessary a world of pains and troubles is to school an intelligence and make it a soul? A place where the heart must feel and suffer in a thousand diverse ways.[29]

This letter addressed to George and Georgiana Keats at this place becomes almost metaphysical and suggests ways for Salvation in a religious sense. Sufferings chasten and purify and prepare one for a nobler life in the face of God.

We may go a little back in time to his letter addressed to John Hamilton Reynolds where he compares human life to a 'large mansion of many apartments' as 'the infant or thoughtless Chamber, and ' the chamber of Maiden Thought'. It is during the second chamber that one comes to the realization:

> That the world is full of Misery and heart break, pain, sickness and oppression – whereby this chamber of Maiden Thought becomes gradually darkened and at the same time on all sides of it many doors are set open – but all dark—all leading to dark passages—we see not the balance of good and evil. We are in a mist. We are now in that state—we feel "the burden of Mystery,"[30]...

Life becomes a 'Mystery' where one can not explain why there is so much of suffering and misery. One cannot do away with this suffering. All that one can do is to bear the 'burden of mystery'. It may be the death of brother or one's own illness. It is only in the

29. *The Letters of John Keats*, p. 335.

30. *Ibid.*, p. 143.

third Chamber that there seems to be a little hope. "Your third Chamber of life shall be lucky and a gentle one – stored with the wine of love – and the bread of Friendship."[31] Here Keats is Lucky that he got the 'love of friends'. In his philosophy of life, friends occupy a central place as they do in that of Ghalib. Friends share suffering but they do not lessen. When he says 'there is something real in the world', he does not refer to any metaphysical entity. To my mind it is the bond between man and man; that alone is real because in man there is an indomitable courage and that binds him to other fellow beings.

In an earlier letter he had talked in highly philosophic tone of life and the real nature of life. "Neither Poetry, nor ambition, nor love have any alertness of countenance as they pass by me : they seem rather three figures on a Greek vase—" Then coming to the world as such he continues:

> This is the world—thus we cannot expect to give way many hours to pleasure—circumstances are like Clouds continually gathering and bursting—while we are laughing the seed of some trouble is put into the wide arable land of events—while we are laughing it sprouts it grows and suddenly bears a poison fruit which we must pluck – Even so we have leisure to reason on the misfortunes of our friends; our own touch us too nearly for words. Very few men have ever arrived at a complete disinterestedness of Mind: very few have been influenced by a pure desire of the benefit of others—in the greater part of the Benefactors to Humanity some meretricious motive has sullied their greatness—some melodramatic scenery has fascinated them—[32]

There is an ironic contemplation in these line – man thinks of some good and enjoys life but at the same time seed of some mischief is being sown. Thomas Hardy developed the same Irony

---

31. *Ibid.*, p. 144.

32. *The Letters of Keats*, pp. 314-15.

working in the world and our Urdu post Ghalib suffered the same Irony in life.

Keats is not only speculative but has become almost philosophical. He quotes Milton who in his *Comus* wrote

> How charming is divine philosophy
>
> Not harsh and crabbed as dull fools suppose
>
> But musical as is Apollo's lute— (ll.476-8)

He concludes his letter that day with his sonnet 'Why did I laugh to night?' The sonnet was written with 'my Mind' and ' a little bit of my heart'. The concluding lines take us to the ultimate in life:

> Verse, Fame and Beauty are intense indeed
>
> But Death intenser—death is life's high mead. (p. 317)

Keats finds death 'intenser'; it needs an explanation. We know he was in love with 'easeful death' because death alone could release him from 'the weariness, the fever and the fret.' The death –wish is to be related to his Grecian Urn and the song of the Nightingale. Death must exhibit 'mad pursuit' and ' struggle to escape'. It must be like the happy love: "all breathing human passion far above." Then alone will it be "For ever warm and still to be enjoyed."

It must become the song of the Nightingale which was heard in ancient days by emperor and clown, by Ruth and by the fairy or princess in the magic casements. Awakening unto life through Forlorn is another name of death—the same misery, the struggle, the pursuit, the high Mead. And that is the beauty of life! "Would it be too bold to say that whenever the poet's soul in Keats touches and unites with the absolute and eternal beauty it is "in love with" death" [33]

It is in the fitness of things to find out points of comparison in the poetic style of our poets.

---

33. A.C. Bradley, " Keats and philosophy", *John Keats Memorial Volume*, (London: John Lane, The Bodlely Head, February23, 1921). p. 54.

7

THEIR POETIC ART

Mirza Ghalib and John Keats were conscious artists: they knew what they were about. When they sat down to compose verses they tried to bring in the best of matter in the best of manner. The finished product is an organic whole which never gives an impression of art or exercise. They took pains with their compositions and the out-put has not only spontaneity but a musical pattern also.

Ghalib: His Poetic Art

The early efforts of Ghalib are highly persianised. A rich Persian vocabulary dominates as he could use Persian like a native. Bedil was too much with him and his early style is marked with Persian idiom and intricate expressions in the manner of Bedil. Some times the whole couplet has just a word of Urdu and if the Urdu word is removed the couplet becomes Persian. The fact is that Ghalib knew that there was a difference between the language of prose and the language of metrical composition. The language of every day speech, in his view, could never become the language of poetry. Then, as Haali observed, "Ghalib always avoided the beaten path and would make a way of his own. He could sacrifice intelligibility to the originality of thought and novelty of expression."[1] He made a conscious effort to avoid the thoughts and expression commonly used by the contemporary writers and poets. His early efforts were disliked for this particular quality of his verse.

By and by he liberated himself from the Persian burden and came to use Urdu in a away that is remarkable for its simplicity, lucidity, intensity, clarity of thoughts and spontaneity of expression. He does not use the language of Delhi or Lucknow: it is his own Urdu that he makes use of. Abdul Rehman Bijnori rightly noted," The poetry of Mirza Ghalib is not circumscribed by the streets of Delhi or lanes of Lucknow: it is an independent Urdu language."[2] He shaped Urdu language, coined new expressions and epithets for better poetic communication.

Mirza Ghalib is fond of simple and beautiful words. He loves fine phrases and goes on creating one after the other. The philosophic ideas, delicate feelings and subtle emotions need an expression peculiar to them. When Ghalib does not find a suitable expression available around him, he creates one of his own. Here are a few compound words and expressions which contain a world of meaning and suggestion:

Mehshar-e-khayal,	*dawat-e-mizgaan,*	*aatish-e-khamosh,*
Khanazad-e-zulf,	*tashna-e-fariyad,*	*aaena-e-intezaar,*
Shaher-e-aarzo,	*dariya-aashna*	*and lazzat-e-sang.*[3]

Ghalib would never stoop to use a simile or metaphor in the way it had already been used by some predecessor or contemporary. He must add a new flavour, colour and meaning and give a new

1. Altaf Hussain Haali, *Yadgar-e-Ghalib* (Lucknow: U P Urdu Academy, 1986), p. 103.
2. Abdul Rehman Bijnori, *Muhasin Kalam-e-Ghalib* (New Delhi: Anjuman Taraqqi-e-Urdu, 1983), p.13.
3. Wherein thousands of ideas gather or riot of ideas; Invitation to eye-brows to come and kill; the quiet fire; residing in the prison – house of tresses; keenly anxious to make an appeal; the mirror of waiting; the city of one's desires; one well-acquainted with the river and the pleasure of being stoned.

shine to it. The rhetorical devices are used by him for meaningfulness, elucidation, suggestion and embellishment. Here are a few couplets to illustrate the point:

1. *Koi weerani si weerani hei*
   Dasht ko dekh ke ghar yaad aaya.
2. *Gham-e-hasti ka Asad kis se ho juz marg ilaaj*
   Shama har rang mein jalti hei sahar honey tak.
3. *Ahl-e-beenash ko hei toofan-e-hawadas maktab*
   Latma-e-mauj kam as saili-e-ustaad nahin.
4. *Nasha-e-rang se hei wa shud-e-qul*
   Mast kab band-e-qaba bandhte hein.

   1. What a desolation it is:
      The wilderness reminds me of my house.[4]
   2. O Asad, none but death
      Can cure the sorrows of this life;
      The candle burns as it must
      Until the break of dawn.[5]
   3. For men of vision, the flood of troubles
      Is but the school of experience;
      The blows of the waves seem
      Like the teacher's slaps on the face. (p.128)
   4. The rose opens when intoxicated with colour;
      The drunk one does not fasten the buttons of the shirt.
      (p.118)

The wilderness of the house is presented in a unique way in couplet 1 and in couplet 2 life is compared to a candle but the way

---

4. It is my own rendring
5. The translation is by Yusuf Husain in his *Urdu Ghazals of Ghalib* (New Delhi : Galib Institute, 1977) p. 106 The subsequent translations are also by him if not otherwise mentioned.

it is done is Ghalib's own. Couplets 3 and 4 are equally unique and rich in suggestion. Majnoon Gorakhpuri noted that "The quality that distinguishes great poets is spontaneous creativity wherein the distinction between nature and art disappears."[6] He found this quality richly present in the verse of Ghalib who uses artistic devices in a way that the expression does not evince any sign of effort or exercise. There are hyperboles and paradoxes and all very natural:

1. *Tum salamat raho hazaar baras*
   Har baras ke din hon pachas hazar.
2. *Har chand ho mushahida-e-haq ki guftugoo*
   Banti nahin hei bada-o-saghar kahe bagher.
   1. Live happily for a thousand years
      Every year should have fifty thousand days.[7]
   2. Even if one speaks
      Of the vision of divine grace,
      One cannot do so without
      Recalling wine and the wine-bowl. (p.92).

Couplet 1 has become very popular and it is on the lips of most of the guests in a Birth-Day party. Couplet 2 has philosophical connotations. You cannot make a mention of Divinity without referring to wine, or 'sharab-e-tahur'.

The poetic art of Ghalib is marked with simplicity, lucidity and spontaneity. There are many couplets and Ghazals which one simply cannot paraphrase. In the best of poetry the distinction between prose and verse disappears as Wordsworth pointed out. Here are a few couplets:

1. *dil-e-nadaan tujhe hua kya hai?*
   Akhir is dard ki dava kya hei?

---

6. Majnoon Gorakhpuri, *Ghalib: Shakhsh aur shair* (Aligarh: Education Book House, 1976),p.75.
7. It is my own rendering.

2. *Haan, bhala kar tera bhala hoga,*
   Aur darvesh ki sada kya hei?
3. *Na suno gar bura kahe koi*
   Na kaho gar bura kare koi.
4. *Rok lo gar ghalat chale koi*
   Bakhsh do gar khata kare koi.
5. *Maut ka ek din moayen hei*
   Neend kiyon raat bhar nahin aati?

   1. O simple heart, what has befallen thee?
      What remedy can there be for thy pain? (p.241)
   2. Yes "do good and good will be done to thee";
      What else is the call of the darvesh? (p.242)
   3. Do not listen if someone talks ill of thee;
      Say nothing if anyone harms thee. (p.249)
   4. If someone goes wrong, then hold him back;
      If he commits a fault, forgive it. (p.249)
   5. The day of death is fixed,
      So why can I not get sleep at night? (p.240)

Ghalib himself was proud of the beauty of his poetic expression because he could bring in appropriate word, an apt simile, a noble thought and a genuine passion: then he could assimilate the ingredients in a way that the outcome was a sublime product. He could rightly call himself the 'ustaad of Rekhta' while acknowledging the authority of Mir Taqi Mir, his predecessor for whom he had great respect.

Rekhta ke tumhin ustaad nahin ho Ghalib
Kehte hein agle zamane mein koi Mir bhi tha.

Ghalib, thou art not
The only Master of Urdu;
They say in former times
There was a man called Mir (p.67)

The reader is simply wonderstruck at the meaningfulness and rich suggestiveness of his verse:

1. *Hum pukarein aur khule yun kaun jaae*
   Yaar ka darwaza paaein gar khula.
2. *Koi weerani si weerani hei*
   Dusht ko dekh ke ghar yaad aaya.

   1. We call and then it opens,
      We won't enter,
      If we find her doors open.[8]
   2. What a desolation it is
      The wilderness reminds me of my house.[9]

In these couplets the English translation does not do justice to the original. Here the suggestion is doubly interesting. Couplet 1 – We will call at the door of the beloved and the door will open. No, no, we won't go like that: she should be sitting there, with doors open, anxiously waiting to receive as. There is one more rich suggestion—we won't enter her house if we find the doors open. Her doors should open only when we call there. It should be closed for everyone else. In the second couplet, (1) the poet wants to run back to his house as the wilderness is too wild for him and (2) when he is in the wild forest, he is reminded of his house as his house is equally wild and deserted. This particular quality we miss in Keats and in most of the poets of the East and West.

It is in the pictorial quality of their verse that our poets go together. We see graphic details of what they put before us and sometimes we have to fill in the blanks—this gives a free play to our fancy and imagination as much as there is free play on the part of the poet. The visual details enlarge the imagery and the reader is transported into a region of romance and sometimes thrown back on the thorns of life:

---

8. My own rendering into English.
9. *Ibid.*

1. *Ji dhondhta hei phir wohi fursat ke raat din*
   Beithe rahen tasawwar-e-janaan kiye hue.
2. *Guncha-e-na shagufta ko mat door se dikha ki yun*
   Bose ko poochta hoon mein munh se mujhe bata ki yun.
3. *Yeh na thi hamari qismat ki wisaal-e-yar hota*
   Agar aur jeete rehte yehi intizaar hota.
4. *Aah ko chahiye ek umr asar honey tak*
   Kaun jeeta hei teri zulf ke sar hone tak.

My soul seeks the same leisure
That it enjoyed before, when for days and nights
I used to sit and contemplate the beloved. (p.217)

Don't show me from a distance
That unopened rose-bud;
I want a kiss from thy lips
To show me that it is like this. (p.110)

It was not our fortune to enjoy
Love's union with the friend;
Had we lived longer, then how
Anxiously must we have tarried? (p.68)

It takes an endless age
For sighs to take effect;
Who could survive until thy locks
Become my captive? (p.105)

The first two couplets take us to the land of beauty and romance but in the last two we are face to face with the grim spectacle of reality . The third one is a picture of an eternal waiting for the beloved who never comes. The fourth one presents another painful aspect – the lover may not live long enough to see the tresses of the beloved spreading on his arms.

The mighty ideas of life and death and of mysticism are also presented through verbal images. Ghalib presents abstract ideas and makes them concrete – the presentation becomes everybody's concern:

1. *Raat din gardish mein hein saat aasman*
   Ho rahega kuchh na kuchh ghabraein kya?
2. *Joo-e-khoon aankhon se behane do ki hei sham-e-firaq*
   Mein yeh samjhoonga ki shamein do farozaan ho gayeen.
3. *Raha abaad aalam ahl-e-himmat ke na hone se*
   Bhare hein jis gadar jaam-o-subo meikhana khali hei.
4. *Latafat be kasafat jalwa paida kar nahin sakti*
   Chaman zangaar hei aaena-e-bad-e-bhari ka.

    1. Day and night without cessation
       The seven skies are in revolution;
       Something will happen, so
       Why be over anxious? (p.73)
    2. Let a stream of blood flow from the eyes,
       For tis the night of separation;
       So I shall think that there
       Two candles have been lit. (p.142)
    3. That the world is full of people, proves
       That there are no more magnanimous ones;
       If the goblet and barrel stay brimful,
       It shows that the taven is deserted. (p.181)
    4. Purity cannot manifest itself
       Without impurity;
       A flower-bed is the rust
       On the mirror of the spring breeze. (p.41)

The planets and satellites are in a constant motion: something is bound to happen –leave every thing to fate and chance. What is the use of crying against the world which is going awry? Life is a game of 'plastic circumstances' – the imagery in this couplet is from heaven and earth and spreads ever a wide perspective. In couplet 2, the imagery is based on a paradox: couplet 4 has an element of mysticism in it. The Eternal Beauty has to manifest itself but it can be done only through some physical phenomenon which by its very nature is uncouth, awkward and may be ugly also. The physical aspect cannot reveal all that the metaphysical or the true Beauty is. The situation is presented through a rare metaphor wherein the garden is the Verdigris on the mirror and the spring breeze is the mirror itself.

Along with the pictorial quality goes the dramatic touch in the verse of Ghalib. The dramatic element can be seen in two ways – in the dialogues and in the portrayal of action. There is a conversational tone as well as action being staged before us:

1. *Harek baat pe kahte ho tum ki tu kya hei?*
   Tumheen kaho ki yeh andaaz-e-guftgoo kya hei?
2. *Poochhte hein wuh ki Ghalib kaun hei?*
   Koi batlao ki hum batlaein kya?
3. *Sanbhalne de mujhe ai na umeedi kya qiyamat hei*
   Ki damaan-e-khayal-e-yaar chhoota jae hei mujh se.

   1. On every word I utter thou dost say
      "What dost thou think thou art?"
      Tell me thyself,
      What is this way of speaking? (p.247)
   2. She is asking "who is Ghalib?"
      Someone please tell me
      What reply should I give
      To such a query? (p.73)
   3. O despair, help me to hold my own;
      What a catastrophe 'tis for me
      That the skirt of the thought of my friend
      Is slipping from my grasp. (p.214)

Music and poetry go together in the verse of Ghalib. Words are suited to thought and emotion and every Ghazal reads like a lyric and can be easily set to music, vocal or instrumental. There is a rich melody and a powerful rhythm and we find that his gazal is not only an organic whole but a fine musical composition also. Take any gazal – *Dil-e-naddan, Nukta cheen hei* or *Yeh na the hamari qismat* and you will see there is a musical pattern all through the composition. Ghalib uses Urdu as it should be used – simply , rhythmically, musically and meaningfully. It is for this felicity of expression that Ghalib is the greatest among Urdu poets.

Ghalib is essentially a poet of sorrow and suffering. Gloom is the main ingredient of his verse and pessimism the main plank. The splendour of his family is gone, the Mughal glory has departed and life has lost its charm and beauty. The 1857 uprising shook the very foundation of life . The old order was changing and the new order with its cruelty was establishing its sway. Ghalib knew there was no alternative, life, with all its misery and suffering , was to be borne. In ghazal after ghazal he presented the pangs, agony and privations that he faced in his life and saw all around in Delhi. The cry of agony still pierces the hearts of the readers and listeners:

1. *Koi ummeed bar nahin aati*
   Koi surast nazar nahin aati.
2. *Ibn-e-Maryam hua kare koi.*
   Mere dukh ki dawa kare koi.
3. *Manhasir marne pe ho jis ki umeed*
   Na umeedi us ki dekha chahiye.

   1. No hope is realized.
      There is no way out. (p. 240)
   2. He may be the Holy Mary's son,
      But he should cure my pain. (p. 248)
   3. One whose only hope
      Depends on death, his helplessness
      Must be a sight worth seeing. (p. 211)

There is no escape, no remedy; one must live till Death comes and liberates the soul. The agony that pierced the heart of Ghalib and visited the hapless capital city of the declining Mughal empire has been presented in universal terms. Sorrow is no more a personal concern with him; it is the lot of mankind. One who is born must taste pain and pass through sufferings to the portals of Death:

1. *Ishrat-e-qatra hei dariya mein fana ho jana*
   Dard ka had se guzarna hei dawa ho jana.
2. *Ranj se khoogar hua insaan to mit jaata hein ranj*
   Mushkilein mujh par pareen itni ki aasan ho gayeen.

    1. To be annihilated in the sea
       Is the delight of every drop;
       When pain exceeds the limit
       It becomes its own remedy. (p. 58)
    2. The man habituated to pain,
       For him pain disappears;
       So many have been my troubles
       That now they are easy to bear. (p. 144)

Saxena pointed out ": That the pessimism and the darkness of pain that is there in the verse of Mirza is mostly contained by his wit and humour."[10] The bright rays of the sun of wit and humour can be easily discerned in his verse. A cheerful or happy smile cannot be expected from one who had so much of suffering around him. But we note that Ghalib knows the art of laughing at himself. He was not happy with the scheme of things so he could laugh at the priests and the angels. He had a sharp dig at the Almighty also.

1. *Hua hai Sheh ka musahib phire hei itrata*
   Wagarna shaher mein Ghalib ki aabroo kya hai?

---

10. Ram Babu Saxena, *History of Urdu Literature*, trans. Mirza Mohammad Askari (Lucknow: Munshi Nawal Kishore, 1929), p. 393.

2. *Kabhi jo yaad bhi aata hoon mein to kehte hein*
   Aaj bazm mein kuchh fitna-o-fasaad nahin.
3. *Kahaan meikhana ka darwaza Ghalib aur kahan waa'z*
   par itna Jante hein kal woh jata tha ki hum nikle.
4. *Hamko ma'loom hei jannat ki haqiqat lekin*
   Dil ke khush rakhane ko Ghalib yeh khayal acchha hai.
5. *Pakre jate hain farishton ke likhe par nahaq*
   Aadmi koi hamaara dam-e-tehrir bhi tha.

   1. Having become the king's companion.
      He puts on airs;
      Else what honour does Ghalib
      Enjoy in the city? (p. 248)
   2. Whenever she remembers me,
      She says to the Company,
      "Today there is no discord
      And trouble in the gathering". (p. 145)
   3. O Ghalib where is the taven door,
      And where is the admonisher?
      We only know that yesterday
      He was going in as we were coming out. (p. 264)
   4. We know the reality of paradise; o Ghalib
      To keep the heart happy, this idea is good. (p. 244)
   5. We stand unjustly accused on the reports
      Of the angels; surely it would be better
      If a man were also present
      When our sins were all recorded. (p. 66)

Ghalib knows that he has a way of his own unmatched by anybody else. His command over language, display of genuine passion, realistic portrayal of human predicament, questioning spirit and wit and wisdom endow his verse with a brilliance that time cannot fade nor fashion tread down:

> *Hein aur bhi dunia mein sukhanwar bahut achhe*
> *Kehte hein ki Ghalib ka hei andaaze-e-bayan aur.*

The Poetic Art of John Keats

Keats realized quite late that he had poetic talents. Ghalib started versifying at the early age of 9-10 while Keats was turning from teens to twenties when it dawned upon him that he was born for the profession of poetry. The awakening came through the good company of his friend Clarke with whom our young poet read some good books like the *Faerie Queene* of Spenser. When the talents were awakened, Keats came to his own. The medical license or the problems of the family could not stand in his way. His readings into Spenser, Homer, Dante, Shakespeare, Milton and others gave him a sure direction. He had a keen sense of appreciation and enjoyed his sojourns into the realms of gold, lands of beauty and regions of romance. Then he sat down to compose because he had the ' poetical character' in him. Writing about 'genius' to his friend Woodhouse, he noted:

> As to the poetical character itself (I mean that sort of which, if I am anything, I am a member;...) it is not itself. . . . It has no self . . . . it is every thing and nothing. . . . It has no character . . . . it enjoys light and shade; it lives in gusto, be it foul or fair, high or low, rich or poor , mean or elevated. . . .[11]

His early efforts can in no way be called remarkable or great but they definitely show a determination — that he has left medicine for 'the beautiful mythology of Greece' and one day he must bring out something beautiful. There are clear signs of immaturity in *Endymion*—the genius is undisciplined, imagination uncontrolled, vocabulary luxuriously burdensome, thoughts and feelings

11. Mauroce Buxton Forman, *The Letters of John Keats* (London: Oxford University Press, 1952), p. 226.

extravagant and style artificial. The unfavorable reviews daunted him not since he knew— "The Genius of poetry must work out its own salvation in a man :..."[12] He composed some sonnets and there is a gradual maturity and perfection in his style. *Lamia, the Eve of St. Agnes and Isabella;* or *The Pot of Basil* reveal a marked development in the poet's art. Then came Odes and Keats found his genius there. The two *Hyperions* further reveal that the poet is on way to some mighty achievement in the domain of poetry. We note that now in Keats there is the restraint and discipline of classicism combined with the ardour and spontaneity of romanticism. It is in his odes that young Keats is ripened to perfection. We find a maturity of thought, sincerity of passion, truth of imagination and perfection of style.

The most striking thing that comes to our mind at the first instant is his love of fine phrases. He uses 'delicious' words and the reader enjoys his words, phrases and epithets as much as the poet might have done. Plain and unadorned words have a beauty of their own but Keats is contented only when he has added an extra brilliance to them. When he is not satisfied with the words available to him, he freely puts forth new coinages and gives us compound words. His early compounds' the sweet lipped ladies', 'milk white lamb', 'leafiness of dales' and 'tasteful nook', are just youthful and the youngman cannot be derided for them. He proceeds further to 'sweet desolation', 'balmy pain', 'rain-scented eglantine' and 'sigh shrilled ladies'. With *Isabella, The eve of St. Anges* and the *Odes* comes the power of liquid diction. Now Keats has come to maturity and we find a superb use of epithets and compound words as 'branched thoughts', 'melodious plot', 'full-throated ease', 'sun-burnt mirth', 'leaf- fringed legend', 'a heart sorrowful and cloyed', 'soft-dying day', and 'wreathed doorway'.

With the coinage of compound words goes the pictorial quality in the verse of Keats. 'Sun-burnt mirth' is not just a compound word: it is a world of beauty and puts before us a vast panorama and so are ' beaded bubbles winking at the brim' and 'purple stained

12. *Ibid*, p.221.

mouth'. These pictures have a powerful telling effect as the verbal becomes visual. Keats creates broad images of delight and beauty with the help of his coinages and makes the abstract concrete. The epithets used by him are extraordinarily rich in suggestion and open up a far reaching perspective before us. *To Autumn* is a living picture of the season with a rich variety of fruitfulness, sights and sounds. Here is the second stanza:

Who hath not seen thee oft amid thy store?
    Sometimes whoever seeks abroad may find
Thee sitting careless on a granary floor,
    Thy hair soft lifted by the winnowing wind;
Or on a half reaped furrow sound asleep,
    Drowsed with the fume of poppies, while thy hook
Spares the next swath and all its twined flowers;
And sometimes like a gleaner thou dost keep
Steady thy laden head across a brook;
Or by a cyder-press, with patient look,
Thou watchest the last oozings hours by hours.[13]

The descriptions are not only visual but colourful also. Keats has a keen eye for the visual detail and an artist's perfection of presenting the most beautiful. *The Eve of St. Agnes* is a visual feast of delight to the reader:

A casement high and triple-arched there was
All garlanded with carven imageries
Of fruits, and flowers, and bunches of knot –grass,
And diamonded with panes of quaint device
Innumerable of stains and splendid dyes,
As are the tiger –moth's ' mong thousand heraldries,

---

13. Miriam Allott, *Keats: The Complete Poems* (London: Longman 1970), pp. 652-53.

And twilight saints, and dim emblazoning,

A shielded scutcheon blushed with blood of queens and kings.

John Keats makes a deft use of similes, metaphors, personifications and other rhetorical devices for the poetic communication of vision of Beauty. As a poetic artist he knows how to blend sensations and thoughts together—it is there in ' the blushful hippocrene' and 'sun-burnt mirth'. His poetic art is greatly coloured by his love of the Greek lore. Moon is always a goddess or a queen to him and the stars are her fairy companions;

And haply the Queen-Moon is on her throne,

Clustered around by all her starry fays; (pp. 527-28)

The visual picture in many cases takes a dramatic turn in the verse of Keats. We may frequently see the visual object presenting a dramatic situation. The *Ode on a Grecian Urn* is a poetic play presenting the intransience of art through certain lasting situations taken from the reality of transience:

Fair youth beneath the trees, thou canst not leave

Thy song, nor ever can those trees be bare;

Bold lover, never, never canst thou kiss,

Though winning near the goal – yet do not grieve:

She cannot fade, though thou hast not thy bliss,

For ever wilt thou love, and she be fair: (p. 535)

In Keats's verse we get a harmony of emotions and verbal presentation. Words are suited to sensation, emotion and thought in such a way that they acquire a lyrical quality. Music is an inseparable part of the poems of Keats. Read his longer poems or shorter ones like *La Belle Dame Sans Merci*, you will see that the poem is a musical composition. The two *Hyperions* have mighty harmonies. The verbal pattern is on a grand scale and Keats does not stoop to low levels. He knows he is talking of the Greek gods and goddesses so the language that he uses has a vigour and freshness of the classical temper. He would not allow his language to be Miltonic; he must come afresh to the topic and he did it valiantly:

Then said the veiled shadow; ' Thou has felt
What 'Tis to die and live again before
Thy fated hour. That thou hadst power to do so
Is thy own.' 'High Prophetess,' said I, 'purge off,
Benign, if so it please thee, my mind's film.'
'None can usurp this height,' returned that shade,
'But those to whom the miseries of the world
Are misery, and will not let them rest.
All else who find a haven in the world,
Where they may thoughtless sleep away their days,
If by a chance into this fane they come,
Rot on the pavement where thou rotted'st half.'

(pp. 666-67)

Keats does not find the world a happy and comfortable place. Like Shelley he does not hope that better times will come. In his poems and letters we frequently read of sorrows, sufferings, heart breaks and misfortunes. The poet does not find any escape from the gloom that envelopes humanity. The profession of a poet alone promises some relief to him as here he would be able to understand the miseries of mankind, and put 'heart easing things' before the people. The third stanza of his *Ode to a Nightingale* is a comprehensive picture of the world which he would very much like to forget and

Fade far away, dissolve, and quite forget
    What thou among the leaves hast never known,
The weariness, the fever, and the fret
    Here, where men sit and hear each other groan;
Where palsy shakes a few, sad, last grey hairs
Where youth grows pale, and spectre-thin, and dies;
    Where but to think is to be full of sorrow
And leaden-eyed despairs;

Where beauty cannot keep her lustrous eyes,

Or new love pine at them beyond tomorrow. (pp. 526-527)

The poet knows that fading and dissolving and quite forgetting the world of reality is not within his power. It is only for a short while that he is allowed to wander into the world of fancy. He must come back to his own world and face the grim reality. Joy is there but it is never 'unalloyed'. In his *Ode on Indolence* he wrote about melancholy:

She dwells with Beauty- Beauty that must die;
    And Joy, whose hand is ever at his lips
Bidding adieu; and aching pleasure nigh,
    Turning to poison while the bee-mouth sips.

(p. 540)

The letters of Keats also present the world as a miserable place where people can not enjoy 'unalloyed happiness'. The lesson that we derive from his letters is that we must learn to live with our misfortunes. "The first thing that strikes me on hearing a misfortune having befallen another is this. ' Well it can not be helped-he will have the pleasure of trying the resources of his spirit,—"[14]

There is manliness about the poet; he does not bow down before the calamities since they are everybody's concern:

> This is the world- thus we cannot expect to give way many hours to pleasure—Circumstances are like clouds continually gathering and bursting—while we are laughing the seed of some trouble is put in to the wide arable land of events—while we are laughing it sprouts, it grows and suddenly bears a poison fruit which we must pluck—[15]

There is a spirit of manly fortitude in the young poet and it makes him dear to his readers. The beauty of his art lies in communicating his misfortune in such an objective and disinterested way that it becomes the suffering of the whole mankind. As a result

---

14. The *Letters of John Keats*, p. 68.

15. *Ibid*, p. 314.

his words prove a balm to the wounded heart of the people of the world : they find an echo everywhere. Then Keats communicates his ideas and feelings in a language which has a freshness and a vitality of its own. He writes English as it should be written simply, rhythmically, musically and meaningfully. It is for his felicity of expression that Keats is one of the greatest among English poets.

We note that Ghalib and Keats go together in communicating their sufferings and those of the people around in an objective way. With their love of fine phrases, condensed expressions, sanity of outlook, romantic brilliance and classical restraint, they say the most 'heart-easing things.' The two poets will provide solace and comfort to readers generation after generation.

In this study of Ghalib and Keats I have tried to present some points of comparison in their lives, themes, thoughts and poetic art. Now I would like to find out the secret of their charm and lasting appeal.

8

THEIR APPEAL

For long the idea "East is East and West is West/ And the Twain shall never meet" dominated the thought of mankind. Now satellite communication and swift means of transport have made the globe a play ground for thinkers, poets, writers and scientists. In place of cultural animosity inhabitants of the globe have started thinking in terms of cultural homogeneity and anthropological invariables. They are coming closer day by day. Cultural delegations and poetry conferences are also a happy step in this direction. It is in the wider interest of life that Men of Letters put their heritage together and give a better feel of life and time to the people at large.

'Nothing is good or bad but thinking makes it so' said the bard. Nothing is big or small but perspective makes it so, say I . How would you like Bharat Muni and Aristotle teaching dramaturgy to our students? How would you like Shakespeare and Kalidas putting the teachings of the Masters to practice adding something of their native talents? And how would you like young Keats holding the finger of Ghalib moving side by side for quite a long distance... ? till Immortality called the one earlier and left the other one in the cauldron of time to become, to borrow the words of Sir Phillip Sideny, ' Food for the tenderest stomach'.

Keats belonged to the Western hemisphere and Ghalib to the Eastern. Now the poet of the West is the part of the syllabus in the East and the Eastern one is a part of the syllabus in the West. They led a poor life, drank to the dregs all dismays and delights, hopes and fears that life could afford, dreamed their dreams, wove webs of facts and fancy and left 'a sheaf of gold' in the hands of mankind before flying high into the Olympian regions.

God does not want that his chosen ones should be nursed and nourished as the mortal millions are. Our poets were orphaned at an early age. Relatives from the side of the mother looked after them. They were granted legacies and pensions and the papers in both the cases were washed in tears – just to multiply their miseries. It is never ' unalloyed happiness' for John Keats and Mirza Ghalib always counts 'dagh-e-hasrat-e-dil' – unfulfilled desires. They were allotted a fairly satisfactory sum of Misfortune to bring out the best in them. "Do you not see how necessary a world of pains and trouble is to school an intelligence and make it a soul?"[1] And the poet of the East wrote that ' the onslaughts of misfortune are in no way less than slaps of teachers on the cheeks of the school-children.'[2] The world of pains and troubles and the slaps of misfortune taught them compose verses of exquisite brilliance to thrill, delight, enlighten and strengthen generation after generation.

They gloried into the past and drank deep the vintage 'cooled a long age in the deep delved earth,' and *came out with a concoction*, a liqueur for you and for me. Homer, Shakespeare, Dante; Firdausi, Amir Khusro, Nizami; our poets had the best of cellars and they being men of taste liked the taste. The drunken-outpourings are sublime:

> *Bak raha hoon junoon mein kya kya kuchh*
> *Kuchh na samjhe khuda kare koi.*
> I know not what nonsense I talk in my madness;
> Would to God that no one understands me.[3]

---

1. Maurice Buxton Forman, *The Letters of John Keats* (London: Oxford University Press, 1952), p.335.
2. '*Latma-e-mauj kam az saili-e-ustaad nahin.*'
3. Yusuf Husain, trans., *Urdu Ghazals of Ghalib* (New Delhi: Ghalib Institute, 1977), p. 249.

Critics and criticasters may not understand but the voice of pain, the cry of agony, and the Beauty of fancy are there for those who have a mind unsullied, a heart wounded and a soul aspiring for a better vision.

Poetry was in their blood—they thought of poetry they knew of poetry and they wrote poetry. It was like breathing to them. Keats said that Poetry should come like leaves to a tree, "It should strike the Reader as a wording of his own highest thought and appear almost a Remembrance."[4] And to the Urdu poet it is the very voice of the heart of the listener—*Meine yah jana ki goya yeh bhi mere dil mein hei*. This is their charm, their appeal.

Ghalib left Agra, his home town, for Delhi and made the capital city his home, though he never had a house of his own there. Keats, when after the death of his father his mother remarried, left for London, and made the capital city his home, though he never had a house of his own there. The homeless ones made a home in the hearts of their readers. Times shuttled them from one house to another but they never left their love—poetry which enshrined them into the Temple of fame.

They are poets of Beauty and Love. They loved Beauty wherever and in whatever from it appeared to them . To them the stars of heaven are beautiful as much as the rose or the face of a woman is beautiful. What is remarkable is the fact that they loved the very arrow that wounded their heart and they welcomed sun and shower alike. Praise or blame had momentary effect on them because they themselves were the best judges of what they wrote. They did appreciate excellence wherever it existed in the works of others but never compromised on the merit of their own composition. They sang of love fulfilled, of love frustrated and of the petty jealousies and mighty motions that love brings in its trail. They never lost sight of other factors of life—sorrows, sufferings, failures, hopes and moral concern, union with the beloved, 'wisal' and separation. Disease and death were regular items in the cup of their sorrow. They touched

4. *The Letters of John Keats*, p.107.

almost every aspect of human life with their magic wand of imagination and endowed the object that they touched with an unfading freshness and unfailing charm. The word came out of their hearts and went to the hearts of the listeners and readers. They have their fingers on the nerves of time. What they sang and wrote is still Beautiful, it still has a charm and an appeal.

As to their poetic art, we know they were conscious artists and knew what they were about. In the early stages they were romantically extravagant and loaded every sentence with beautiful burdens. They could judge what was beautiful and what was burdensome. Soon there comes a classical restraint. Words are chosen both for sound and sense. Ornamentation is there but it becomes 'fine excess' to give an extra aesthetic delight to the readers and extra meaningfulness to the *cymini sectores.*

They use similes, metaphors and other figures to the best advantage and put sensation and thoughts together in phrases like 'blushful Hippocrene' and 'mehshar-e-khayal'. You more than read their poems, you see delightful pictures—'beaded bubbles winking at the brim'. 'Hair soft-lifted by the winnowing wind' and

Dekho to dil farebi-e-andaaz-e-naqsh-e-pa

Mauj-e-kharam-e-yaar bhi kiya qul katar gayee.

Look at the heart-alluring way of her

Footprints; the wave of her graceful walk

Plucked petals from the roses and

Spread them on the ground.

Then there is drama enacted before the eyes of the readers:

What mad pursuit? What struggle to escape?

What pipes and timbrels? What wild ecstasy?

(Ode on a Grecian Urn, 11. 9-10)

and

The bald-head philosopher

had fixed his eye, without a twinkle or stir

Full on the alarmed beauty of the bride,
Brow-beating her fair from, and troubling her sweet pride.
(Lamia II 11. 245-48)

You can find the same dramatic element in the verses of our Urdu poet:

1. *Rau mein hei rakhsh-e-umr kahan dekhie thame*
   Ne haath bag par hei ne pa hei rakab mein.
2. *Tujh se to kuchh kalam nahin hei par ai nadeem*
   Mera salaam kahiyo agar namabar mile.

The steed of age is galloping,
Let us see where it will stop;
The hand does not hold the rein
And the foot is not in the stirrup.[5]
My boon companion, I have no complaint
To make to thee; but if thou dost meet
The messenger that thou did'st recommend.
Just wish him well, on my behalf.[6]

Our poets began with a romantic exuberance, came to a classical restrain, loaded every rift with ore and perfected their style to a liquid diction and felicity of expression. They charged their words with beauty, meaning and rich suggestion.

Keats and Ghalib won the hearts of their readers not because they were highly philosophical or profoundly learned and deeply contemplative; they won the hearts of the people because they talked of the common human experience in a language richly suited to the task. Their art lies In presenting the common human experience in a way that the reader is willy nilly transported to the world of beauty and the land of romance. 'A thing of beauty is a joy

---

5. Yusuf Husain, *Urdu Ghazals of Ghalib*, p. 137.
6. *Ibid.*, p. 238.

for ever....' Is every body's concern as much as ' *Ishq par zor nahin hei yeh woh aatish Ghalib'* is every body's treat. They tell the plain truth about this world of ours 'Where men sit and hear each other groan' and our helplessness in the scheme of things—

Raat din gardish mein hein saat aasman,

Ho rahega kuchh na kuchh ghabraaein kya.[7]

Ghalib had a longer life, he was allowed a larger share of suffering and experience. As a result he has a wider sweep and a deeper probe:

1. *Hai kahan tamanna ka dusra qadam ya rab*

   Ham ne dasht-e-imkaan ko ek naqsh-e-pa paya.

2. *Hei aadmi bazaat-e-khud ek mehshar-e-khayal*

   Ham anjuman samajhte hein khilawat hi kiyon na ho.

Where is the next step of desire?

We find that the desert of potential existence

Is a mere foot- print.[8]

Man himself is a tumultuous

Riot of ideas; even when alone

We consider ourselves

In very fine company.[9]

Then Ghalib had his studies into the sufi tradition which enabled him to have a mystic vision of life. He presents illusion and reality of life with the eye of a detached observer as in the following couplet:

Haan khaiyo mat fareb-e-hasti Asad

Harchand kahein ki hei, nahin hei.

Be not deceived by existence;

However, they may say it is, yet 'tis not so.

---

7. Yusuf Husain, *Urdu Ghazals of Ghalib*, p. 73.
8. *Ibid.* , p. 267.
9. *Ibid.*, p. 148.

Ghalib had a wit and humour which was denied to our young poet. He laughed at himself, at others, at angels and could cut jokes even with God:

Pakre jate hein farishton ke likhe par nahaq

Aadmi koi hamara dam-e-tahrir bhi tha?

We stand unjustly accused on the reports

Of the angels; surely it would be better

If a man were also present

When our sins were all recorded:[11]

His sufferings have made him bold towards God:

Kya wuh Nimrood ki khudai thi?

Bandagi mein mera bhala na hua.

Was it to the divinity of Nimrud offered—

That my devotion has been unrewarded?[12]

Ghalib and Keats are great poets. The two walk together and cover quite a long distance. The powers- that-be called the one earlier—Keats left with us a great work and a greater promise. Ghalib marched on buffeting the blows of unkind times and left with us a work expected of him. Keats is a promise; Ghalib is a promise fulfilled.

Our poets thought of doing some good to the world. They had no resources to feed the hungry or clothe the naked. They had an art of their own. Ghalib thought in terms of feeding the hungry of his town and wandering all over the world with a knapsack on his back.[13] He could not afford that. In one of the letters Keats wrote, "I find there is no worthy pursuit but the idea of doing some good for the world – some do it with their society—some with their wit—some

10. Yusuf Husain, *Urdu Ghazals of Ghalib*, p. 221.
11. *Ibid*., p. 66.
12. *Ibid*., p.74.
13. Ale Ahmad Saroor, ed., *Aks-e-Ghalib* (Aligarh: Aligarh Muslim University, 1973), p. 38.

with their benevolence—some with a sort of power of conferring pleasure and good humour on all they meet and in a thousand ways all equally dutiful to the command of great nature—"[14] Our poets were endowed with a 'sort of power of conferring pleasure and good humour on all.' This is the secret of their popularity and herein lies their charm and appeal. Ghalib and Keats are our poet-kings who simply tell ' the most heart-easing things'. With the passage of time and the progress of ages the charm of their work will not decrease. Keats is among the greatest in the West and Ghalib is one of the greatest in the East. The two suffered at the hands of time and out of their sufferings they put forth works of beauty which shall remain a friend to man generation after generation and provide consolation and stay to the people in the East as well in the West.

14. *The Letters of John Keats*, p. 133.

SELECTED BIBLIOGRAPHY

JOHN KEATS

Primary Sources

1. Allott, Miriamm ed. *Keats: The Complete Poems*. London: Longman, 1980.
2. Garrod, H.W. ed. *The Poetical Works of John Keats.* London: Oxford University Press, 1956.
3. Murry, John, ed. *Poems of John Keats*. London: Peter Nevill,1948.
4. Scharf, George. Illust. *The illustrated Poetry of Keats with a Memoir by Richard Monckton Milnes*. London: Chancellor Press, 1984.
5. Forman, Maurice Buxton, ed. *The Letters of John Keats*. London: Oxford University Press, 1952.

Secondary Sources

6. Abrams, M.H. ed. *English Romantic Poets: Modern Essays in Criticism.* London: Oxford University Press 1960.
7. Bate, Walter Jackson *John Keats*. New York: Oxford University Press, 1966.
8. Bowra, Sir Maurice, *The Romantic Imagination*. London: Oxford University Press, 1961.

9. Gittings, Robert, *Joihn Keats: The Living Year.* Melbourne: William Heinemann, 1954.

10. ————, *The Mask of Keats: A Study of Problems.* Melbourne: William Heinemann, 1954.

11. ————. *John Keats* . Harmondsworth: Penguin Books, 1971.

12. Hayden, John O., ed., *Romantic Bards and British Reviewers.* London: Routledge & Kegan Paul, 1971.

13. Inglis, Fred. *Keats.* London: Evans Brothers,1966.

14. Kumar Shiv K., ed., *British Romantic Poets : Recent Revaluations,* London : University of London, 1966.

15. The Keats House, Committee. *The John Keats Memorial Volume.* London: John Lane The Bodley Head, 1921.

16. Murry, John, Middleton. *Keats and Shakespeare.* London: Oxford University Press, 1925, rept. 1958.

17. MacGillivray, J.R. *Keats: A Bibliography and Reference Guide with an Essay on Keats' Reputation.* Canada: University of Toronto Press, 1949.

18. O'Neill, Judith, ed., *Critics on Keats.* London: George Allen & Unwin, 1967.

19. Ward, Aileen, *John Keats: The Making of Poet.* London: Secker & Warburg, 1963.

MIRZA GHALIB

Primary Sources

20. Haq, Mufti Mohammad, Anwarul, ed., *Diwan-e-Ghalib Jadid al Maroof beh Nuskha-e-Hamidia.* Lucknow: Uttar Pradesh Urdu Academy, 1982.

21. Raza, Kalidas Gupta, ed., *Diwan-e- Ghalib Kamil Tarikhi tartib Se Bombay*: Sakar Publishers, 1988.

22. Husain Yusuf. Trans *Urdu Ghazals of Ghalib.* New Delhi: Ghalib Institute, 1980.

23. ————, *Persian Ghazals of Ghalib.* New Delhi : Ghalib Institute, 1980.

24. Askari, Mirza, Muhammad, ed., *Adabi Khutut-e- Ghalib.* Karachi : Mubarak book Depot, 1970

25. Saroor, Prof. Ale Ahmad., ed., *Aks-e-Ghalib.* Aligarh : Aligarh Muslim University, 1973.

Secondary Sources

26. Arif, Akhlaq Husain. *Ghalib aur Fan-e-Tanqeed*. New Delhi: Ghalib Academy.

27. Askari, Jafar., ed., *Jadid Adab: Manzar Pas Manzar*. Lucknow: Uttar Pradesh Urdu Academy, 1982.

28. Bijnori, Dr. Abdul Rehman, ed., *Mahasin-e- Kalam-e-Ghalib*. New Delhi: Anjuman Taraqq-e-Urdu, 1983.

29. Fatehpuri, Niaz. *Mushkilat-e-Ghalib*. Lucknow: Nasim Book Depot, 1961.

30. Gorakhpuri, Majnoon. *Ghalib : Shakhsq aur Shair.* Aligarh: Educational Book House 1976.

31. Haali, Altaf Hussain. *Yadgar-e-Ghalib*. Lucknow: Uttar Pradesh Urdu Academy 1986.

32. -do-, *Muqaddama Shair-o shairi*. Lucknow: Uttar Pradesh Urdu Academy, 1988.

33. Hasan, Mohammad Aziz. *Tasawwarat-e-Ghalib*. New Delhi: Ghalib Academy, 1987.

34. Husain Intizar. *Alamaton Ka Zawal*. New Delhi: Maktaba Jamia, 1983.

35. Husain, Yusuf., ed., *International Ghalib Seminar*. Urdu Vol. New Delhi: Ghalib Centenary Committee, 1969.

36. -do-, International Ghalib Seminar. Eng. Vol. Ghalib Centenary Committee, 1969-70.

37. -do-, *Ghalib aur Ahang-e-Ghalib*. New Delhi: Ghalib Academy, 1971.

38. Ikram, Shaikh Mohammad. Ghalib Namah Ya Aasar-e-Ghalib. Lucknow: Ehsan Book Depot, n.d.

39. Kashmiri, Dr. Hamidi. *Iqbal aur Ghalib*. Srinagar: Idara-e-Adab, 1978

40. Mahmud, S. Fayyaz, And Iqbal Husain, *Tanqeed-e-Ghalib ke sau sall*. Lahore: University of the Punjab,1969.

41. Meher, Ghulam Rasool. *Ghalib*. Lahore: Sheikh Mubrak Ali, 1941.

42. Mohani, Fazlul Hasan Hasrat. *Arbab-e-Sukhan*. Lucknow: Uttar Pradesh Urdu Academy, 1982.

43. Mujeeb, M. *Ghalib*. New Delhi, Sahitya Academy 1983.

44. Ram, Malik. *Fasana-e-Ghalib*. New Delhi: Maktaba Jamia, 1977.

45. Ram, Malik. *Mirza Ghalib*. New Delhi: National Book Trust, 1980.

46. Russell, Ralph., ed., *Ghalib: The Poet and His Age*. London: George Allen & Unwin, 1972.

47. Sattar, Qazi Abdul. *Ghalib: A Novel.* Aligarh Educational Book House, 1986.

48. Sayyal, Mirza Mohammad and Hayat Khan. *Ahwal-o-Naqd-e-Ghalib.* Lahore Nazar Sons, 1967.

49. Sud, K.N. *Selections from Ghalib and Iqbal.* New Delhi: Sterling Publishers, 1978.

50. Verma, Pawan, K. *Ghalib: The Man, The Times.* New Delhi: Penguin Books, 1989.

51. Zaman, Dr. Masihul. *Urdu Tanqeed Ki tarikh.* Lucknow: Uttar Pradesh Urdu Academy, 1987.

52. Saxena, Ram Babu. *History of Urdu Literature.* Trans. Mirza Mohammad Askari. Lucknow: Munshi Nawal Kisore, 1929.

53. Faiz Ahmad Faiz. " *Ghalib ki ek Urdu Ghazal*". Ajkal 32, VII, February, 1974, pp.16-17.

54. Farooqi, Khwaja Ahmad., ed., *Urdu-e-Moalla, Ghalib Number,* Vol. X, 1969.

55. Siddiqi, Ejaz., ed., *Shair, Ghalib Number,* 40, II & III, February-March,1969.

General Books

56. Mohan, Chandra., ed., *Aspects of Comparative Literature.* New Delhi: India Publishers, 1989.

57. Amirthanayagam, Guy., ed., *Writers in East-West-Encounter: New Cultural Bearings.* London: MacMillan, 1982.

58. Saintsbury, George. *Loci Critici.* Boston: Cine & Selected Company, 1931.

59. Chopra, D.K., ed., *Literary Criticism: An Anthology.* Meerut: Loyal Book Depot, 1974.

60. Handy, William, J. & Max Westbrook., ed., *Twentieth Century Criticism: The Major Statements.* New Delhi: Light & Life Publishers, 1976.

APPENDIX-I

C-504, Defence Colony
New Delhi-110024
18-05-1985

Dear Dr. Zaheer Hasan,
Adaab,

Thank you for your letter of 14th May.

1. What to talk of any research paper on Keats and Ghalib, I have not yet seen any petty article. Truly speaking, both have a different taste and manner, quite different from one another. Keats is a romantic poet of beauty and love. On the other hand, the element of thought, insight and philosophy is prominent in Ghalib.

2. There are many books on the Life and Poetry of Ghalib, e.g., *Hayaat-e-Ghalib* (Ikram), *Yaadgaar-e-Ghalib* (Haali), *Ghalib* (Meher), *Zikre-e-Ghalib* (Malik Ram). There may be several useful books in English.

3. *Nuskha-e-Arshi* is the best of all the Urdu Kalaams of Ghalib. Other Diwans are also good enough for the common reader.

Yours,
Malik Ram

APPENDIX-II

30-08-1985
Mumbai-5

Dear Sir,

It is in response to your letter of 14th May, sorry for the delay.

1. Long back, an article on Keats & Ghalib was published. I'll try to send you a Xerox copy of it.
2. *Zikr-e-Ghalib* written by Malik Ram is very popular.
3. *Ahawal-e-Ghalib* and *Naqd-e-Ghalib* will be available in Delhi: both the books were published from Aligarh.
4. *Fikr-e-Ghalib* is by Khalifa Abdul Hakim; to be read again and again. I have published 19 articles on Ghalib till now. One book *Ghalib Shenasi* is 2 volumes was published by Anjuman Taraqqi-e-Urdu. It will be available with Makhtaba-e-Jamia.

Yours,
Zoe Ansari

INDEX